HEALTH, ILLNESS AND DISEASE

Also by Havi Carel and published by Acumen
Illness: The Cry of the Flesh

Also by Rachel Cooper and published by Acumen
Psychiatry and Philosophy of Science

HEALTH, ILLNESS AND DISEASE
PHILOSOPHICAL ESSAYS

Edited by
HAVI CAREL and RACHEL COOPER

ACUMEN

© Editorial matter and selection, Havi Carel and Rachel Cooper, 2013.
Individual contributions, the contributors.

This book is copyright under the Berne Convention.
No reproduction without permission.
All rights reserved.

First published in 2013 by Acumen

Acumen Publishing Limited
4 Saddler Street
Durham
DH1 3NP, UK

ISD, 70 Enterprise Drive
Bristol, CT 06010, USA

www.acumenpublishing.com

ISBN: 978-1-84465-543-4

British Library Cataloguing-in-Publication Data
A catalogue record for this book is available from the British Library.

Typeset in Warnock Pro by JS Typesetting Ltd, Porthcawl, Mid Glamorgan.
Printed and bound in the UK by MPG Books Group.

CONTENTS

Acknowledgements vii
Contributors ix

Introduction 1
Havi Carel and Rachel Cooper

Part I: Concepts of health and disease

1. The opposition between naturalistic and holistic theories of health and disease 23
   Lennart Nordenfelt

2. Health and disease: social constructivism as a combination of naturalism and normativism 37
   Elselijn Kingma

3. Towards autonomy-within-illness: applying the triadic approach to the principles of bioethics 57
   Antonio Casado da Rocha and Arantza Etxeberria

4. The concept of "mental disorder" 77
   Valérie Aucouturier and Steeves Demazeux

Part II: The experience of illness

5. What is phenomenology of medicine? Embodiment, illness and being-in-the-world 97
   Fredrik Svenaeus

6. Beyond the wounded storyteller: rethinking narrativity, illness and embodied self-experience 113
Angela Woods

7. Transitions in health and illness: realist and phenomenological accounts of adjustment to cancer 129
James Brennan

8. Pain as illness 143
Elisa Arnaudo

Part III: Illness and society

9. Intersex, medicine and pathologization 161
Melanie Newbould

10. Stigmatizing depression: folk theorizing and "the Pollyanna Backlash" 181
Charlotte Blease

11. Doing health: a constructivist approach to health theory 197
Britta Pelters

12. Beauty and health as medical norms: the case of Nazi medicine 211
Sophia Efstathiou

Bibliography 229
Index 253

ACKNOWLEDGEMENTS

This volume started its life in a conference funded by the UK Arts and Humanities Research Council (AHRC). The conference was part of a Research Networks Project on Concepts of Health, Illness and Disease that was run by us. We are grateful to the AHRC for funding the project. We also wish to thank the University of the West of England (UWE), Bristol, who hosted the conference and provided support for the AHRC project. Thanks also to the Leverhulme Trust for awarding Havi Carel a Research Fellowship in 2011–12, which enabled work on the volume. We are also grateful to Steven Gerrard, who initiated and supported the project, and to Camille Bramall, Hamish Ironside and Gina Mance for their excellent work on the manuscript. Finally, we would like to thank the contributors to this volume, who were both meticulous and prompt, and wrote the excellent contributions that you are about to read.

CONTRIBUTORS

Elisa Arnaudo is a PhD student in science, technology and humanities, Department of Philosophy at Bologna University, Italy. Her thesis is on "Pain as the Object of Biomedical Knowledge".

Valérie Aucouturier is a postdoctoral fellow in philosophy at the Research Foundation (Flanders) at the Free University in Brussels (Leo Apostel Center). Her publications include "'An Originality That Belongs to the Soil, Not the Seed': Wittgenstein on Freud" in *Ungesellige Geselligkeiten/Unsocial Sociabilities*, an edited volume on Wittgenstein (2011).

Charlotte Blease is a teaching assistant in philosophy in the School of Politics, International Studies and Philosophy, Queen's University, Belfast. Her recent publications include "Mental Health Illiteracy? The Unnaturalness of Perceiving Depression as a Disorder" (2012) in *Review of General Psychology* and "The Principle of Parity: The Placebo and Physician Communication" (2011) in *The Journal of Medical Ethics*.

James Brennan is a consultant clinical psychologist at the Bristol Haematology and Oncology Centre (NHS) and St Peter's Hospice, Bristol, and an honorary senior lecturer in palliative medicine at the University of Bristol. He is the author of *Cancer in Context: A Practical Guide to Supportive Care* (2004).

Havi Carel is a senior lecturer in philosophy at UWE, Bristol and teaches at Bristol Medical School. Her research examines the experience of illness and of providing and receiving health care. She is the author of *Illness* (Acumen, 2008), shortlisted for the Wellcome Trust Book Prize 2009, and of *Life and Death in Freud and Heidegger* (2006).

CONTRIBUTORS

Rachel Cooper is a senior lecturer in philosophy at Lancaster University. Her publications include *Classifying Madness* (2005) and *Psychiatry and Philosophy of Science* (Acumen, 2007).

Antonio Casado da Rocha is a permanent research fellow at the University of the Basque Country (UPV/EHU), Spain. His books include *Bioética para legos* [*Bioethics for Lay People*] (2008). He serves as secretary in the Health Ethics Committee at the Donostia Hospital, San Sebastian, Spain.

Steeves Demazeux is a postdoctoral fellow at the CeRMeS3 (Research Centre of Medicine, Sciences, Health, Mental Health and Society), CESAMES team, Paris-Descartes University.

Sophia Efstathiou is a researcher in an integrated, philosophy and systems biology project at the Norwegian University of Science and Technology (NTNU). She studies how everyday ideas can become scientific ones, as detailed in "How Ordinary Race Concepts Get to be Usable in Biomedical Science: An Account of Founded Race Concepts", forthcoming in *Philosophy of Science*.

Arantza Etxeberria is an associate professor at the University of the Basque Country (UPV/EHU), Spain. Her research is in philosophy of science, in particular the philosophy of biology and medicine. She is part of a research group in Donostia-San Sebastián (IAS-Research Centre for Life, Mind, and Society) exploring the notion of autonomy from biological and ethical perspectives.

Elselijn Kingma is a Wellcome Research Fellow in the Centre for Humanities and Health and the Department of Philosophy, King's College London, and Socrates Professor of Philosophy and Technology in the Humanist Tradition at the Technical University of Eindhoven, the Netherlands. Her main research interests are concepts of health and disease and medical epistemology.

Melanie Newbould is a consultant paediatric histopathologist at the Royal Manchester Children's Hospital. She is also undertaking a PhD in bioethics and medical jurisprudence at the University of Manchester. Her thesis is entitled "Legal and Ethical Issues Concerning Genital Surgery in Children".

Lennart Nordenfelt is a professor of philosophy of medicine and health care at the Department of Medical and Health Sciences, University of Linköping, Sweden. He is the author of *On the Nature of Health* (1987;

2nd rev. edn 1995), *Action, Ability, and Health* (2000), *Health, Science and Ordinary Language* (2001), *Rationality and Compulsion* (2007) and *The Concept of Work Ability* (2008). From 2001 to 2004 he was president of the European Society for the Philosophy of Medicine and Health Care.

Britta Pelters is a postdoctoral visiting fellow at the Department for Gender Medicine at the University of Linköping. She is a social science researcher with a background in educational science and human biology. Her dissertation, *Doing Health in the Community: Breast Cancer Genes between Societal, Familial and Individual Health Norms*, will be published by Transcript Verlag.

Fredrik Svenaeus is a professor at the Centre for Studies in Practical Knowledge, Södertörn University, Sweden. His main research areas are philosophy of medicine, bioethics, medical humanities and philosophical anthropology. His books include *The Hermeneutics of Medicine and the Phenomenology of Health: Steps towards a Philosophy of Medical Practice* (2000).

Angela Woods is a lecturer in medical humanities at the Centre for Medical Humanities, Durham University. She is the author of *The Sublime Object of Psychiatry: Schizophrenia in Clinical and Cultural Theory* (2011). Her study of the role of narrative in the field of medical humanities is continued in articles published in *Narrative Inquiry* and the BMJ journal *Medical Humanities*.

INTRODUCTION

Havi Carel and Rachel Cooper

At both a social and individual level, securing health acts as a motivating goal for many of us. Public health education schemes tell us we should drink less, use condoms and eat more fruit. Screening programmes aim to catch the early signs of disease while it is treatable. Hand-washing schemes in hospitals aim to stop the spread of infection. At the individual level, too, many of us believe that "health is the most important thing". We aim to look after ourselves and those we love. Come New Year we join gyms and those of us who still smoke give up smoking, at least for a while. Overall, many (although by no means all) individuals are willing to do much for the sake of their health.

We agree that health matters, but disagree when it comes to determining exactly what counts as health or ill-health. Conditions such as AIDS, cancer and tuberculosis stand out as being fairly clear-cut cases of disorders, but many of the conditions that cause us suffering do not look much like such paradigmatic cases. Increasingly, the conditions for which we seek treatment are not those that straightforwardly lead to suffering and death. Some are "risk factors" – nebulous conditions that might be linked to future ill-health. Certainly we are motivated to reduce our risk factors for disease if the change in habits is something as simple as taking a pill; for example, there are millions of people worldwide who use medication to control their cholesterol level or blood pressure. We are less inclined to reduce our risk factors by cutting back our alcohol consumption. And that is because the risk and the potential disease are often understood by patients as remote and statistical risks, and the link between risk factors and actual disease is sometimes difficult to demonstrate and badly understood. It still sounds wrong, at least to some, to call conditions such as high blood pressure "disease"; and yet it also seems wrong to consider persons with high blood pressure completely healthy. So how do we decide when a risk factor becomes a disease?

Other conditions that challenge the attempts to define disease include ambiguous states, such as feeling down or losing one's interest in sex, that some regard as a normal part of life's ebb and flow, and some view as medically treatable conditions. Thinking about such states is a complex and difficult task. Some welcome the possibility of medically treating such problems. Others, who are critical of the increasing medicalization of our lives, claim that "problems in living" are coming to be reconfigured as disorders in ways that are problematic. For example, some argue that bereavement, which can share the symptoms of depression, has unjustly come to be seen as disease if it continues beyond a period of mourning considered "normal" (Horwitz & Wakefield 2007).

Thus we find ourselves at an odd point in history. Seeking health acts as a motivating force (for some) more strongly than ever; our understanding of disease processes and the availability of new treatments is growing; the percentage of gross domestic product (GDP) spent on health care is higher (in many Western countries) than at any other point in history. At the same time the concepts of health and disease have become problematic in ways that are unprecedented, and further complicated by technological advances and growing possibilities for health and performance enhancement. We know that we want health, but are unsure what health is. We want to avoid disease and disease risk, but find the definition of these terms inconsistent and baffling. In this context there is much work in clarification and elucidation for philosophers of medicine and researchers in other fields who engage with these issues.

THE DEBATES TO DATE

The philosophy of medicine subjects the concepts and methods employed in medicine to philosophical analysis. Philosophers of medicine ask questions such as: how should we understand concepts of health, disease and illness? By what methods can medical knowledge be gained? How can we gain understanding of the experience of illness? With the exception of medical ethics, which has been well developed over the past fifty years, other areas of philosophy of medicine have only recently been investigated and much work remains to be done. While the use of pathological cases to exemplify a more general philosophical view is not uncommon in philosophy (e.g. Bayne & Levy 2005; Schroeder 2005; Ratcliffe 2008), there have until recently been few philosophers who specialized in the philosophy of medicine. As such until the late 1970s the philosophy of medicine consisted of little more than a handful of articles focusing on the concept of disease, and no body of literature had been established for other areas within the field. Indeed, some areas such as the experience of illness were almost entirely neglected. All this is now changing. In the last decade or so the philosophy of medicine has begun to establish itself as a recognized sub-discipline, with its own journals and conferences, and a corpus of work that is fast developing. The chapters in this volume tackle recent developments in the philosophy of medicine, broadly construed. Work in medical ethics is plentiful and easy to find and will not be reviewed here. In order to orient the reader we begin with a review of the other major debates in the philosophy of medicine to date.

DEFINING HEALTH AND DISEASE

Much of the work in the philosophy of medicine has aimed at providing an analysis of our concepts of health and disease. When seeking to define disease, it has been common to take the term "disease" (or "disorder", or occasionally "malady") to be an umbrella term that includes all those conditions that make us unhealthy – diseases, disabilities, injuries, and so on. The primary task that philosophers have set themselves is to provide an analysis of this umbrella concept, to try and capture what they all have in common. "Disease", "disorder", or "malady" have been taken to be diametrically opposed to and mutually exclusive of health – that is, the disease-free, and only the disease-free, are healthy. We can immediately see (and this will be brought out in detail in many of the chapters in this collection) that such an approach might be considered problematic. In lumping all medical conditions together, work in the philosophy of medicine has certainly overlooked much detail. There are surely important differences between somatic and mental disorder, and between chronic and acute conditions, for example. The limitations of the "lumping approach" should be balanced by its advantages, however, and one of us (R.C.) has engaged in the "lumping approach" herself, and continues to think it justified when considering certain issues (R. Cooper 2002a). For many questions of practical importance (should this person be eligible for sickness benefit? Do they have an excuse for handing in their essay late?) the key question is whether a condition should be considered to be pathological or healthy. In order to deal with such issues we do need a general umbrella concept of disease and seeking to analyse this general concept remains a worthwhile project, even if for certain other types of question it might be hoped that philosophers of medicine will become more sensitive to the important differences between different types of medical conditions.

Working within the framework that takes "disease" as an umbrella term that includes all states that reduce health, two major camps have developed. These are often referred to as the descriptive (or naturalistic) approach and the normative approach, and are sometimes also referred to as the "value-free" and the "value-laden" approaches to disease, respectively (Agich 1983; DeVito 2000). However, the opposition is somewhat contrived. While "descriptive" approaches basically come down to the account proposed by Christopher Boorse (1975, 1976, 1977, 1997, 2011), normative or value-laden approaches do not form a unified opposition to the descriptive approach, but differ radically among themselves. All value-laden accounts agree that "disease" is a value-laden concept and that diseases are essentially bad, but as authors disagree in their accounts of what is bad, and what other criteria might be essential for a disease, this agreement hides much disagreement.

When considering concepts of health and disorder, the classic account, to which all theorists compare their own, is the descriptive and value-free account proposed by Boorse. Boorse first presented his account in a series of papers written in the 1970s, but has more recently reaffirmed it (1997, 2011) and still adheres to the broad outlines of his original account. Boorse sees medical theory to be applied biology. On his account, whether a condition counts as a disease is a matter of straightforward biological fact. Boorse thinks of the human body and mind as made up of numerous subsystems. Bodily subsystems may be solid organs, such as the kidney and heart, or more diffuse systems such as the nervous system or the circulatory system. At the psychological level, there is no reason why "mental modules" (if such exist) should not be conceived of as Boorsian subsystems (though for reasons that are somewhat obscure Boorse himself has on occasion shied away from applying his account to mental disorders; Boorse 1975, 1977). Boorse holds that each subsystem of the body or mind has a natural function. For example, the function of tear ducts is to produce tears to protect and lubricate the eye. Descriptions of these natural functions can be found in physiology textbooks. The function of each subsystem is whatever it normally does in organisms of a particular type that contributes to the organism's overall goals of survival and reproduction. In order to count as healthy, all of one's subsystems must achieve functioning within the statistically normal range as compared with other organisms of the same reference class, for example sex and age (for a critique of Boorse's use of reference classes, see Kingma 2007).

Boorse's picture has much to recommend it and, for the most part, classifies conditions as diseases or non-diseases in ways that accord well with our intuitions. Consider conditions that affect our vision, for example. On Boorse's account we can say that the function of our eyes is to enable us to see. This is what eyes are supposed to do, helping human beings to survive and reproduce. If there is a problem with our eyes, such that our eyesight falls below what is statistically normal for those of our age, then we count as having a disorder. On Boorse's account all of this is a straightforwardly factual matter. I can have my eyes tested, and if the results fall outside the normal range, I can be said to be short-sighted or long-sighted. Questions about values and subjective experience – whether I'm upset about my eyesight, what the meaning of seeing is for me, and so on – may come to prove important for practical purposes, such as figuring out the best way to persuade me to wear glasses, but on Boorse's account they do not enter into the question of whether or not I have a disorder.

Opposition to Boorse's account has centred on two main issues: (a) Is his account of normal function adequate? (b) Is a value-free account of disorder acceptable?

Some have raised concerns about Boorse's account of function (Amundson 2000; R. Cooper 2002a; Wright 1973). Within the philosophy of biology the literature on function is vast. Boorse is not alone in holding the account of function that he adopts. Many, however, prefer evolutionary accounts of function, and hold that the function of a biological subsystem is whatever it has been selected to do (see Gammelgaard 2000 or Garvey 2007: chapter 7 for a critical account). In many cases the two accounts of function will agree on the function that should be attributed to a subsystem; but when a subsystem that evolved for one purpose is now used for something else, they come apart. For our purposes here it is sufficient to note that those who are opposed to Boorse's account of normal function, but who think some other account is acceptable, can still adopt a descriptive account of disease as dysfunction, and merely replace Boorse's account of function with their preferred account.

More radical disagreements exist between Boorse and those who think that the concept of disease is essentially a value-laden concept such that diseases have to be harmful (R. Cooper 2002a; Fulford 1989; Nordenfelt 1987, 2000, 2001; Reznek 1987; Stempsey 2000; Wakefield 1992a, 1992b). The view that diseases are essentially harmful came to prominence during the debates of the 1960s and 1970s about homosexuality (for an overview of the controversy, see Bayer 1981). Boorse, and others who adopt descriptivist accounts of disease, are forced to accept that homosexuality might turn out to be a disease. If it turned out that some mental module has the function of making sure that humans are sexually attracted to members of the opposite sex in order to ensure reproduction, and that dysfunction in this system produced homosexuality, they would have no alternative but to declare homosexuality pathological. To many involved in the debates about homosexuality, however, arguments about the biological causes of homosexuality appeared largely irrelevant. Those who insisted that homosexuality is not pathological took this line not because they had some particular theory about the evolution of homosexuality, but rather because they thought that homosexuality is not a harmful condition, even if it is a dysfunction on a Boorsian analysis.

In the light of such debates, Jerome Wakefield's value-laden account of disease according to which diseases are harmful dysfunctions became popular (1992a, 1992b). On such an account, even if homosexuality turns out to involve some biological dysfunction, insofar as it is not harmful, it will not count as a disease.

Wakefield's account is one among many "normativist" or "value-laden" accounts. Other normativist accounts include R. Cooper (2002a), Fulford (1989), Nordenfelt (1987, 2000, 2001), Megone (1998, 2000), Reznek (1987) and Wakefield (1992a, 1992b). Of particular note is Lennart Nordenfelt, one of the major figures responsible for developing holistic accounts of disease. His is a kind of normativist account that focuses on the idea that the healthy person is in a bodily and mental state such that he or she has the ability to achieve his or her vital goals (goals that are essential for an individual's well-being; Nordenfelt 1987, 2000, 2001, 2008). As noted earlier, such accounts should not be thought of as providing a unified opposition to Boorse. Accounts are diverse, with authors disagreeing about the account of harm that should be adopted, and also disagreeing about other criteria that a condition might need to meet to count as a disease.

Determining the correct account of harm is, of course, a huge problem; the issue is the flipside of determining what counts as the good life – one of the perennial philosophical problems. In the philosophy of medicine it has been commonplace for authors to state that diseases must be harmful without going into detail about what counts as harm. But depending on how one conceives of harm, very different accounts of disease will ultimately be produced. To give some idea of the range of possibilities, let us consider the account of harm that will be provided by an Aristotelian as compared with the account that will offered by those who think that agents themselves should judge whether they have been harmed. For the Aristotelian, whether an organism has a good life is an objective matter. Each type of creature is naturally suited to a particular way of living and flourishes if it lives in accordance with its nature (Aristotle 2004; Foot 2001). Thus, gerbils, to take an example, are naturally desert-dwelling, tunnel-digging, sociable creatures. For this reason, a domestic gerbil will be happiest with friends and in a tank where it can dig, and it is cruel to keep one in other conditions. For the Aristotelian, humans, too, are naturally fitted to live in particular ways – humans are sociable, rational beings, and do best in environments where they are able to live in accordance with their nature. On an Aristotelian account, a human who spends all his time watching daytime television is missing out on living the sort of good life that is right for a human – he has a poor life, even if he claims to be happy.

Other accounts of the good life are quite different and take the views of the affected agent to be authoritative. On desire-satisfaction accounts, a life is good insofar as an agent achieves her desires. The differences are brought out sharply if one considers what each would say about particular cases. Let us take the case of an anorexic woman who says that she values a way of life that centres around an aesthetic of control and extreme thinness. She values being thin and being able to reject food. She claims to accept the risk of death as a necessary component of her values. Those who hold that disorders are essentially bad and who hold a desire-satisfaction account of the good life will struggle to explain what is wrong with such a woman's life. She claims to be happy; none of her desires are frustrated, so she has a good life. The Aristotelian sees things quite differently; whatever the woman says, her way of living does not correspond to the sort of good life that is natural for a human being – she has a poor life of hunger rather than moderation and regardless of how she rates her well-being, she still fails to flourish. The Aristotelian and desire-satisfaction accounts of the good life are, of course, not the only options (see Griffin 1986 for an overview), but they bring out clearly how different value-laden accounts of disorder will be depending on the account of the good life that is used to underpin them.

Further diversity among value-laden approaches emerges as many theorists will add extra criteria that a condition must satisfy in order to count as a disease. Value-laden accounts of disease agree that diseases are bad things, but of course there are many bad states that are not diseases (illiteracy, selfishness, homelessness) and so value-laden accounts have to say something about which sorts of bad state they consider in particular to be diseases. Some accounts hold that a condition is a disease if it affects some internal part of the organism in such a way that harm either results or can be anticipated (Megone 2007). Other accounts add other criteria – for example, that the condition must be appropriately medically treatable, or statistically unusual, or the sufferer must be unlucky (Reznek 1987; R. Cooper 2002a).

It is worth adding to this already diverse picture that some theorists have suggested that to seek to provide an account with necessary and sufficient conditions for disease is a mistake. Instead they hold that "disease" is a family resemblance term (Lilienfeld & Marino 1995). Wittgenstein pointed out that many concepts cannot be characterized by sets of necessary and sufficient conditions, but are instead held together by networks of family resemblances. He uses "game" as an example (Wittgenstein 1953: §66). Many, but not all, games are fun. Most have rules, but some do not. Many are played with others, but some are solitary. Although there are no criteria that all and only games meet, we can recognize something as a game when we see it – a new board game is close enough to accepted examples to count as a game. Those who hold that disease is a family resemblance term similarly think that whether a condition should count as a disease depends not on it satisfying some formal criteria, but on it being similar enough to accepted central examples. Work on the concepts of health and disease continues, and a number of chapters in this collection examine these issues further.

PHENOMENOLOGY OF ILLNESS

Possibly the most important aspect of disease is that it causes pain, suffering and sometimes death. The conceptual approaches described above have only touched on this issue tangentially, when trying to define what it means to say that a condition is harmful. To address this, a body of philosophical work that focuses on the experience of illness has developed in recent years. The contrast it wishes to draw is between disease, referring to biological processes taking place in a diseased organism (the ill person's body), and illness, which refers to a person's first-hand experience of the disease. Indeed, we can easily think of disease without illness (e.g. early non-symptomatic stages of undiagnosed cancer). We can similarly think of illness without disease (perhaps some cases of minor depression, that give rise to symptoms but where no clear disease process is present). Some have added also the notion of "sickness" to disease and illness, using the term "sickness" to denote the social attitudes and perceptions of a disease (Hofmann 2002).

The phenomenology of illness turns attention to the person experiencing illness and how best to philosophically describe the experience of illness, which is universal (at least in the sense that all human beings experience disease symptoms at some point) and often life-changing. In work dating from the late 1980s onwards some phenomenologists have taken the experience of illness as their central theme and applied different phenomenological approaches to it. Some aimed to describe the essential ("eidetic") features of illness (Toombs 1988). Others characterize illness existentially as a feeling of being not at home, being disoriented (Svenaeus 2000a, 2000b). Yet others describe illness as a breakdown of the body's normally transparent and smooth function (Carel 2008, 2013). What these approaches share is the importance they accord the first-person perspective and the unique insights it may give us about what illness is like for the person undergoing it, an area that has been overlooked by the philosophy of medicine.

S. Kay Toombs's seminal article "Illness and the Paradigm of Lived Body" (1988) applies Merleau-Ponty's distinction between the body as lived and the biological body to the case of illness, demonstrating the problems and limitations arising from understanding illness as merely a disruption of biological function. Rather, Toombs argues, illness disrupts the lived experience of one's body, leading to an overarching existential disruption of the ill person's way of being in the world and their life world. Toombs's work also explores temporal experience in illness, using Sartre and Husserl, as well as examining the patient–clinician encounter through a phenomenological lens (Toombs 1987, 1990). She also uses phenomenology to characterize the general features of chronic illness and disability, weaving together examples from her life with multiple sclerosis and phenomenological analysis (Toombs 1993, 1995).

Toombs's work was then followed by Fredrik Svenaeus and Havi Carel, among others. Svenaeus published a series of articles developing a Heideggerian analysis of illness as an "unhomelike" experience. He describes medicine's role as showing the patient the way home, back from an uncanny experience (2000a, 2000c). His work was further developed in a book entitled *The Hermeneutics of Medicine and the Phenomenology of Health*. In this book Svenaeus develops a unique account of medicine's aim, using a hermeneutic phenomenological approach to describe medicine as an interpretive practice (2000b). This emphasis on hermeneutic aspects of the patient–clinician encounter, as well as on the interpretative work involved in diagnosis and in other epistemic aspects of medical work, draws on Gadamer's account to provide a view of illness as based in social and interpretative practices of generating meaning.

Carel's book *Illness* uses Merleau-Ponty and Heidegger to provide a description of the first-person experience of illness (2008). The book confronts the tendency of philosophy to work from a third-person perspective and criticizes the central debate in the philosophy of medicine, between those advancing a naturalistic value-free description of illness and those claiming that illness is fundamentally a social and normatively laden concept. Carel argues that this debate excludes the actual experience of illness, which is highly relevant to the concept of illness. She suggests augmenting this gap by providing a phenomenological account of the first-person experience of illness, examining the personal, social, physical, temporal and existential dimensions of illness.

The phenomenological approach is not limited to exploring the patient's lived experience of their illness. It can also be used to explore the experience of carers and family members, and the experience of health care professionals providing medical care (e.g. Raingruber & Kent 2003). The approach also has practical applications and uses, for example in teaching and training of medical and health care staff. Another application is the proposal to use phenomenology as a resource for patients. Carel (2012) has developed a patient toolkit, which uses phenomenological concepts such as thematization and being in the world to assist patients in making sense of their illness and providing a method for describing and ordering their experiences.

Recent years have seen a dramatic increase in the number of conferences, research projects and journal articles devoted to the phenomenology of illness, written by and for philosophers. This recent growth bodes well for this approach, which has so far been under-utilized in philosophy and in medical teaching and training. A number of chapters in this collection employ phenomenology to understand health and illness.

METAPHYSICS AND EPISTEMOLOGY OF MEDICINE

The chapters in this collection do not address issues in the metaphysics or epistemology of medicine. However, excellent work in these areas has been produced over the last few years. Among the issues currently being examined, a body of work examines how one might understand disease causation and the role of mechanisms in causation and explanation in medicine (e.g. Campaner 2011; Russo & Williamson 2007, 2011; Dragulinescu 2012). Other work focuses on philosophical problems associated with the ways in which medical knowledge is gained. Miriam Solomon has explored the epistemology behind medical consensus conferences, in which experts are brought together in an attempt to reach agreement about a particular treatment (2011). The methodologies employed in randomized controlled trials have been a particular focus of concern (see Worrall 2007 for an introduction to the problems involved). Other areas of medicine that have recently come under philosophical scrutiny include epidemiology (Broadbent 2009), medical ontology (Simon 2010), evidence-based medicine (Borgerson 2009) and placebos (Howick 2009). In all of these areas philosophical intervention has proved fruitful and a useful dialogue between philosophers and medical researchers and practitioners has developed.

Philosophers have illuminated methodological and conceptual issues in medicine, but recent challenges to medical practice and some of the norms underlying it have put into question some views in the philosophy of medicine. Here are a few of the recent developments.

CURRENT CHALLENGES TO PHILOSOPHY OF MEDICINE

Challenge 1 – disability studies and the rise of the social model of disability

Philosophers of medicine have largely ignored the growing body of work in disability studies and tend to treat disability as one variety of pathological condition that can be lumped under the umbrella term "disease", alongside diseases in the narrow sense, wounds, injuries, and so on (but exceptions include Amundson 1992; Kristiansen *et al.* 2009). A now-powerful tradition in disability studies opposes this move (Finkelstein 1980; Oliver 1990).

According to the social model of disability, disability should not be considered as being primarily a medical problem at all. On this model, a woman whose legs will not support her weight is disabled not by the deficiencies of her body but by the presence of stairs, which make wheelchair use cumbersome. If the built environment were changed so that ramps became more commonplace, the wheelchair user would no longer be disabled (indeed since wheelchairs are faster over certain surfaces than human legs, in certain environments humans who depend on their legs would be disabled). Associated with this model of disability is a demand that disability not be lumped together with medical conditions such as diseases and wounds. While those with diseases and injuries are thought to need medical help, those with disabilities are not considered legitimate targets of medical care; they merely require the removal of social and material barriers that make it harder to live well with differently abled bodies.

The social model of disability poses a direct challenge to much work in the philosophy of medicine. Philosophers of medicine have tended to treat disability as much of a muchness with medical conditions, and thus the insistence that it is different challenges the attempt to provide an umbrella concept of disease. The social model of disability also raises interesting philosophical questions: what does it mean to say that disability is "caused by" environmental barriers rather than the deficiencies of bodies? If disability is thought of through the social model, what are the implications for thinking about chronic illness and the infirmities of old age? These conditions shade into, or cause, disability, but at the same time they also shade into acute disorders that are paradigmatically the legitimate targets of medical care.

Challenge 2 – the rise of patient voices

Alongside the rise of the disability rights movement, patients with a wide range of conditions have become organized and now demand to have their views taken into account in medical and policy decisions. In some cases patients have quite different views of their conditions than do the health professionals who treat them. Consider chronic fatigue syndrome/myalgic encephalomyelitis (ME), for example. This condition is characterized by general fatigue and various pains. It has no known cause, and is often extremely debilitating, with some patients confined to their homes or even beds for years. Among health professionals the condition has, on occasion, been treated with suspicion; some have claimed that some patients are malingering or that the condition is psychosomatic. Patients groups, on the other hand, insist that the condition has an organic cause and lobby to have the genuineness of their disease status recognized (for further discussion of these debates, see R. Cooper in press). Such movements raise questions about the status of medical experts and medical knowledge versus patient expertise and patient knowledge. Insofar as the philosophy of medicine has tended to take for granted that the views of health professionals are authoritative, the patient rights movement challenges not only medicine but the philosophy of medicine also.

A case in point is the patient lobbying for fast-tracking approval for HIV drugs. The tension between the standard drug approval procedures (carried out by the US Food and Drug Administration) and the vociferous demand of lobby groups for "drugs in bodies" exploded in the late 1980s and has permanently changed the way in which medical expertise is perceived. Medical expertise and knowledge and medical judgement are no longer seen as objective, value-neutral and fact-based, but as embedded in a complex system of social perceptions, political pressures and conflicting demands of different stakeholders (Mukherjee 2011).

Challenge 3 – the expanding and changing domain of medicine

Much philosophy of medicine is written on the assumption that the primary aim of medical care is to deal with the acute disorders of otherwise healthy young adults. The assumption is that a disease afflicts a patient, interferes with their life for some time, and then, with luck and medical care, goes away. In such a world, the condition is taken to be well defined and understood, and the expertise unquestionably lies with the medical staff. The only question is the practical one: how best can we deal with the condition? Increasingly, however, the conditions that afflict us do not look much like such prototypical cases. Rather than treatable acute conditions, we suffer from conditions that are problematic in some way or other – we go to doctors with chronic problems, risk factors, addictions, genetic dispositions and conditions that may not be disorders at all. Conditions that are chronic raise different issues as patients become adept in their self-care, find ways of living (or even living well) with their impaired health and come to challenge the medical opinions that they are given.

Figuring out how to conceive of "risk factors" is also problematic. Those who are considered "at risk" fall into a grey area: they are neither clearly diseased nor clearly well, as Britta Pelters discusses in her chapter in this volume (Chapter 11). And yet much literature in the philosophy of medicine has taken health and disease to be exclusive and opposed concepts; that is, everyone is either diseased or healthy, and there is no room for in-between states (but see Nordenfelt in Chapter 1 of this volume for a contrasting view). Finally, increased medicalization of Western societies has led to the reconfiguring of various conditions that would previously have been considered "problems in living" as disorders. In recent decades, we have seen the impotence of male middle-age rebranded as "erectile dysfunction", fidgety children turned into the sufferers of attention deficit hyperactivity disorder (ADHD), and shyness transformed into social phobia. Such cases raise problems about the limits of disorder – are such states disorders or not?

Challenge 4 – critiques of medical expansion

As sociologists of medicine such as Peter Conrad have done so much to show, medicalization has diverse causes and consequences (Conrad 2007). When a problem becomes thought of as a medical problem this is taken to imply that health professionals should be the proper experts to treat it, and that the suffering individual should be treated for it rather than blamed. Medicalization increases the markets that are available for medical products, and correspondingly diminishes the domain of "ordinary human living" that people feel competent to deal with themselves. In some cases interest groups have worked to medicalize conditions. Sometimes health professionals gain status by developing new medical areas; sometimes suffering individuals (or their parents) lobby to have their conditions recognized as disorders and thus to be eligible for the legal and economic benefits that accompany a diagnosis of a bona fide disease. Much medicalization has been fuelled by the marketing campaigns of pharmaceutical companies. Those who wish to sell us drugs find it profitable to make us think that we are ill and need them, when we might otherwise think of ourselves as merely experiencing the ups and downs of a normal life. Thus drug companies fund research into new conditions (such as social phobia) in order to establish their legitimacy as medical afflictions and then fund "patient education programmes" that aim at increasing the perceived prevalence of the condition (Healy 1997).

While medicalization has broadened the medical domain into some areas, the influence of medicine has decreased in other areas. Homosexuality offers the clearest example of a condition that was once thought to be a medical disorder and is now considered a normal mode of sexuality. Other sexual preferences and acts that were traditionally considered "perversions" to be treated by health professionals are now widely seen as non-pathological. Examples include cross-dressing, trans-sexualism and sexual promiscuity. The rise of disability rights movements has also led to questioning as to whether certain states are pathological or merely testament to the normal variety of human life. When it comes to conditions such as dwarfism, deafness or intersexuality, prominent voices claim that there is no medical problem at all; such persons are not ill, but merely differently normal. Feminists, too, have lobbied with some success for "women's problems" to be taken outside the domain of medicine. Many now assert that birth and menopause are not in themselves medical problems and should not come under the control of the medicine establishment, unless such control is explicitly sought.

Medical expansion is not only challenged by various rights movements, but is also increasingly limited by a shortage of funds. In recent decades the percentage of national wealth spent on medical care has risen by unsustainable levels in all developed countries (Organisation for Economic Co-operation and Development 2011). Continuing to increase spending at these rates is impossible, and in areas experiencing financial difficulties, cuts in health spending will prove necessary. Seeking to place firmer boundaries between the "deserving disordered" and those whose problems should not be deemed to be disorders is partly motivated by the need to ration health care and control health spending.

The increased understanding of the engines of medicalization and de-medicalization poses a challenge for much work in the philosophy of medicine. Philosophers of medicine have tended to test proposed accounts of disease against our intuitions regarding various conditions. They have sought an account that classifies conditions we consider to be diseases as diseases, and classifies those states we think of as non-pathological as normal. This method only makes sense if we think that our intuitions are trustworthy. Insofar as shifts in the perceived disease status of various states can be shown to be a consequence of marketing campaigns and lobbying, the use of such philosophical methods is thrown into serious doubt. If our intuitions are shaped, at least in part, by market forces, advertising, pressure groups, campaigns and the media, why should we trust these intuitions to uncover the true meaning of the terms "disease" and "health"? Future work in the philosophy of medicine must thus seek to be more sensitive to the findings of those who study medicine using the social sciences.

With key debates in the philosophy of medicine to date explained, let us now turn to the chapters included in the collection.

AN OVERVIEW OF THE CHAPTERS

We have split the chapters into three parts, with four chapters in each part. Part I explores the concepts of health and disease, Part II focuses on the experience of illness, and Part III examines the tensions and connections between ill health and society. Here is an overview of the chapters in this collection.

Part I: Concepts of health and disease

The volume opens with a contribution from Lennart Nordenfelt, who developed a holistic account of disease. In his chapter, Nordenfelt makes clear the important differences between his and Boorse's account. He then goes on to consider possible worries for each. A major worry for Boorse's account is that it links the notion of disease too closely to an organism's survival. An advantage of the holistic account, Nordenfelt thinks, is that diseases can manifest themselves via interfering with our achieving any number of important goals apart from merely staying alive. Nordenfelt then goes on to consider some objections that are commonly raised against the holistic account and shows how he can respond adequately to them. Concerns that Nordenfelt deals with are that the holistic account makes the concept of disease too expansive; that it cannot deal with the problematic test cases of grief and pregnancy; and that it struggles to account for animal and plant diseases. Nordenfelt concludes that the holistic account remains at least as promising as Boorse's account of disease.

In Chapter 2 Elselijn Kingma argues against the dominant approach, which has seen naturalist and normativist accounts of disease as being opposed to each other. Kingma argues that the supposed opposition between naturalist and normativist accounts of disease has been over-emphasized. As she points out, even Boorse, the paradigmatic naturalist, allows that when it comes to practical matters such as deciding who to treat, values are important (Boorse holds that "disease" is a purely value-free concept, and holds that some of the diseased may be happy and thus not need treatment). Kingma uses Ian Hacking's work on social construction to show how social constructivism can be used to provide a way of combining key insights from both the naturalist and normativist analyses of disease (Hacking 1999). Following Hacking, Kingma characterizes the social constructivist as insisting that the concepts we employ are historically contingent. Both normativism and naturalism about health and disease are consistent with this claim. The normativist can insist that values play a role in explaining why we have the concepts of health and disease that we do. At the same time the naturalist can insist that the categories that we employ reflect a natural structure and can be described in value-free terms. Kingma concludes that a long-standing debate in the philosophy of medicine is something of a red herring – we should not see naturalism and normativism as being opposed. Furthermore, social constructivist accounts of health and disease potentially offer an attractive way of thinking about these concepts and should be developed further.

To a great extent work on concepts of health and disease, and work in bioethics, have developed independently. In Chapter 3, Antonio Casado da Rocha and Arantza Etxeberria show that this is a mistake. In particular they focus on the *principlist* approach to bioethics that has held that ethical decision-making in medicine should aim to respect the principles of beneficence, non-maleficence, justice and respect for autonomy. Casado da Rocha and Etxeberria argue that a major problem with this approach is that it has ignored the fact that patients suffer from illnesses and are therefore in a very different situation to those who do not. In particular, the discussion of the importance of autonomy in bioethics has proceeded as if the autonomy of patients was like the autonomy of healthy people. This is a problem, as ill people may feel poorly and be vulnerable in ways that make modelling their decision-making on that of healthy autonomous agents problematic, and a richer notion of autonomy must be developed for bioethics. Casado da Rocha and Etxeberria argue that reflecting on what it means to be diseased, ill or sick will enable a richer understanding of the principles of medical ethics.

In developing accounts of disease, philosophers working in the Anglo-American tradition have tended to rely on the method of conceptual analysis. The standard approach has been to develop an account of disease and then to test it against intuitions about how particular conditions should be classified. For example, homosexuality, pregnancy and early-stage symptomless cancer have regularly featured as test cases. The reason for using such test cases is the view that an adequate account of disease should correctly classify homosexuality and pregnancy as non-pathological, and symptomless cancer as pathological. In Chapter 4, Valérie Aucouturier and Steeves Demazeux show that different views of conceptual analysis have been employed by different philosophers, and that at least some proposed uses of conceptual analysis are problematic as they depend on mistaken views about language. The chapter then goes on to consider a further problem. Those who have used conceptual analysis have tended to work within the Anglo-American analytic tradition of philosophy, a tradition that is famously insensitive to the nuances of history and context. The working assumption has been that conceptual analysis is a method that can be expected to yield the same results regardless of the context in which a philosopher is working. Using a historical review of philosophical and psychiatric work aimed at defining and analysing "mental disorder" in a period stretching from the 1970s to the 1990s, Aucouturier and Demazeux show that it is more plausibly the case that accounts of disorder have developed in ways that are responsive to the concerns of particular historical moments. They conclude that those who would use conceptual analysis would do better to be more sensitive to the historical and political context in which they are working.

Part II: The experience of illness

A useful philosophical method for the study of the experience of illness is phenomenology. In Chapter 5, Fredrik Svenaeus presents this method and its usefulness for understanding the experience of illness as it is lived by the ill person. He begins with an overview of phenomenology, which he defines as seeking the foundations of ontological and epistemological questions by returning to lived experience. The starting point for phenomenology is not the world of science but the meaning structures of the everyday world, what the phenomenologist calls the "life world". Thus a phenomenological view of medicine may see it as a meeting of health professional and patient in an interpretative attempt to help and treat the ill and suffering one. Svenaeus provides an account of illness using phenomenological ideas such as the centrality of embodiment to human experience, the rejection of mind–body dualism and the importance of the first-person perspective. His particular account of illness sees it as "being not at home", or an experience of uncanniness. In illness, he claims, the homelike feeling of health, which is transparent and taken for granted, is replaced by a feeling of disorientation and being not at home. On this view, the role of medicine is to help the ill person find their way back to a feeling of belonging to a world, a homelike feeling.

In Chapter 6, Angela Woods critically examines Arthur Frank's account of illness narratives as emblematic of the enthusiastic adoption of narrative as core to illness experience by some of those working in medical humanities. She suggests that this positive embrace of narrative as pivotal to the project of (re)humanizing medicine should be tempered by a more critical view of narrativity. Using Galen Strawson's article "Against Narrativity", she argues that it is not at all obvious that we are "narrative selves" and that the best or most healthy way to respond to illness is through narrative. However, Woods also discusses the limitations of Strawson's approach that can be revealed by taking a phenomenological stance. She concludes by suggesting that alternative approaches to narrative medicine, such as phenomenology, may be useful for understanding the experience of illness. Woods finally proposes that a closer look not at narrative but at its opposite, silence, may also provide an alternative to the emphasis on narrative in medical humanities.

James Brennan is a clinical psychologist specializing in providing support for cancer patients. In Chapter 7, he uses quotations from patients who kept diaries as part of their therapy to explore the meaning of the transition from health to illness, and (sometimes) back to health again, for the ill person. Brennan develops a model of adjustment that accounts for both positive and negative responses to major life transitions such as illness and recovery. He argues that the transition from health to illness is not captured merely in the direct physical effects of disease and its treatment, but in the threat they pose and the havoc they cause to people's lives. This can be explained by seeing illness as a radically new situation, which our most deep-seated assumptions fail to adequately make sense of, leaving us disoriented, afraid and potentially traumatized. Adjustment involves reorienting our assumptions and such a successful reorientation may result in a feeling of well-being, even though the disease itself has not been resolved.

Pain is a unique medical phenomenon and a fascinating philosophical topic. First, it is severely debilitating and undoubtedly harmful to the person feeling it. As a medical symptom, it relies almost entirely on first-person reports and is therefore often considered to be entirely subjective. In philosophy, the feeling of pain has often been taken to be a paradigmatic case of something that cannot be doubted, of certainty (Wittgenstein 1974). Elaine Scarry contrasts the experience of pain, which gives us absolute certainty (it makes no sense to ask someone in pain how they know, or whether they are certain, that they feel pain), with the experience of witnessing pain, which gives absolute uncertainty (the person may be an actor, or might be faking her pain behaviour; Scarry 1985). This gives rise to some interesting problems in the medical understanding of pain as a disease. In Chapter 8 Elisa Arnaudo provides an overview of the medical attempts to define, categorize and understand pain as a medical phenomenon. She explores the medical framework within which pain was understood, and contrasts it with the complexity of pain. Arnaudo discusses the variable relationship between stimulus and pain perception, and highlights the contribution of psychological factors to pain perception. She describes the difficulties facing those charged with finding a definition of pain, given its highly subjective and variable nature. Arnaudo also criticizes the problematic understanding of chronic pain as a disease, particularly in relation to individual accountability in maintaining pain behaviour when psychological factors are judged to play a role in the persistence of pain.

Part III: Illness and society

Intersex people have ambiguous sexual characteristics. They may have genitalia that do not match their chromosomes, or external genitalia that are neither distinctively male nor female. In Chapter 9, Melanie Newbould argues that medical treatment has developed on the assumption that when an infant is born who is neither clearly male nor female this is a medical problem that needs medical treatment (e.g. via the use of hormones and surgery). Newbould points out that it is not clear that intersex conditions have to be conceived of as medically pathological. In themselves, intersex conditions do not cause suffering or death (although sometimes intersex conditions do occur as part of syndromes with negative effects on health) and intersex people may be happy as they are. Normally we think of medicine as aiming to offer interventions for conditions that are independently considered to be in need of treatment, but Newbould argues that in the case of intersex conditions this relationship has often been reversed. Rather than treating a pre-existing problem, medical practices have sometimes constructed intersex conditions as pathological. Newbould's argument echoes views that have been recently been voiced regarding many other conditions (e.g. Amundson 2000). Not only intersex conditions, but conditions such as Asperger's syndrome, dwarfism and deafness might be better thought of as types of normal human variation rather than pathological states requiring medical care.

Despite educational campaigns, depression remains widely stigmatized. Both onlookers and depressed people themselves tend to doubt that depression is a legitimate illness, and often suspect that it is some sort of character flaw or malingering. In Chapter 10 Charlotte Blease aims to provide an explanation for the deep-seated nature of this stigmatization. She suggests that the thinking of lay people can in many cases be thought of as analogous to the thinking of scientists. In Thomas Kuhn's (1962) famous account of the structure of scientific change, scientific communities are highly resistant to the acceptance of anomalies (i.e. phenomena that their favoured theory struggles to accommodate). Blease argues that lay people also tend to cling to their (lay) theory of the world, and respond to challenges to their view by dismissing evidence that does not fit their theory. Blease says that a central component of our worldview is the belief that the world is largely benevolent and that the self is competent. Depression poses a problem for this view, because the depressed expressly deny these two beliefs and behave in ways that do not fit them. In an attempt to maintain our positive worldview despite this evidence, we seek to deny the plausibility and acceptability of the depressed worldview. This is done by either downplaying the suffering caused by depression ("it's not so bad, she's just seeking attention") or by arguing that the patient is somehow responsible for their condition ("she needs to pull herself together"). Blease contends that, like scientists, the "folk" attempt to ignore or reinterpret anomalous data, and this explains the deep-seated roots of the stigma of depression and why this stigma has been so resistant to public education campaigns.

So far we have touched upon health and disease concepts. However, how do we classify someone who is neither healthy nor diseased? For example, someone who carries a gene that disposes them to develop a certain disease may be offered medical counselling, frequent screening and particular tests that are not offered to non-risk groups. This seems to indicate that those who carry the gene may be considered different to those who do not. But how does this difference play itself out in an individual's health-related self-definitions? In Chapter 11 Britta Pelters examines the case of women who are BRCA-positive (BRCA includes two genes, BRCA1 and BRCA2, associated with hereditary breast and ovarian cancer). How do these women conceive of themselves? Do they think of themselves as healthy or diseased, or perhaps both? Notions of "the healthy sick" and of "the perpetual patient" have been developed to address this issue. Pelters uses this case study to demonstrate the shortcomings of Boorse's biostatistical theory of disease, as well as holistic theories of health, such as Nordenfelt's. She then proposes a constructivist approach to health, which refrains from using an external marker for the evaluation of health, considers health as an embedded concept, and favours a personal view of health.

In Chapter 12, Sophia Efsathiou examines the complex interplay between concepts of health and beauty in Nazi Germany. Efsathiou shows how the Nazis portrayed those they considered to be threats to the racial health of the German people – the mentally ill, the disabled, Jews and other groups – as ugly. Through invoking feelings of disgust, such people were dehumanized and their brutal treatment legitimized for those exposed to this propaganda. At the same time, healthy Aryan bodies were portrayed as beautiful and many purportedly progressive (if piecemeal) public health policies were put into place. Through her historical case study Efsathiou shows how difficult it can be to disentangle our concepts of health and beauty, and also how dangerous this entanglement can be. Her argument remains relevant. It is still the case that in much current thinking health and beauty tend to be equated. Public health campaigns present diseases as being ugly; consider the images of smokers' lungs that have been used in anti-smoking campaigns, for example. Disabled bodies have only recently been considered fit subjects for art. Figuring out whether and how concepts of health and beauty can be kept apart remains a challenge.

PART I
CONCEPTS OF HEALTH AND DISEASE

1. THE OPPOSITION BETWEEN NATURALISTIC AND HOLISTIC THEORIES OF HEALTH AND DISEASE

Lennart Nordenfelt

INTRODUCTION: TWO THEORIES OF HEALTH

A central problem in the philosophy of health is to adequately characterize the notions of health and disease and at the same time to establish the nature of the relation between these notions. Are the two notions completely tied to each other, so that health is the total absence of disease, or is there a much looser connection? Is health something over and above the absence of disease? Is health even compatible with the existence of disease?

We seem to have varying intuitions in this regard. We seem also inclined to interpret health slightly differently in different contexts. I have discussed these issues in earlier publications (Nordenfelt 1987/1995, 2000, 2001, 2007). In this chapter I wish to continue this discussion by raising some crucial points that have recently come to the fore. I will advance and scrutinize certain arguments for and against some central current theories in the philosophy of health. In order to do this I have to present these theories as clearly and concisely as I can.

I will present two theories of health: a biostatistical theory of health (BST) and a holistic theory of health (HTH). The clearest version of the BST has been proposed by the American philosopher Christopher Boorse, first in 1977 and later in a more developed presentation in 1997. The HTH has appeared in several versions, presented by authors such as Caroline Whitbeck (1981), Ingmar Pörn (1993), K. W. M Fulford (1989) and myself (1987/1995). The theory of Fredrik Svenaeus (2000b) has strong affinities to the HTH but does not have the same emphasis on the notion of ability. In order to simplify matters for my present purpose I will present my own version of the HTH.

Observe that my formulations in the following are not direct quotations. This holds in particular for my presentation of the BST. I have chosen to reformulate the ideas somewhat (keeping the semantic content intact) in order to see more easily the similarities and differences between the two types of theories.

Christopher Boorse's BST (1977; 1997) can be formulated in the following way:

> A is completely healthy if, and only if, all organs of A function normally, i.e. if they, given a statistically normal environment, make at least their statistically normal contribution to the survival of A or the reproduction of A.

The concept of *disease* in the BST can be formulated in the following way:

> A has a disease if, and only if, there is at least one organ or other part of A that functions subnormally (i.e. does not make its statistically normal contribution to the survival or the reproduction of A) given a statistically normal environment. The disease is identical with the subnormal functioning of the organ or other part.

Observe that the term "disease" is here used in an inclusive sense, covering also injuries and defects. Some authors prefer the term "malady" for this generic concept.)

The characterization of health given in my version of the HTH (1987/1995; 2001) is the following:

> A is completely healthy if, and only if, A is in a bodily and mental state such that A has the ability, given standard or otherwise reasonable circumstances, to realize all his or her vital goals.

The concept of disease (or malady) given in my version of the HTH is:

> A has a disease if, and only if, A has at least one organ or other bodily part that is involved in such a state or process as tends to reduce the health of A. The disease is identical with the state or process itself.[1]

Let me make three brief comments on these latter definitions. First, observe that the criterion of health is compound in the following sense. Health is not *identical with* a certain kind of ability. The criterion says: A is in a *bodily and mental state* which is such that A has an ability to realize vital goals. For instance, A's physiological condition is adequate and A is feeling well, and thus A is able to realize his or her vital goals. Second, "vital goal" is a technical concept in the sense that people's vital goals are not completely identical with their intentionally chosen goals. The class of a person's vital goals is the class of conditions that are such that the fulfilment of them is necessary for the person's long term minimal happiness. Thus all people, including babies, persons with dementia and others who do not consciously set any goals in life, have vital goals. Third, the phrase "tends to reduce the health of A" is selected because not all diseases actually do compromise health in the holistic sense of being able to realize vital goals. Some diseases are aborted; that is, they disappear before they have influenced the person as a whole. Others are latent; yet others are so trivial that they are never recognized by their bearer (for comprehensive discussions of all these conditions, see Nordenfelt 1987/1995 and, in particular, 2001).

The presented versions of the BST and the HTH are clearly quite different theories of health. The differences can be summarized thus:

(a) In the BST health is exclusively a function of internal processes in the human body or mind and their relation to reproduction and survival. In the HTH health is a function of a person's abilities to perform intentional actions and achieve goals.
(b) In the BST health is a concept to be defined solely in biological (or perhaps also psychological) and statistical terms. In the HTH the concept of health presupposes extra-biological concepts such as "person", "intentional action" and "cultural standard".
(c) In the BST health is identical with the absence of disease. In the HTH health is compatible with the presence of disease. The concept of disease is, however, logically related to the concept of ill health also according to the HTH. A disease is defined as a state or process that tends to negatively affect its bearer's health.

My procedure in the following will involve advancing some critical arguments against both these basic positions in the philosophy of health. My arguments will mainly be directed against the HTH. This means that I will put my own view of health and disease to severe tests; that is, I will perform a piece of self-criticism in the Popperian sense. However, I will first raise a criticism against the BST with regard to its criterion of survival. I consider it counterintuitive to connect the concept of health so completely to the concept of survival. Second, I will raise a criticism against the HTH to the effect that its concept of health is too expansive. Third, I will discuss two conditions whose status as diseases has been disputed and briefly analyse how the HTH can handle these disputed cases. Fourth, I will discuss the relationship between human and animal health and illness. It is often maintained that the BST is the only viable theory of the two when it comes to characterizing the health and disease of non-human animals. Finally I will conclude that the HTH in my version can satisfactorily answer these criticisms.

ON PROBABILITY OF SURVIVAL AS A KEY CRITERION OF HEALTH: A CRITICISM OF THE BST CONCEPT OF DISEASE

In the BST definition, a disease is constituted by the subnormal function of an organ or some other bodily part. This entails that the organ or bodily part in question does not make its statistically normal contribution, given a statistically normal environment, to the survival of the individual or the species (for the sake of simplicity I will here only discuss the case of the survival of the individual).

It is not altogether easy to interpret this criterion. And in particular it is not easy to measure it. How do we know that a certain organ does not contribute to survival with statistically normal efficiency? It is clearly not sufficient to say – and this is a common misunderstanding of the BST – that the function of the organ happens to fall outside a statistically normal scope. The pulse of an athlete, for instance, can be abnormally low, say thirty-five beats per minute. His or her pulse is then well below the normal frequency scope, which lies between sixty and eighty beats a minute. However, we would clearly say that the function of the athlete's heart is perfect. The function is indeed supernormal in that, as we believe, it makes more than a normal contribution to the survival of its bearer.

I will here leave the problem of measurement aside and in my discussion use the following interpretation of the BST analysis of disease. I will propose that a person who has a disease has a slightly lower probability of survival than the completely healthy person. Through the dysfunction it involves, the disease lowers the probability of the bearer's survival. Of course, this does not mean that every instance of a disease is life-threatening. It can only mean that there is a marginal reduction of the bearer's probability of survival (for the sake of simplicity I leave out the criterion of reproduction here).

The traditional understanding of this idea is that a disease reduces the probability of survival solely via the body's physiology and biochemistry. Through the dysfunction of the organ in question the function of the whole body (or mind) is becoming weaker. As a result the body (or mind) becomes vulnerable to more fatal processes that in the end might lead to premature death. Many diseases (in particular infections, but also cardiovascular diseases and endocrine diseases) have such known complications. A mild infection can develop into serious meningitis or a general sepsis that may be fatal. Angina may develop into a myocardial infarction, diabetes may give rise to a stroke, and so on. Such examples, then, give the basic idea concerning probability of survival some plausibility.

It seems, however, much less plausible to generalize this intuition to cover all kinds of such diseases as are conventionally accepted as such. Not all diseases, in particular not the ordinary trivial ones like headache or eczema, or injuries like a bruised leg, really lower the probability of survival. And, if so, in what terms could we understand such a probability?

What seems to be universal, and that is exactly what the HTH claims, is that there exists, with all diseases, the probability of certain phenomenological consequences or some limitation of agency. Persons who have a disease are often ill, in the sense of having negative sensations. They do not feel "at home" (to put it as Fredrik Svenaeus does; Svenaeus 2000b), or are disabled. It is true that some people having a disease do not *yet* have any negative symptoms. On the other hand, it is plausible to say that there is a high risk of their having such symptoms. If there is no risk of suffering or disability at all, it is legitimate to ask what reason there would be for calling the state a disease in the first place.

It seems therefore that we have come up with a reasonable criticism of the basic BST idea of connecting disease to reduced probability of survival. On the other hand there is a point to make here and to be explored in defence of the BST along the following lines. (As far as I know, however, neither Christopher Boorse nor anyone else in the BST camp has ever in fact made this point.) The BST protagonist might claim that a disease always lowers the probability of survival but *not necessarily directly* by making the body (or mind) vulnerable to other, fatal, biological or mental processes. The disease may lower the probability of survival by *disabling* the person. Persons who are disabled in vital respects (being blind, deaf or partly paralysed, to take some extreme examples) have difficulty in finding their way and supporting themselves. They may require assistance in order to move around or indeed to obtain such basic commodities as food and shelter. Moreover, they are more vulnerable to accidents of various kinds than if they had been healthy.

One might maintain that this argument also holds for mild diseases such as the common cold. Although the cold in itself may be mild in its disabling consequences, it still often prevents its bearers from performing their normal tasks to some extent. Such consequences entail some, although often very slight, reduction in the probability of survival of these persons, according to the argument I am expounding. Hence there seems to be a case for maintaining that all diseases (or all maladies) increase the probability of death, as the BST maintains.

But again, it is highly debatable whether this is a universal phenomenon. There are many diseases, in particular if we move outside the somatic sector, which have no known fatal complications and which need not in any other sense increase the risk of death. For instance persons with a mild paranoia have a disease, because they are prevented from living a well-balanced life and fulfilling much of their potential. On the other hand these persons may – indeed *because of* the disease – be highly alerted to risks and thereby become quite careful persons who in a sense have a higher survival potential than ordinary healthy persons.

My conclusion is therefore that even if we improve the arguments of the BST, and include disability among the potential causal factors of death, we cannot satisfactorily sustain the BST concept of disease in this regard.

ON THE SCOPE OF THE CONCEPT OF HEALTH ACCORDING TO THE HTH AND THE BST: THE RISK OF TOO EXPANSIVE A CONCEPT OF HEALTH ACCORDING TO THE HTH

It is frequently claimed that a holistic concept of health such as that of the HTH (also in my version of it) risks being too inclusive and vague. Or, to be more specific, the most acute risk is that the converse concept, ill-health, will include too much. If every person who is somewhat disabled in relation to his or her vital goals turns out to be ill according to the HTH conception, then we might come up with too many sick-listed persons. The HTH concept of health would then turn out to be unreasonable and of little practical use in health care. (I may mention that I have caused worry during two conferences on insurance medicine in Europe where many persons in the audience interpreted my presentations as opening the floodgates and letting in altogether too many conditions among diseases or maladies.)

An interesting version of this criticism has been put forward by the German philosopher Thomas Schramme (2007). He formulates the following crucial purpose for a fruitful theory of health: it should be able to function as a gatekeeper against medicalization. Schramme claims that Boorse's biostatistical theory of health fulfils this purpose whereas mine doesn't. For example Schramme says the following:

> Consider Lily, an athlete, who struggles, for her whole adult life so far, to become an accomplished high-jumper, but does not succeed ...We may agree that it is one of Lily's vital goals to succeed, because not to succeed means that she is not minimally happy but actually quite angry and sad ... Lily is unable to realize at least one vital goal, therefore she is not healthy according to Nordenfelt's definition. (Schramme 2007: 14)

Schramme says that we certainly would not call Lily unhealthy in this case. We would only do so if she really suffered from a disease in the ordinary sense of the word. The consequence of the HTH is thus, he says, counterintuitive.

I have already in a reply to my critics (Nordenfelt 2007) given an answer to this argument and I wish now to develop it further. I say first that Schramme presupposes that I consider the concepts of health and illness to be contradictory in the strong sense that wherever we do not have complete health we have some degree of illness. In fact, for me health is a dimension ranging from a state of complete health to a state of complete illness. So, when Lily does not achieve what she has striven for so intensely – and this goal qualifies as a vital goal in my sense – the assessment is not automatically, I claim, that she is ill in the sense that her state of health is on the negative half of the scale. The result is only that Lily's health is somewhat reduced. Her health is probably in general very good since she is capable of achieving most or all of her other vital goals.

I think it is reasonable to claim that Lily's health is somewhat reduced, but that does not necessarily entail that she has a disease or that there is reason for her to seek ordinary health care. The "cure" for her reduced health might instead be that she attempts to set more realistic goals for herself.

My answer to Schramme also entails a rebuttal of the biostatistical theory as an adequate one in this regard. I claim that the BST risks including too little. If we require that there is a disease in the biostatistical sense (that is, a specific bodily or mental state that causes a subnormal function in relation to survival) to claim that a person has reduced health or in order to characterize this person as ill, then one can wonder about the future for many people who are now normally (and I think legitimately) sick-listed. In many of these cases we cannot detect any biological (nor any obviously mental) malfunction in the BST sense. Should we say that these people do not (or should not) come within the scope of medicine or psychiatry?

The HTH is clearly capable of handling such cases more easily than the BST. First, it does not, as I have said above, relate disease to the bearer's probability of survival. But the HTH can also talk about ill-health without invoking the notion of disease. According to the HTH a person with burnt-out syndrome is clearly ill without there necessarily being a specific somatic or, for that matter, mental condition behind the syndrome that we should be inclined to call a disease. So, to repeat, according to the HTH there can be reduced health and thereby ill-health without disease.

TWO TEST CASES: GRIEF AND PREGNANCY

I will now consider two conditions that are sometimes considered to be test cases for the different proposals of health and disease definitions, namely the conditions of deep grief and pregnancy. Does either of these conditions emerge as a disease according to the different theories? And if so, is this an argument for saying that such a theory is deficient? The argument sounds particularly plausible with regard to the HTH, and I shall here limit myself to discussing it in that regard.

Grief and pregnancy have continuously been crucial cases in the context of insurance medicine. People have questioned whether it is reasonable to sick-list and pay benefits to persons just because they grieve at the loss of a close relative, for instance. Similarly, should a doctor sick-list a woman who is pregnant and who at some stage of the pregnancy feels nauseous and is incapable of working? Does the pregnant woman have a disease? We know that the authorities in some countries, including my own country (Sweden), have from time to time regarded persons in such circumstances as ill and thereby eligible for state benefits, but they have often also expressed unease about this. In Sweden we are now in a political situation where it is much more difficult than previously to label persons in these conditions as having a disease (there is a proposal that they be covered by other kinds of insurance but not under the disease label; SOU 2009).

On the other hand it seems to be a fact that many persons in deep grief suffer and are often incapable of doing much. They normally stay at home and are absent from their workplace, at least for a short time. Likewise a pregnant woman may, in the early phases of pregnancy, feel quite nauseous and be prevented from doing any work. And, in particular towards the end of the pregnancy, she may be in pain or have other symptoms that are highly disabling.

Persons in these conditions therefore seem to fulfil the criteria of being unhealthy according to the HTH. Such people, it may be claimed, are incapable of realizing their vital goals. Should the HTH then also say that grief *in itself* and pregnancy *in itself* are diseases? And is this not a *reductio ad absurdum* – that is, a fatal blow to the whole theory?

Before giving an answer let me qualify the underlying critical argument somewhat. The argument does not have as much force as it may initially seem to have. Consider first grief. It is simply not true that all persons in deep grief are highly disabled. Although it is true that grieving persons typically abstain from taking part in ordinary social life, including going to work, this is more the result of a decision than of pure disability. Persons who grieve at the loss of a close relative typically *choose* to withdraw from their daily affairs, either in order to pay respect to the deceased person or to reconsider their future life. In a standard sense of the word "ability" the typical grieving persons are still able to perform their normal duties. We also consider the grieving person's choice to withdraw from the world for a brief period to be very reasonable and I think it should be supported in one way or the other by the state's insurance authorities.

It is a different matter that grief may in some cases, or even frequently, turn into something else. There are indeed grieving persons who literally *cannot* go to work. They may be so overwhelmed by their personal catastrophe that they become disabled. And this may be a condition that lasts for a long time. In such cases we might be inclined to say that grief has turned into something different, namely depression. And depression is also conventionally understood as a disease, or rather an illness. Whether it qualifies as a disease in the BST sense is less clear (see my observations above regarding diseases as increasing the probability of death).

Similar reasoning can be proposed for pregnancy. Ordinary pregnancy is certainly not a disease, either conventionally or according to either of the types of theory. Ordinary pregnancy does not entail suffering or disability. On the contrary, pregnancy is normally a state that has been chosen for the sake of realizing a goal that is vital for most people, namely having a baby. Therefore we must be talking about special complications of pregnancy. Among these are the nausea that is related to the early stage of pregnancy and symphysiolysis, which can occur in the later stages. These can be highly disabling conditions and they involve a lot of pain and discomfort. But again, such conditions are accepted as pathological conditions, or at least should be so, in conventional medicine and thus when they emerge as maladies according to the HTH this is in line with both ordinary and medical intuitions.

However, I don't think my answers are entirely satisfactory, in particular as regards grief. It seems as if there are grieving persons who are, for a period of time, indeed suffering and are highly disabled, without deserving the label of depression. I think we should acknowledge this fact and look upon such cases of grief as genuine exceptions to the general characterization of disease and illness. The interesting question then is: why should disabling grief (that is, not genuine depression) be considered as such an exception? I think there is a plausible answer to this, which I have suggested already in my book *On the Nature of Health* (1987/1995: 112–17).

Grief is an emotion, and emotions, including negative ones, are sometimes, as we say, *adequate* and *justified*. When we grieve at the loss of a close relative we have an emotion that we *should* have. It is highly morally justified or even morally commendable to feel grief in such a situation. Similarly it is highly morally justified and morally commendable to feel happiness at the success of a loved one.

In fact it is, or should be, included in our moral training to acquire some emotional sensitivity, that is, a disposition for experiencing both positive and negative emotions. Thus it should be included in a young person's moral training to become disposed to certain negative emotions in certain kinds of circumstances, for instance feeling deep grief at tragic personal events. And deep grief normally involves a certain amount of suffering and disability.

There are no similar circumstances surrounding the paradigm cases of diseases and illnesses. We do not train ourselves for "pathological sensitivity" in a sense similar to the training for emotional sensitivity. And most importantly, there is no moral obligation for such training. Hence grief and certain other negative emotions, when they are adequate responses to tragic situations, should not, although they are disabling, be classified as diseases or illnesses.

ON ANIMAL AND HUMAN HEALTH

I turn now to my final case. It could be argued that the HTH is basically a theory of *human* health. As I have noted, the holists have introduced notions and arguments that are particularly applicable to human conditions. All my examples so far have concerned humans who suffer or are disabled. On the other hand the notions of health and disease are used also with regard to the lives of non-human animals and even plants. It is also obvious that there is some connection between our ordinary uses of the terms "health" and "disease" across all living domains. The illness of a person and the illness of a dog, for example, are considered to be similar phenomena.

From this point of view the BST seems to have a clear advantage as a theory the crucial notions of which – the ones that deal with survival of the individual and the species – easily cover the whole domain of animals and plants. Therefore, within the BST, health and disease can be defined according to the same formula across the whole living world. It seems more dubious, however, to say that holistic notions such as feelings, actions and intended goals can be attributed to all kinds of animals. Is this then a salient weakness in the holistic theories of health and disease?

I will briefly argue here that the HTH (at least when slightly generalized) is applicable – in some respects even more so than the BST – in the analysis of the concept of health in respect of animals. I will argue for this thesis in some detail for the case of higher-level animals, but I will also suggest how the further reasoning can be performed with regard to lower-level animals (a more full-fledged discussion is to be found in my book *Animal and Human Health and Welfare*, 2006).

A first crucial difference between humans and animals, which may constitute a problem for the HTH, is the following. There is in the case of animals, even higher-level animals, no subject that can consciously present a problem using a language like the human one. Moreover, there is no animal subject that by itself approaches a doctor and explains what the problem is. Can a holistic concept of illness, then, be used at all in the animal context?

It is true that most animals (as far as we understand) do not embrace a full-fledged language. On the other hand, most other elements present in the human story of illness can be present in a parallel animal story. All animals can have problems. Many of them, I wish to argue, can suffer and can express their suffering. In their wordless way they can ask for help. If the animals in question are in close contact with humans, which is the case with pets and livestock, the humans can interpret the call for help and can try to respond to it.

I have argued with regard to the human case that it is unreasonable to define disease or pathology simply in terms of malfunction in relation to survival and reproduction. I think the case is similar on the animal side. Animals, like humans, can be ill without there being any obvious threat to survival and reproduction. They can be ill in the sense that they feel malaise and have a reduced capacity, as humans can. We can easily observe when our pet dog is not feeling well, when it drags its tail or even whines in pain. A horse can have a disease that reduces its capacity to run in a race. This is a reduction in relation to a goal, but this goal is not identical with the survival of the horse.

But can we make this move as easily as this? Can we substantiate the claim that animals have feelings? Can animals suffer? This is a complex story. There are still a few animal scientists who doubt the possibility of animal feelings altogether (Barnard & Hurst 1996). On the other hand the overwhelming majority of veterinarians and animal scientists base their whole work on the presupposition that many animals can feel pain, nausea and fatigue in much the same way as humans. Why should there otherwise be so much concern about animal welfare (Dawkins 1990; Duncan 1996)?

But can animals feel anything but simple sensations? Is there any point in introducing the more complex vocabulary of feelings? Common sense certainly points in this direction. My dog can clearly show deep affection to myself and my family. This is an emotion of love or friendship. My dog can show a high degree of expectation and hope when I move towards the door, and thereby indicate that I may be going out for a walk. And certainly my dog can be sad and depressed about the fact that I am leaving home and abandoning him for a while.

Moreover, these common-sense conceptions of the diversity of feelings of animals are substantially supported by specialists in animal science. Donald Broom (1998) is one of the animal scientists who have systematically characterized a variety of complex animal feelings, including both emotions and moods. Broom discusses in some detail the emotions of fear, grief, frustration and guilt in animals. He notes that fear is an extremely common emotion in vertebrates, one that has an obvious role in the animal's coping process. Concerning grief, Broom notes that there are many reports of pets, especially dogs and monkeys that show the same sort of behaviour that humans show in such circumstances.

One may seriously doubt, however, that all animals have cognitions, sensations and emotions. What about worms, cuttlefish and indeed amoebae? Although I think that they must all have some minimal perception (i.e. some mechanism to get information from the outside), it is probably true that the most primitive ones lack most other mental properties. For one thing they have only a rudimentary neurological system or, in the case of amoebae, none at all. But such an observation is a problem only to those holistic theorists who base their idea of illness *totally* on suffering. Higher animals may suffer, but not all animals do. A theory of health and illness regarding these lower-level animals cannot depend, then, on the notion of suffering or on the general feeling of not being at home.

A holistic theory like the HTH, which is primarily based on abilities, would then be in a better position to cover the animal world. And we seem to be able to transplant the idea of vital goals to the animal world. Animal science clearly shows that animals have goals. Many animal theorists claim that the model of animals as stimulus–response automata should be replaced by that of animals as goal-seeking systems (Toates 1987). And researchers such as Marion Stamp Dawkins (1990) and Ian Duncan (1996) have devised sophisticated experiments putting animals in situations of choice in order to determine the goals of the animals. They have demonstrated that many animals can make informed choices based on earlier experiences. We can, they say, ascribe a desiring faculty to most animals. A predator wants to get its prey; the predated animal wants to escape. All animals (that reproduce in a sexual way) want to mate and have offspring.

Thus it is not only humans that perform intentional actions, although we hardly ever use the term "intentional action" in the animal case. However, we would not understand the "doings" of many animals if we did not use our own mental language and the associated action language. So, ascribing intentional actions to many animals is almost unavoidable. Therefore there is nothing incoherent in ascribing goals to them.

But what about *vital goals* in my technical sense? Neither a dog nor a worm embraces the concept of a vital goal. No, but neither does a baby nor a senile person, nor for that matter most other people. The notion of a vital goal is a theoretical notion; it is not tied to any hierarchy of preferences in a psychological sense (although I contend that most vital goals among humans are also strongly preferred in a psychological sense). A goal is vital to an animal, according to my theory, if, and only if, its realization is a necessary condition for the animal's long-term happiness. And there is nothing unrealistic in using these concepts with reference to a large part of the animal world.

But again of course a problem crops up. I may have argued convincingly for the case that the *higher*-level animals can have vital goals in my technical sense. But what about the lower-level animals? We may perhaps say about all of them that they have goals and that they pursue goal-directed "doings". But how can they have *vital* goals in my sense, since such goals are, per definition, related to long-term happiness? How do we characterize the happiness of a worm or an amoeba?

My answer to this is that we need for the present purpose a more general notion than that of happiness. The notion I propose is that of *welfare*. And in order to substantiate the idea that lower animals can have welfare, let me turn to the philosophy of nature presented by Paul Taylor in his *Respect for Nature* (1976).

Taylor presents what he calls the *biocentric* outlook in order to develop an environmental ethics that is not dependent on human interests. This outlook on nature entails a certain way of perceiving and understanding each individual organism. Each is seen as being a teleological centre of life, pursuing its own good in its own unique way. Consciousness may not be present at all, and even when it is present the organism need not be thought of as intentionally taking steps to achieve goals it sets for itself. Rather, a living being is perceived as a unified system of organized activity, the constant tendency of which is to preserve its existence by protecting and promoting its well-being.[2] (Here I summarize from P. Taylor 1976: 156–8.)

In my brief discussion about feelings above I admitted that we have little evidence for talking about feelings in the case of animals with rudimentary or non-existent neurological make-ups. Here I also think that the holistic characterization of health must use a more generic concept. When the goal of a worm is frustrated, then the worm, as far as we know, does not feel pain. However, something negative has happened to this worm. The welfare of the worm or the quality of the worm's life has been reduced. We can infer this from certain behaviours or non-behaviours on the part of the worm. It may make stereotyped and unsuccessful movements, for instance with regard to reaching a goal that it has started to try to reach. Or it may not move at all. We may also compare this worm with another worm crawling just beside it. The latter worm is lively, it moves around quickly, it is bigger and it seems to be thriving. The first worm, we say, must have some problem. It is ill.

My suggestion for a systematic and general characterization of health and illness in the case of animals is, then, very briefly, the following. An animal A is healthy if, and only if, A has the ability to realize all its vital goals given standard circumstances. A vital goal of A's is a necessary condition for the long-term welfare of A. In the case of the higher animals the criterion of welfare is the happiness of the animal. In the case of lower-level animals and, for that matter, plants, we must find other criteria, such as the vitality of the animal or plant.

CONCLUDING REMARKS

In this paper I have scrutinized some arguments that can be directed against the two types of theory labelled as BST and HTH. First, I have discussed the claim that the criterion of survival of the individual, which is a central element in the BST, does not seem to be a universally applicable criterion. On this point I have argued that the criticism would remain valid even if one were to improve the BST idea by including disability as a condition that reduces the probability of survival. Second, I have discussed the statement that the HTH is too inclusive, since it seems to entail that all reductions of complete health should be labelled as ill-health and call for health care. My answer here is that the HTH is not bound to consider mild deviations from optimal health as illness or ill-health. People can be in good health even if they cannot fulfil all their vital goals. Third, I have put the HTH to the test by considering how it handles two conditions, grief and pregnancy, which have often been disputed in the context of health insurance. And fourth, I have considered how the two types of theory can deal with the general concepts of health and disease that pertain not only to humans but also to animals and plants. In both these cases I have argued that the HTH is at least on a par with the BST when it comes to characterizing health and disease.

NOTES

1. All these specific formulations of the BST and the HTH were first presented in Nordenfelt (2004).
2. Taylor suggests that the well-being of the organism is a means for preserving its existence. This may look as if he might in the end support a Boorsian theory of health. However, what is crucial for my argument is that there is a notion of well-being of a lower-level organism that is *not defined* in terms of survival. There is no indication that Taylor proposes such a definition.

2. HEALTH AND DISEASE: SOCIAL CONSTRUCTIVISM AS A COMBINATION OF NATURALISM AND NORMATIVISM

Elselijn Kingma

What is health? What is disease? Thirty years of literature has failed to deliver an answer. Instead a protracted debate has been carried out over one single question: are the concepts of health and disease value-free? Naturalists ardently argue in favour, whereas normativists equally vehemently oppose. It is time for a different approach.

In sociology, a firmly held doctrine maintains that health and disease are socially constructed (Nettleton 2006), but this claim has not been philosophically unpacked. In this chapter I begin that task. I first give a brief and general characterization of social contructivism as the claim that a social construct is not *fixed* or *inevitable*, but is the contingent result of social and historical processes. I then present one main argument in favour of a social constructivist approach to health and disease: social constructivism provides a novel and particularly promising way of combining naturalist and normativist lines of thought. This argument is supported, first, by a brief discussion of the problems for and promises of naturalist and normativist analyses and, second, by a demonstration that social constructivism explains the strengths and weaknesses of either approach, and can unite them in a manner that retains the former while avoiding the latter.

HEALTH AND DISEASE: THE DEBATE SO FAR

Why have philosophers attempted to find out what health and disease are? Because it is thought that this would answer other questions. Most people, for example, agree that our health service should treat *diseases*, and finding out what diseases are, therefore, might help us decide the often-difficult question of who to treat (e.g. Daniels 1985; Cooper & Megone 2007). Another common thought is that treatment can be permissible where enhancement is not. An understanding of the difference between enhancement and treatment is predicated on understanding the difference between health and disease. Finally, an understanding of what health and disease are might help us understand the proper scope or goal of clinical medicine.

The concepts "health" and "disease" in these contexts, and in the philosophical literature as a whole, are artificial concepts that do not quite map onto medical or practical usage. Disease, in this context, is an umbrella term that covers not only what we ordinarily call diseases or illnesses (e.g. pneumonia, diabetes and malaria) but also a wealth of other unhealthy conditions (e.g. traumata such as broken legs, bruises, or wounds; disabilities such as blindness or the inability to walk; and other conditions such as infertility, genetic syndromes or congenital deformations). I take no stance on whether this is or is not a legitimate interpretation of our use of medical concepts, nor should I be taken to condone any implicit assumptions contained within it, such as the assumption that disabilities are always a form of non-health (see Amundson 1992; Nettleton 2006). I merely report that presenting health and disease as mutually exclusive concepts, and using "disease" as an umbrella term for all unhealthy conditions, is a running approach in the literature from which I will not deviate in this chapter.[1]

An alternative view of the naturalist–normativist opposition

Answers to the question of what health and disease are have come in two opposing kinds. First, naturalism maintains that health and disease are objective, empirical, value-free notions (Boorse 1975, 1976, 1977, 1987, 1997; Kass 1975; Kendell 1975; Scadding 1988, 1990; Szasz 1960; and most recently Schramme 2007).This approach attempts to define health and disease in terms of biological function, where disease is usually dysfunction.[2] The second view is normativism, which maintains that health and disease are essentially value-laden concepts (Agich 1983; Clouser *et al.* 1981, 1997; R. Cooper 2002a; Engelhardt 1976, 1986; Goosens 1980; Margolis 1976; Nordenfelt 1987, 2001, 2007; Reznek 1987; Whitbeck 1978).[3] Most if not all of the literature on health and disease has been devoted to the naturalist–normativist opposition, and has attempted to answer the question of whether health and disease are value-free concepts. But there are good reasons for thinking that this opposition, and hence the focus on this question, is deeply misguided.

Naturalism is often characterized as maintaining that health and disease are completely value-free concepts, but this characterization is incorrect; it overlooks that naturalists offer a two-layered account of medical concepts.

Disease, according to this account, is a value-free first-layer concept, which features predominantly in theoretical medicine but has no direct relevance for our actions or application in society. In order to apply this concept it has to be augmented with values and social attitudes, to arrive at second-layer, partially evaluative "*disease-plus*" concepts: for example, "diseases that should be treated", "diseases that are serious" and "diseases that excuse you from legal responsibility". Naturalists contend that these *disease-plus* concepts, rather than the naturalistic first-layer concept on its own, are relevant for decisions about treatment and other practical applications. They therefore do not defend that applied health and disease concepts are value-free, but only that a component of these concepts is.[4]

Normativists as a rule have failed to realize this more restricted commitment of naturalists, and as a result most normativist arguments against naturalism go astray: they have criticized naturalists for defining a concept that has no real relevance to us, or to medical practice (e.g. Agich 1983; Engelhardt 1986: 171; Margolis 1976). But this argument pertains to applied disease concepts only, and naturalists already agree with normativists that applied "diseases-plus" concepts, namely the disease concepts we should use for social and ethical purposes, are value-laden. There is, then, no *prima facie* incompatibility between naturalist commitments and the normativist claim that health and disease are value-laden. Insofar as it pertains to applied concepts, the debate and supposed opposition between naturalists and normativists can largely be put to rest.

But there is much more to say about naturalism, normativism and the relationship between them.

Naturalism

Although naturalists do not claim that applied disease concepts are value-free, they do claim that the core component of these concepts is. This claim been defended in great detail by Christopher Boorse (1975, 1976, 1977, 1987, 1997). But there are good reasons to think that it cannot be supported. First, it appears that the naturalist component of Boorse's account of disease, which is an account of biological dysfunction, cannot accommodate certain core classes of diseases, which are diseases that are the direct result of an environmental factor. Examples include infections, trauma and toxic stress (Kingma 2010; but see Hausman 2011 for a response). Second, and more importantly for this chapter, *even if* Boorse were successful in providing an account of disease as biological dysfunction, that does not make his account value-free. Here is a brief summary of the latter argument (see Kingma 2007 for more detail).

Our best naturalist theory of disease, Boorse's BST, has to make some basic assumptions. For example, it has to make the assumption that typical men and typical women, who are biologically different in some ways, form separate categories that are both healthy. Once these assumptions are made, a fairly successful value-free description of health and disease can be provided. However, if we change these underlying assumptions, quite a different account would be generated. If we assumed, for example, that people with and people without Down's syndrome formed separate categories or reference classes that were both healthy, then a value-free description of health and disease would be generated in which people with Down's syndrome were healthy.

If naturalists want to claim that their account of disease is truly value-free, they have to provide a value-free justification for assumptions implicit in their accounts, such as assumptions about what reference classes are normal, healthy and therefore permissible (i.e. age, sex and race) and which ones are not (i.e. having Down's syndrome, height and – according to Boorse – sexual orientation). No such justification can be provided; the obvious answer that these latter reference classes are not permitted because they indicate ill-health, is circular and therefore inadmissible (Kingma 2007). Boorse has no other answer, however, therefore the supposedly naturalistic account offered by Boorse is not value-free.

It is important for the rest of this chapter to note what this particular argument does and does not establish. It does *not* give us a reason to suppose that (components of) the health and disease concepts cannot be described in value-free terms (as normativists argue). And it therefore does not provide a reason to reject outright naturalist accounts of disease and accept normativist ones instead. It does, however, give a strong reason to think not only that *applied* accounts of disease as offered by naturalists are value-laden (as naturalists already conceded), but that the supposed theoretical and value-free *components* of their accounts are too. And that latter, new finding is very damaging. For if the supposed value-free part of their account is really value-laden, then the naturalists' main aim, which is to demonstrate that at least part of our disease concept is value-free, has been thoroughly, and fatally, undermined.

Normativism

It might seem, then, that normativism wins – on multiple fronts! But that conclusion is too quick. For so far all that normativists have won is a very general claim that applied disease concepts are value-laden, which naturalists never denied, and the claim that *if* naturalist or value-free descriptions of disease are possible, that does not show the concept to be value-free – which is a claim only ever submitted by me (Kingma 2007). And for reasons that will become clear in this chapter, I would hesitate to characterize myself as a normativist.

Both claims fall short, however, of the agenda that most normativists have committed to. Normativists have not merely argued that health and disease are value-laden, but have wanted to use that conclusion, first, to reject naturalist accounts and, second, to support their own alternative accounts that reductively define health and disease in evaluative terms and tend to lack any form of appeal to the biological sciences.[5] Neither of these two moves follows: the first is not supported because the observation that applied concepts of health and disease are value-laden is not only compatible with a two-layer account of health, but, following Kingma (2007) may even be true of the supposed value-free components of these accounts. The second is not supported because this gives us no reason to think that the value-ladenness of applied concepts of health and disease will particularly favour normativist over naturalist accounts.

Normativists have also offered other arguments in favour of their accounts. Of these I want to briefly mention two – not because I consider them successful arguments either against forms of naturalism or in favour of normativist accounts, but because they bring insightful observations to the table that will be relevant for my discussion of social constructivism later on.

The first aspect of the concepts "health" and "disease" that has been stressed by normativists is the observation that our concepts of health and disease are intimately related to medical practice and to the provision of treatment. Such an argument is endorsed by many but not all normativists, and is offered in its strictest form by Engelhardt: "choosing to call a set of phenomena a disease involves a commitment to medical intervention" (Engelhardt 1975: 137) and "the concept of disease acts ... to enjoin action" (Engelhardt 1975: 127). Goosens (1980: 103–5) successfully undermines this claim by arguing, first, that not every disease is always a disvalue and, second, that it would therefore be undesirable and dangerous to let our actions depend entirely on the ascription of disease; a decision to treat should always depend on an evaluative assessment of a total picture, and not merely, and blindly, on the presence of disease. For example, we should not blindly treat infertility *because* it is a disease; people may wish not to have children and thus not suffer from that condition (see also Kopelman 1975; Whitbeck 1978).

Goosens seems correct in rejecting Engelhardt's proposal as too strict, but a weaker version of his observation survives: most normativists agree that there is at least some conceptual connection or relationship between the concepts of health and disease and the practice of medicine, or between the concept of disease and social actions, obligations and entitlements; to label something a disease is to *prima facie* qualify a condition for treatment. Goosens (1980), for example, recognizes a *conditional* obligation to treat, and Kopelman (1975) concedes that treatment is the usual goal of medicine. See also Margolis (1976: 242) and Wartofsky (1975: 69).

Second, many normativists have emphasized that diseases are both known to us and cared about because of their disvalued effects:

> By "disease" we aim to pick out a variety of conditions that through being painful, disfiguring or disabling are of interest to us as people. This class of conditions is by its nature anthropocentric and corresponds to no natural class of conditions in the world.
> (R. Cooper 2005: 22)

> The concept of disease may be a basically heterogeneous concept standing for a set of phenomena collected together out of ... social interest, not on the basis of the recognition of a natural type or a common conceptual structure. (Engelhardt 1975: 127; see also Engelhardt 1975: 136, 1976: 226; R. Cooper 2002a: 271; Margolis 1976: 242)

Nordenfelt (2007) places this observation in the context of a putative history of the concepts "health" and "disease": people took an interest in their conditions as *medical* conditions not because they had a biological dysfunction but because they had a condition that they strongly disvalued, such as pain, discomfort, an inability or incapacity. These disvalued conditions have shaped our concepts of health and disease, shaped the scope of medical practice, and eventually led to medical scientific enquiry that investigated and defined health and disease further. See also Goosens (1980: 106): "persons seek aid partly because they believe states to be disvaluable, and the concepts of medicine arise from, respond to and have their content fixed by this kind of interaction".

None of the above observations, I contend, compel us to accept normativist accounts or reject naturalism: many of our classifications and concepts may have been motivated originally by observations or normative concerns that are no longer explicitly reflected in their definitions. Our concept "water", for example, will have been shaped originally through concerns to do with potability, liquidity, transparency and other properties that made water salient to us as users. Yet many people think that water is properly defined not in terms of its watery properties, but in terms of its chemical structure (e.g. Putnam 1973; Kuhn 1990). A naturalist could similarly accept the normativist observation that people came to know about diseases because they are nasty conditions, and that people cared about this classification because they want them treated, yet maintain that that was only our first engagement with nature: science has now found out what health and disease really are, accounts of which can be given at least in part in terms of dysfunction. Alternatively put, medical science investigated the causes of disvaluable states, which are dysfunctions or diseases (see also Schramme 2007).

I am not here interested, however, in evaluating the above observations as argument in a debate between naturalism and normativism – which I suggest we abandon sooner rather than later anyway. Instead I am interested in the above observations because they emphasize that the concepts "health" and "disease" do not operate in a vacuum, but are applied by people, in social frameworks, and for a reason; our evaluative concerns interact with, shape and motivate the development of medical practice and science. These observations will be important later on in this chapter.

SOCIAL CONSTRUCTIVISM

It is extremely difficult to give a strict definition of social constructivism, in part because of the breadth of the field (ranging from sociology to history and philosophy), and in part because social constructivists present quite varied, sometimes vague, and occasionally even competing interpretations and commitments. Social constructivism has been claimed about race, gender, quarks, technological systems, white women, female refugees and a host of other topics (see Hacking 1999 for these and other examples). The only thing that seems to unite all of these is the loose claim that they are, to some degree, the product of social processes.

Some forms of social constructivism are highly unpopular: "constructivism has generated a body of work whose breadth and depth is rivalled only by the degree of animosity it has provoked from scientists and others with more traditional epistemological sensibilities" (Costelloe 2001: 469; see Sokal & Bricmont 1998 for an example of such animosity). A discussion of or defence against those allegations is beyond the scope of this chapter.

Recent work has put forward social constructivism as a useful approach to understand the interaction between our social and scientific concepts, our social practices and institutions, and in particular the formation and classification of *human* kinds (Hacking 1991, 1995, 1998). An example of this is the application of social constructivism to discussions about race (Andreasen 2000; Appiah 1998; Mills 1998; Piper 1992; Root 2000). Here the interesting question is not whether a biological or scientific correlate of race might be identified, but, rather, how such scientific practices interact with and have effects upon the concepts, practices, structures and people that live in our societies (e.g. Mallon 2004; Kitcher 2007). It is within this latter tradition that my sympathies lie, and that is where I would like to place my analysis. This means that Foucault (1961, 1963), who offers an early and influential but quite different approach to the social construction of medical science, will not be considered.

What is social constructivism?

There is a substantial debate on what can and cannot be legitimately called constructivism. André Kukla (2000) recognizes at least eight forms of constructivism in the philosophy of science alone, and makes additional distinctions between metaphysical, semantic and epistemological constructivism (see also Hacking 1999; Mallon 2007). I will deliberately avoid taking a position in that debate. Instead, given the breadth of social constructivist theses and the controversy surrounding them, I will only give a general and very inclusive gloss on social constructivism. In this characterization I draw heavily upon Hacking (1999).

A general description of social constructivism is that for a particular thing x, if x is socially constructed then x is at least in part the product of social processes; different processes would have meant that x would have been different, therefore x is not inevitable. In order to understand social constructivism, Hacking advises us to not "ask for meaning" but to "ask what [i]s the point" (Hacking 1995: 5). The point of arguing that x is a social construction is often to argue against something else. This "something else" is the received view that x is inevitable, or that x is determined or fixed by the structure of nature.

Take for example gender roles. There is or was a received view that gender roles are *not* the contingent result of human activity. Gender roles are or were seen as the result of human biology or God's intent, and therefore inevitable: had human activity been different, human biology and/or God's intent would have been the same and therefore so would gender roles. A social constructivist about gender roles might argue against this view: he might contend that gender roles are the result of contingent social processes, and that different processes would result in different gender roles (and different ideas of what gender roles are appropriate).

What, then, are the subjects of socially constructed theses? Here a distinction can be made between ideas and objects (Hacking 1999: 21–4). Take, for example, race. We might make a distinction between the *object* "race" – that is the existence of groups of people that share some (biological) differences, such as a difference in skin colour or ancestry – and the *idea* "race", that is the practice of using certain physical characteristics to sort people into groups, and to use this classification for various purposes. The idea of race is the idea that sorting people into groups by, for example, skin colour, is a relevant means of classification.[6]

At first glance, the thesis "race is a social construction" could be about either the object "race" or the idea of race. But on second glance, it is probably a thesis about the *idea* of race. A social constructivist about race does not, generally, defend the view that the biological differences that exist between groups of people – for example differences in skin colour, differences in ancestry, or patterns of genetic variation – are the product of (intentional) human activity.[7] The social constructivist thesis about race is therefore not about the *object* "human groups that share biological characteristics". Instead, the social construction is the *idea* of race; the social constructivist holds that using *racial characteristics* (skin colour, ancestry, genetic variation) as a means of classifying people is contingent upon (intentional) human activity. Whereas those racial characteristics, these biological differences, may be inevitable, it is not inevitable that we take them to mark *salient* differences between people.[8] Grouping people according to these markers is a human activity, a socio-historical process, and the *idea* "race" is a result of this. That idea was not inevitable and we certainly did not have to use this idea for the many, often harmful, purposes for which it has been and is being used.

Why, however, should we be so concerned about ideas? Why should we *care* that concepts are the result of human activity, and could have been otherwise? This, to my mind, is where the real bite of social constructivism comes in: the reason we should care about ideas, concepts and classifications is that they have effects.

The idea of gender, for example, influences the things that women and men are allowed to do in a society. It also influences what men and women *expect* to do, who they choose as their role models, what they think and desire. It affects how they grow up, what they are exposed to and what they consider suitable for themselves. Ideas about gender affect how people perceive themselves, and it affects the choices they make. Ideas about gender affect who and what people are.[9]

The same point can be illustrated by the example of race. Our idea of race – our practice of grouping people by, for example, skin colour – has affected and does affect real people, and real lives: it affects how people think about each other and how they treat and have treated each other; how people perceive their relationships to each other and who they identify with; and it affects the expectations people form of themselves and others, where and how they live, the jobs, houses and benefits people want and get, and how these jobs and benefits are handed out. Our concept "race" affects who people are; it allows people to form a racial identity (Appiah 1993).

These effects of our ideas on identity are important. They demonstrate that the effects of our ideas do not just spread outwards, to other objects and ideas, (such as role models, social expectations and dress codes) and to social and material institutions (such as jobs, universities and housing arrangements), but also spread back in. The ideas of gender and race affect how people develop, what they expect, think, want and hope, and how they construe their identity. Hacking calls this process *looping* (Hacking 1995). Our concept "gender", or our *idea* "woman", has affected what and who the objects – actual women – *are*. It has affected the ways in which men and women differ. This means that in some ways the *objects* "women" (and "men") have also been socially constructed: men and women are constructed *as a certain kind of person*.

To understand the observation that ideas and objects interact, I find it useful to adopt Hacking's idea of the matrix:

> Ideas do not exist in a vacuum. They inhabit a social setting. Let us call that a *matrix* within which an idea, a concept or kind is formed ... The matrix in which the idea of the women refugee is formed is a complex of institutions, advocates, newspaper articles, lawyers, court decisions, immigration proceedings. Not to mention the material infrastructure, barriers passports, uniforms, counters at airports, detention centers, courthouses, holiday camps for refugee children ... [T]his contingent classification, and the matrix in which it is embedded, changes how some women refugees feel about themselves, their experience and their actions. (Hacking 1999: 10–11)

The idea of a matrix illustrates *why* ideas or concepts are important and *how* they can have such large effects; ideas, concepts and classifications do not exist on their own. They are *embedded* in a network of social ideas, expectations, social practices and institutions, and have effects precisely because they are embedded in such a social setting.

Realism and constructivism

I now turn to focus on one main objection to – or rather, as I will demonstrate, misinterpretation of – social constructivism. This is the objection that social constructivism denies its subjects any form of mind-independent reality. I briefly discuss a possible defence against this objection that will, first, illustrate a way of cashing out social constructivism and, second, be relevant to the project of integrating naturalism and normativism in the third section of this chapter.

Given that water is H_2O, a famous argument establishes that our concept "water" refers to H_2O necessarily (Kripke 1972). But now imagine Twin-Earth (Putnam 1973). On Twin-Earth there is a substance that falls from the sky as rain, sustains life as water does on Earth, and has every other superficial property of water. Rather than being H_2O, however, this substance has molecular structure XYZ. Could we have had a concept that referred to both H_2O and XYZ? Some philosophers argue that we could have had such a concept – and if so, this example could be used as a basis for a social constructivist account of the concept water. Our concept "water" was not inevitable; we could have had a different concept that referred to H_2O *and* XYZ. This would not show, however, that water, or H_2O, is not real.

Rather than hang my case on this example, however, I would like to consider some other examples, which are a bit less outlandish.

Consider the following story (Donnellan 1983; LaPorte 1996: 117–20; 2004): in 1920 scientists travelled to the planet Pluton, where they discovered a substance that seemed a lot like water, although on closer investigation subtle differences from water were found. After chemical analysis, scientists announced the discovery of a new element – plutrogen (Pg) – which is similar to hydrogen but has an (extra) neutron in its nucleus. Plutonian water is plutrogendioxide (Pg_2O), and further investigation revealed very small quantities of Pg_2O in Earthian water. Chemical classification and theory adjusted to accommodate this new element.

Contrary to XYZ, Pg_2O is not a made-up substance – but nevertheless history progressed differently. No-one travelled to Pluton, but "plutrogen" was discovered on Earth in 1931 as deuterium, an isotope of hydrogen. And plutrogen dioxide, or deuterium dioxide, is not considered a separate substance, but rather an uncommon form of water (heavy water).

The story suggests that we could have had an alternative way of classifying isotopes. The lesson I wish to draw from this is that *if* the chemical concepts we have depend in part on how and when we encountered particular substances and that *if* we could have had concepts with a different extension that still "cut nature at its joints", as the above story suggests, then we have a very simple basis for a social constructivist account of water, that is not antirealist. The concept of water that we have, which reflects a real substance, water, was not inevitable but is a contingent result of social and historical processes.

The world seems to present few "twin substances" – substances virtually identical in surface properties but radically different in chemical structure – that provide a real world analogue to H_2O and XYZ. The case of jade, however, has received attention in the literature because it presents precisely such an example (Hacking 2007; LaPorte 2004: 94–100; Putnam 1975: 241; I take my details from Hacking).

Jade is a gemstone that comes in two distinct chemical varieties: jadeite and nephrite. Whereas "jade" refers to both now, this may not always have been the case. In China, where jade has been traded for millennia, samples christened "yu" were predominantly nephrite whereas Europeans first encountered jade as (Mesoamerican) jadeite. Chinese jade (nephrite) "met its XYZ" (jadeite) when China annexed Burma in 1784 and large amounts of jadeite were found. While many new names evolved, jadeite was accepted as being of the same generic stuff, yu (or jade), as nephrite. In Europe the two different chemical structures were discovered and named in the nineteenth century. European, particularly British, quibbles about the meaning of the generic term "jade" were resolved by Chinese trade practice and business; both jadeite and nephrite are now jade in European languages too.

The thing to emphasize about this example, again, is that the history of jade can be seen as an example of social constructivism: our concept "jade" was not inevitable, but was the result of social and historical processes. In this case the social processes are particularly salient. Imagine that the Chinese had not succeeded in annexing Burma and that jadeite had not formed the spoils of victory but rather the economic motor of an enemy regime; or that Burmese jadeite had not predominantly ended up in the hands of the Imperial court, as it did (Hacking 2007), but had become the main means of certain classes to imitate traditionally more respected social groups; or that not China but Britain had controlled the jade trade. Although this is all speculation, it is more than conceivable that such or similar contingent social and historical processes would have caused nephrite and jadeite to be treated and classified differently. This would have resulted in a different concept of jade and hence, we could say, the concept of jade is socially constructed.

The above stories can be used to illustrate various points. First, they illustrate that the concepts we have depend (in part) on social and historical contingencies. In the case of Jade in particular, considerations concerning value and imperial conquest – social forces and historical events – determined the fate of the concept "yu". In Europe the debate was similarly decided by business considerations.

Second, they provide a reply to those who believe social constructivism would suggest that things are not real. Social constructivism is not committed to this: it only claims that our concepts could have been different – that they were not inevitable – and this has no implications for realism: nothing in the above examples suggests that water and jade are not real. Objecting that something is *not* socially constructed *because* it is real is therefore not a good objection, and misconstrues social constructivism (as does the claim that something is not real *because* it is socially constructed).

In fact, the above examples illustrate a further claim: not only are water and jade real, but both the actual and alternative possible classifications of them appear to classify nature along existing, *real*, discontinuities. Being social constructivist about jade is therefore not the same (as some seem to suppose) as claiming that we could have drawn lines anywhere, or that everything is relative; it is not to claim that these concepts are the product of social and historical processes *alone* or that any concept would have been possible or is equally probable. The structure of nature, in the above example, did provide some constraints: it provided several salient lines or discontinuities for classification. History then determined which lines were cut. One can therefore be a social constructivist about kind-concepts and a realist about kinds.[10]

Third, the above examples illustrate the embeddedness of concepts, and how they affect how we structure our world. If we take the case of jade, where social processes were particularly salient, then a world where the concept of jade, or yu, would not have included jadeite would not be a world that merely differs semantically – a world where labels or names only were different – but one where practices, such as what gets traded, and attitudes, such as what we consider valuable, are also different. The concept "jade" is embedded in – that is, interactively related to, part of and shaped in conjunction with – social practices, attitudes, values and institutions. And an alternative world would be one where our practices and institutions – in particular the organization of trade and perhaps certain other aspects of Chinese society – would be different too.

SOCIAL CONSTRUCTIVISM AS A COMBINATION OF NATURALISM AND NORMATIVISM

The final section of this chapter is devoted to an assessment of the relationship between a social constructivist approach and naturalism and normativism. In contrast to the received view, which considers constructivism a version of normativism, and therefore incompatible with naturalism, I will demonstrate that social constructivism is not only compatible with both naturalism and normativism, but can offer a way of combining these positions that retains the good elements of both and illuminates and resolves problems discussed earlier in this chapter.

This chapter is limited in focus, and therefore does not do the following. First, it does not provide a defence of the position *that* health and disease are socially constructed and it gives no details about *how* health and disease have been constructed. To do the latter would fill a library. Instead I will simply proceed on an assumption: the assumption that if one could argue that some version of social constructivism is true for water and jade, an analogous argument will be defensible for health and disease. What the details of that argument are will remain unanswered for the moment, but the literature in history and sociology suggest not only that the assumption is very plausible for health and disease, but also that many details of the relevant story are already known (see Nettleton 2006 for an introduction). Second, the chapter will not work out in any detail what the consequences of a social constructivist approach to health and disease would be. All I do here is open up that investigation, and demonstrate that given the problems of naturalism and normativism, and given existing arguments in the literature, it is an extremely promising way to go.

Let us assume, then, that health and disease are socially constructed; that is, that the concepts "health" and "disease" that we have and employ are not inevitable or dictated to us by the structure or the world, but are both the contingent result of our actions, choices, intentions, and so on, and are embedded in a matrix of other concepts and social structures, practices and attitudes.[11] How does this position relate to naturalism, and how does it relate to normativism?

Social constructivism and naturalism

A main conclusion about naturalism made earlier in this chapter was that even if naturalists could provide a successful account of components of health and disease in value-free terms, this would fall short of demonstrating the naturalist claim that that health and disease are value-free concepts. The reason was that any account of function must adopt assumptions – reference classes in the case of the BST for example – for which there is no value-free, empirical justification.

This conclusion and the argument supporting it show remarkable similarity with the discussion of social constructivism in the previous section. The discussions of jade and water demonstrated that a classification, for example the classification of jadeite and nephrite into the one category of jade, can *both* reflect a realist natural structure that is describable in value-free terms *and*, through being a consequence of them, reflect social choices, values and attitudes. We can tell a story of how the classification "jade" was determined by social processes, but we can also give an account of what jade is by presenting the conjunction of two chemical formulae – which is about as value-free a description as one can get. Kingma's (2007) argument makes a similar point about disease: Boorse's reference classes may result in a naturalistic account of health and disease, that is, a value-free description of health and disease, but this does not mean that those concepts are not social in origin or implicitly reflect norms and values. Just as we could give a value-free definition of jade, we can give a value-free definition of reference classes. And just as this did not preclude us from giving a social explanation for the classification of jadeite and nephrite into one category, in which values play an important role, this should not stop us from giving a social or evaluative explanation for the reference classes Boorse relies on, in which values play an important role. Thus even if the BST succeeds as an account of disease, a social constructivist approach still strongly supports as well as explains the claim made in this chapter: that all naturalism has managed to do is present a concept that is the product of socio-historical processes in naturalistic, value-free terms. And this, I argue, is not sufficient to justify the naturalist claim that health and disease are value-free concepts.

Rather surprisingly, then, social constructivism is thoroughly compatible with naturalistic accounts of health and disease (in the sense that it is compatible with naturalistic descriptions and/or accounts of disease-as-dysfunction, even if it is not compatible with the naturalist's claim that health and disease are value-free concepts.) It is worth stressing briefly quite how crucial this point is; the literature has generally presented constructivism either as a form of normativism, and certainly as radically opposing any form of naturalism; social constructivism, it was supposed, showed that disease is whatever we think it is, or that "disease has no true existence" (Ruse 1997: 139). This chapter demonstrates those views to be misguided: social constructivism opposes neither naturalism nor realism about disease.

Social constructivism and normativism

Earlier in this chapter I offered two conclusions. First, we should accept the normativist claim that health and disease are value-laden but that gives us no reason to reject a naturalist and accept a normativist *account* – that is a reductive account that defines health and disease in terms of values. Second, normativists have contributed worthwhile observations about health and disease, such as the observation that to label a condition a disease is to make a *prima facie* statement about the need for treatment and the observation that diseases are salient to us as a group *because* we dislike them.

The first of these claims is related to social constructivism in the way just discussed: a classification can reflect or originate in social and evaluative considerations, but can nevertheless be described in naturalistic, value-free or empirical terms. Therefore an acknowledgement or argument that a classification is social or evaluative in origin, or reflective of values or social norms, does not commit to or even give a strong reason for rejecting a naturalist and/or accepting a normativist account.

The second of these claims has close connections with a different element of constructivism: the social embeddedness of concepts. According to constructivism concepts form part of and have meaning within a matrix of social practices, institutions, ideas and expectations; develop as part of and in conjunction with this matrix; and interact through this matrix in multiple, complex and sometimes intractable ways. What social constructivism suggests, then, is that those aspects of health and disease that normativists have most consistently and successfully emphasized and that we should be happy to take on board, such as their relation to value, medical treatment and the development of medicine, *are* the matrix of which health and disease are part. Health and disease as concepts did not develop in isolation, but in conjunction with the development of medicine, medical science and – more recently – the social organization of health care. Social constructivism can explain, therefore, the attraction of the normativist observations.

Normativists take these observations as evidence for a reductive definition of disease in terms of disvalue and/or medical treatability (e.g. R. Cooper 2002a; Reznek 1987). Social constructivism, however, undermines such reductive definitions: the embeddedness of the concepts of health and disease supports that our values, attitudes, social processes and institutions affect the concepts we end up with, that is what health and disease are, but it also supports that these concepts affect our values, attitudes, social processes and institutions in turn. Such looping effects do not give clear support to a reductive normativist definition of health in terms of values or vice versa. Social constructivism therefore gives an explanation of normativist observations not in terms of an *account* of what health and disease *are*, but in terms of a richer explanatory account of how concepts and society *develop*.

This implicit and different kind of analysis of the relationship between the concepts of health and disease and social and evaluative concerns that social constructivism offers – a relation of embeddedness rather than reduction – is why I like to distinguish between normativism and constructivism. Again, this may seem surprising: constructivism and normativism are often viewed as the same thing (e.g. Kitcher 1996: 208–9; Murphy 2008). But that view should be rejected. For beyond the general claim that applied concepts of health and disease are value-laden, normativists are committed to the claim that health and disease should be *defined* in terms of values. They are thus committed to a particular kind of account of disease. Constructivists as characterized by me do not share that commitment. They contend only the much more minimal claim that whatever account of health and disease we give is not inevitable, but the contingent result of socio-historical processes (and thus implicitly reflecting them). This also explains why I hesitate to call myself a normativist: despite maintaining firmly that health and disease are value-laden – even if described naturalistically – and are the result of social processes and evaluative judgements, I do not share the crucial normativist commitment: I do not believe that any of this shows that health and disease should be described entirely or even primarily in evaluative terms.

The relationship between naturalism and normativism revisited

Naturalism and normativism can in principle be combined by following the two-layer model employed by Wakefield (2002) and Boorse (1977, 1997), which defines a core concept of disease in scientific or biological terms to which values are added as a second layer. But this approach keeps naturalist descriptions and normativist considerations largely separate. Social constructivism, I suggest, can provide a much better and more interesting way of reconciling naturalism and normativism because it gives an *interactive* account of how naturalistic accounts and normativist considerations relate: naturalistic descriptions, or accounts of disease as dysfunction, are the result of the social processes that normativists have emphasized.

To illustrate, consider the judgement that homosexuality is *not* a disease. An account of disease as dysfunction might bear this out by accepting homosexuality as a separate reference class. To be more precise, this view would accept homosexuality as a normal polymorphism of human sexuality, just like blue eyes and brown eyes are normal polymorphisms of human eye colour. But what explanation can we give for an account of dysfunction in which homosexuality is a normal polymorphism, rather than one in which homosexuality is a dysfunction? Such an explanation cannot be purely naturalistic, because the natural world does not arbitrate between alternative accounts of dysfunction (although the resulting disease concept can be described in value-free terms; Kingma 2007). Rather, an explanation of a naturalistic account of dysfunction which includes homosexuality as a normal polymorphism should appeal to social developments that have resulted in, or rather that have interacted with and been part of, our acceptance of homosexuality as a normal form of love and partnership (as well as, I submit, our unearthing scientific data and interpreting them in such a way that they support this). These social processes include elements that normativists have highlighted, such as a change in our evaluation of homosexuality. But they also include many processes that normativist accounts do not reflect, such as the secularization of society, changes in our perception of the appropriate role and purpose of sex, the loss of status of the institution of marriage, the active lobbying of homosexual groups, and so on (e.g. Bayer 1981). Importantly, and in contrast to the reductive normativist picture that suggests that a change in value judgement unidirectionally changes what is a disease, these values, attitudes, social developments and the concept of disease interact, change and develop in conjunction. All of these processes have affected many aspects of our world, and only one of these is the naturalistic account of biology, sexuality, disease and/or dysfunction that we have come to adopt. Therefore, although this account may be given in naturalistic terms, as a result of social processes that include normativist concerns, it is also a reflection of those social processes and normativist concerns – and is such a reflection in a far richer and more complex way than a reductive normativist account that defines disease in terms of values.

Whether or not we retain the two-layer model in addition – and we may have good reasons for doing so because it may be a good way of accommodating slightly different disease concepts that have a role in different situations – social constructivism improves upon it. It teaches us that normativist considerations – and in fact a far richer conception of normativist considerations than normativists have presented – do not just play a role at the second level of this model, but also at the first level, which was limited to naturalistic or scientific descriptions only. Using a social constructivist approach we can add an account of the *interaction* between naturalistic descriptions and normativist considerations, and an account of the *origin* of naturalistic descriptions, which the literature has lacked so far.

CONCLUSION

This chapter has argued for a radical restructuring and reconceptualization of the literature: the received views that naturalism and normativism are opposed and that social constructivism is (a version of) normativism should be rejected. Instead social constructivism should be investigated as a promising, realist and realistic new approach to the analysis of health.

I demonstrated, first, that naturalism and normativism do not disagree on what is perceived as the important question, the value-ladenness of applied concepts of health and disease. This means that this long-standing debate can be put to rest. Second, even if naturalists could provide a successful account of components of health and disease in value-free terms, this would fall short of demonstrating that health and disease are value-free concepts as long as they did not provide a justification for our using those accounts rather than others. Third, despite the apparent triumph of the normativist claim that health and disease are value-laden concepts, there is as yet little reason to think that we should therefore either accept normativist accounts – that is accounts of disease that explicity appeal to values – or reject naturalist ones that attempt to define disease (partly) in biological terms. I then sketched an outline of a social constructivist approach to health and disease and provided an argument in favour of it: social constructivism is compatible with strong elements in both naturalism and normativism while avoiding their weaknesses, and provides a more interactive, accurate and explanatory method for unifying naturalism and normativism than currently exists in the literature.

This chapter is limited in its aims; it has not given a defence that health and disease are socially constructed – but has only argued that this is an approach worth pursuing – and it has not investigated implications of the view that health and disease are socially constructed. The very purpose of this chapter is to pave the way for that latter investigation. Among philosophers, social constructivism is now hardly taken seriously as an approach to health and disease, and I hope to have shown that this can change: social constructivism can form a starting point for innovative investigation and conceptual thinking about health and disease that is long overdue.

NOTES

1. See, for example, Boorse (1975) and R. Cooper (2002a). Not all have used the same term: some prefer to speak of malady (Clouser *et al.* 1981, 1997), disorder (Wakefield 1992) or pathological condition. I will stick with disease throughout.
2. The disease-as-dysfunction approach is defended in most detail by Boorse (1977, 1997) and Wakefield (1992a).
3. See Simons (2007) for an overview and comparison of different normativist positions.
4. It is worth stressing this point because it has been so universally overlooked: Kass (1975) denies that health is the highest good, and claims that medicine should serve other ends as well. Both Kendell (1975) and Scadding (1988, 1990) consider it appropriate for medicine to treat certain non-diseases. Finally Boorse, who has been the most heavily attacked on this point, is also most elaborate in his insistence that the concept he defines has no bearing on treatment or legal and social categories, unless it is augmented with values. See Boorse (1975: 54–5, 60; 1977: 544; 1997: 11, 12–13, 55, 95–9).

   I do grant that there is a semantic difference here: Boorse, for example, calls the naturalistic concept "disease" and the applied concept "disease-plus", whereas Wakefield reserves the term "disease" for the applied concept only. But I am not interested in semantics; given the use of an umbrella concept, any labelling is already a somewhat artificial departure from ordinary usage. What matters is the commitment of these authors and the content and consequences of their claims, not the labels used.
5. Rachel Cooper (2002a) provides the clearest example of this strategy.
6. I would like to distinguish the idea "race" from what Appiah calls *racialism*. Racialism is the view that members of groups share "heritable physical, moral, intellectual and cultural characteristics with one another that they did not share with members of any other race" (Appiah 1998: 54). Racialism is false; races do not

share moral and intellectual characteristics (Mallon 2004). When I discuss either the idea or object "race", I only refer to *thin* racial endowments: "thin racial endowments are thin clusters of properties that include one's genotype, and more or less genetically determined phenotypic features such as skin colour, eye colour, and body morphology that have traditionally been associated with racial categories. Include also in one's thin racial endowment various relational properties including one's ancestry that are extrinsic to the individual, but are heritable" (Mallon 2004: 647). Having this idea of race is a precondition for racialism, but it does not entail racialism.
7. With the exception, of course, of human migration and human reproductive choices.
8. See Kitcher (1999, 2007) and Andreasen (1998, 2000) for a defence of (a) a respectable biological reality of race (the object) and (b) the view that race (the idea) is socially constructed. Of course there are also people who deny that there is *any* biological reality to race.
9. See Fine (2010) for a recent empirically informed summary.
10. See Dupré (1993) for a pluralist ontology that supports this, and Andreasen (2000) and Kitcher (2007: 298) for a similar statement about race.
11. It is worth making a distinction here: the claim is not that these concepts are the result of our contingent encounter with diseases in the first place, or contingent in the sense that individual instances of disease are the result of contingent human action (eating hamburgers, falling off a cliff, or a contingent sexual encounter). Rather the claim is that *given* the people and conditions that exist, the conceptual classification of them is contingent.

3. TOWARDS AUTONOMY-WITHIN-ILLNESS: APPLYING THE TRIADIC APPROACH TO THE PRINCIPLES OF BIOETHICS

Antonio Casado da Rocha and Arantza Etxeberria

INTRODUCTION

The notion of autonomy has been crucial in the development of bioethics and, particularly, the ethics of health care. Generally speaking, autonomy refers to the capacity of individuals to act in the world in a self-regulated way, "the having or making of one's own laws" (*Oxford English Dictionary*). In this sense, agents are autonomous if their actions are truly their own. In ancient Greece the term was applied to the *polis*, referring to the self-government of city-states; later, modern philosophy extended this to the ethical and political self-determination of human beings (Schneewind 1998). The idea of autonomy as moral freedom already appears in the writings of Rousseau and is central to Kant's philosophy, for which the autonomy of the will is a necessary condition for moral action, and the moral principles or laws that dictate how we must act originate in reason. In this sense, autonomy is understood as the capacity to act in accordance with internal norms, not controlled by others, but also as the obligation established by one's duty to consider others as autonomous beings; that is, their right to be respected as such and therefore, not to be externally manipulated (Etxeberria & Casado 2008). In the field of bioethics, most scholarship has focused on this second meaning of autonomy. In this chapter, however, we argue that the first sense of the term, that is, the *capacity* to be autonomous, needs to be re-examined within a naturalist approach so as to explain what it means for an agent to be autonomous.

For mainstream bioethics, which largely developed after the work of Beauchamp and Childress ([1979] 2008), autonomy is a pivotal element in a four-principle account of the ethical issues surrounding health care (the other principles being: beneficence, non-maleficence and justice). Although Beauchamp and Childress consider all four to be of equal weight, for many authors the principle of respect for autonomy is *first among equals* (Gillon 2003), implying that patients' right to make decisions on issues affecting their health should prevail at the end of the day.

However, in considering the obligations that respect for autonomy entails, a large part of the literature has been more concerned with the legal and juridical aspects of the principle of autonomy involved in how to protect a "right", than with the personal subjective aspects that underlie patients' capacity to act autonomously. To take this into account, philosophical analysis and research should address the experience of patients and physicians, and the needs arising from it (Tauber 1999). Thus, in fact, we contend that, to a certain extent, the principle of autonomy developed by mainstream accounts of bioethics has been shaped according to an idealized capacity for autonomy, based on the image of healthy adult individuals who are self-sufficient citizens and are entitled to rights that protect their ability to act. What this view has neglected to address, however, are the particularities that characterize the situation of ill people who are more dependent on others. A better understanding may arise from a perspective focused on how the capacity to be autonomous is grounded in biological, psychological and social factors.

In this chapter we question the validity of the notion of autonomy underlying the mainstream doctrine of the four principles of bioethics, and propose to expand it. Our strategy will be to appeal to the philosophy of medicine and the debate therein on the nature of health and disease so as to work out a richer conception of autonomy-within-illness. If ailments, generically, are conditions that are judged to be "bad" or evaluated as non-healthy, the triadic approach distinguishes between *disease* (an ailment as considered by the medical profession), *illness* (the ailment from the subjective experience of the ill person) and *sickness* (the ailment from the perspective of society's institutions).[1] Of course, an ailment can be considered as a disease by the ill person herself, for example when she is looking at X-rays, or deciding on which chemotherapy to go for, but in that case her judgement is shaped by medical knowledge (something that has been increasingly made possible in our society, where lay people can sometimes access very specialized knowledge) and not limited to her subjective experience. One could also say that sickness and disease overlap, because the medical and health care institutions are part of society's institutions, but although both science and the political system can be considered from an institutional perspective, science and the economic system generate different evaluations of ailments.[2]

A framework similar to the one we adopt was first proposed by David Thomasma and Edmund Pellegrino (1981), who argued that medical ethics must be based on philosophy of medicine. These authors advocated that *beneficence* is the most important principle of medical ethics, and that the triadic model, which pays equal attention to how disease is experienced and conceptualized subjectively by patients, how it is clinically objectivized by medicine and physicians, and how it is variously viewed by, and embedded in, society, is a good way of emphasizing the variety of relevant aspects involved in beneficence. It is evident that a consideration of this kind requires a change in the classical perspective of autonomy. As the paragraph below shows, Thomasma's inspiration was taken from the work of Karl E. Rothschuh:[3]

> Health and disease are building blocks of medical logic, but this logic is not exclusively scientific. In fact, as Rothschuh indicates, disease is a *relational structure* between sickness, the sick person, the physician, and society. *The ill person enters three relations – one to the self, another to the physician, and still another to society and environment – all of which are governed by the need for help.* The physician also enters three relations – one of responsibility to the sick person, another to the disease (what is the case? what to do?), and another to society. Society is also involved with individual good for the patient, the common good, and a relationship of aid, prevention, and research on the causes and effects of disease. Rothschuh therefore defines disease as *the presence of a subjective, or social need for help in persons whose physical, psychic, clinical, or psychophysical balance of boundaries in the organism is disrupted*. Health, or well-being, on the other hand, is characterized by the presence of order and balance in the organism and no perceived or actual need for help. This analysis recognizes the primary referent of health and disease as conditions of the body. (Thomasma 2000: 253, emphasis added)

Thus, according to these authors, the philosophical analysis of the notions of health and disease obliges us to adopt a triadic perspective and, as regards the relationship between bioethics and the philosophy of medicine, this means that the former cannot be based on a simple account of disease as conceived by the medical profession, but rather upon a careful consideration of other implications also.[4]

Unfortunately, although in a later book Bergsma and Thomasma (2000) provided an account of autonomy in light of the changes that had taken place in health care worldwide, such a comprehensive philosophy of medicine has not yet been completed (Sulmasy 2005: 487–8). Thomasma died in 2002, and few other sustained efforts have been made to link bioethics to the philosophy of medicine, and particularly to the debate on the concepts of health and disease. This chapter aims to make a contribution to this line of research at the intersection between medicine, philosophy and ethics. We claim that bioethics needs to be grounded in the philosophy of medicine and we present an analysis of the problems encountered when analysing some philosophical aspects of the principle of autonomy. We contend that the principle of respect for autonomy requires that the practice and experience of being autonomous in health and illness be taken into account, and that the triad helps conceptualize the complex aspects involved.

The argument presented in this chapter starts with the triadic approach to the concept of disease in relation to debates in the philosophy of medicine regarding the definition of health and disease. In the next section, the "four principles" account in bioethics is considered in light of the triad. Although relationships are found between disease and the principle of non-maleficence, between sickness and the principle of justice, and between illness and the principle of respect for autonomy, the "four principles" model has not been sufficiently informed by the multidimensional perspective of the triad. In particular, the principle of respect for autonomy needs to be reformulated to account properly for the illness dimension. The final section focuses on the concept of autonomy, and we offer a partial explanation of the reasons why it is unable to make sense of the complexity inherent to the triadic approach if it is understood as in mainstream bioethics, and suggest a new approach.

HEALTH AND THE TRIAD: *DISEASE, ILLNESS AND SICKNESS*

One of the main topics in the philosophy of medicine concerns our understanding of the notions of health and disease; the on-going debate concerns the two different naturalist and normativist views in medicine. For naturalists, disease needs to be described in accordance with natural science (biology), in an objective and reductionist manner, whereas for normativists, judgements on disease cannot be purely objective, since they involve norms and evaluations. Boorse's (1977, 1997) account, typical of the naturalist side, conceives health as the normal statistical functioning of an organism, and disease as an atypical deviation from that normality. For normativists, such as Nordenfelt (1987), health is a matter of well-being, judged according to the standards of the patient. Naturalists and normativists differ also on whether medicine is science or art, understanding that as a science, medicine focuses on studying the nature of disease and possible interventions, whereas as an art, it is concerned with the practical ability to apply that knowledge to individual patients or populations. Medicine has sought legitimacy in laboratory-based science, sometimes at the cost of being less able to pay full attention to the physician–patient relationship (Tauber 1999: 13). Another related issue to consider is whether medicine requires an exhaustive knowledge of the organic nature of diseases (providing that such knowledge is possible), or whether it should limit itself to the practical search for efficacious therapeutic interventions. Although this debate has been going on over recent decades, some authors have recently argued that it has now reached a stalemate that needs to be overcome (Khushf 2007: 27).

A possible way out of the opposing naturalist and normativist positions might be found in an understanding of ailment based on a triad of notions (disease, illness and sickness), capable of encompassing the medical, personal and social aspects of the phenomenon. This triadic conceptualization would not be committed to either naturalism or normativism, but may accommodate features of both. Indeed, disease is usually defined in naturalistic terms, but illness and sickness incorporate insights from the normativist position, thus recognizing the relevance of subjective and social values. In Bjørn Hofmann's (2002) characterization the triad offers a comprehensive way of addressing the conflicting views of basic concepts in health care. His distinction between illness, disease and sickness corresponds to the social structure of health care, since it represents the perspectives of the main stakeholders involved. Furthermore, it genuinely connects evaluative and epistemic aspects, clarifying how these complex issues emerge and can be tackled. This is how Hofmann (2002) defines the triad:

- Disease is a negative bodily occurrence as conceived of by the medical profession.
- Illness is a negative bodily occurrence as conceived of by the person himself.
- Correspondingly, sickness is a negative bodily occurrence as conceived of by society and/or its institutions.

As said before, although the style of thinking of each vortex as disease, illness and sickness could be reproduced by other parties (e.g. patients thinking of their condition in terms of disease), the triadic model tries to characterize the knowledge generated according to the authority that motivates each different system of evaluations.

Hofmann concurs with other authors, such as Nordenfelt (1987), in that both health and disease are evaluative concepts, since values play a role in constituting the concept of "health care". Yet, in contrast to Nordenfelt (1987, 1994) and Twaddle (1994), for whom the starting point is a general or positive notion of health, Hofmann maintains that negative concepts, such as disease, illness and sickness, can be used independently, as they are informative enough. He argues that as a matter of fact, these concepts do exist, even in the absence of a general theory of health; they are not mere names for different "health problems", as Twaddle contends, or "disabilities", as Nordenfelt says, but rather the terms capture three different perspectives on human ailment that are the main focus of medicine and health care.

In Hofmann's view, the triadic distinction between illness, disease and sickness is fruitful both theoretically and practically. For instance, he argues that the term "health care" should be replaced by terms such as "disease control", "illness care" and "sickness rights ascription". Indeed, such conceptual differentiation would correspond better to the different perspectives and would be more explicit regarding how to act and what to expect from the practice of medicine, even if we doubt that it could ever be implemented in practice. The term "health care" has been used for a long time and will be very difficult to substitute. But this is not the most interesting aspect of his use of the triad. When combined, the three perspectives provide an understanding of "normal" or typical health care scenarios, as opposed to ethically problematic situations or "cases". The paradigm of a normal scenario in health care is when a person feels *ill*, the medical profession is able to detect *disease*, and society attributes to him the status *sick*. Illness explains the person's situation from their point of view, disease permits medical attention, and sickness frees the person from ordinary duties of work and provides the right to assistance.

In the typical or normal scenario, negative bodily occurrences, as conceived of by the individual, correspond to those recognized by the medical profession and by relevant social institutions. In other cases, however, conditions deviate from this standard and may be judged as falling under one or two aspects of the triad, but not all three of them (Hofmann 2002: 10–12).[5] Thus, an instance may be judged to be both disease and sickness, but not illness (for example, some mental diseases in which the person does not personally feel afflicted by any condition, or diseases that are asymptomatic for the patient but potentially harmful to others, such as some cases of human papillomavirus, or HPV, infections). It may also be the case that a condition is understood as both disease and illness, but not sickness (the common cold or dental caries could fall into this category as far as their social consequences are null), as the individual in question would suffer ailment and be in need of mild medical assistance, but this would not affect their social identity. Other instances could be occurrences of illness and sickness, but not of disease (a typical example of this used to be fibromyalgia, a condition of vast social and personal consequences that for a long time went unacknowledged by the medical system). Currently, we may consider some conditions, such as low and moderate hypertension or lactose intolerance, to be examples of disease, but not of either illness or sickness; other negative bodily occurrences (such as melancholia, feelings of dissatisfaction, unpleasantness or incompetence) might be personally experienced as illnesses even though they are not socially understood as medical conditions (neither disease nor sickness); and some situations may be considered by society as sickness, although they are not counted as either disease or illness (Hofmann mentions in this respect some cases of delinquency, dissidence or homosexuality in certain societies).

An interesting aspect regarding our use of the triad is linked to the significance assigned to the body. Hofmann's formulation tries to avoid the notion of "the body", using the expression "occurrences" to mean processes, states or events. This might be because he wants to avoid difficulties in relation to mental health and illness. But, as we see it, an emphasis on "bodily" aspects is necessary in order to stress that whenever there is disease/illness/sickness, someone is afflicted by it: these concepts predicate an embodied organism. In other words, if we consider, quoting Epicurus, that illness is about "the cry of the flesh", there must be some bodily flesh in order for there to be illness.[6] All disease, be it mental or physical, is embodied.[7] Thus, the triad appears able to integrate controversial cases discussed in the literature (R. Cooper 2002a, 2002b) and to offer a more comprehensive framework for assessing ailment and analysing difficult cases involving conflicts of moral values and principles.

The triad comprises biopsychosocial elements and possibilities in a holistic approach. In particular, it attempts to address elements of personhood that have no firm objective basis – the social, the emotional, the moral – in a picture of the organism as an integrated, functioning whole, according to which medicine should be holistic in orientation. A similar argument is offered by Alfred Tauber, who claims that the basic purpose of medicine is to recover "the full personhood of the patient to again become an autonomous free-living individual"; therefore, by its very nature, medicine "demands a holistic understanding of the organism and a holistic approach to the care of the patient" (Tauber 2002: 262, 268). Indeed, respecting and promoting the autonomy of patients seems to be connected to the very idea of fighting human ailment in its complexity.

In the next section, we analyse the "four principles" account of bioethics formulated by Beauchamp and Childress in order to observe the relationship between the triadic approach in philosophy of medicine with this bioethical perspective and the notion of autonomy that underlies it.

THE PRINCIPLES OF BIOETHICS AND THE TRIAD

The mainstream doctrine or standard model in biomedical ethics is the well-known "four principles" approach developed by many authors after 1979, when it was introduced by the first edition of *Principles of Biomedical Ethics* (Beauchamp and Childress [1979] 2008). The four principles are respect for autonomy, non-maleficence, beneficence and justice; they were proposed as mid-level norms mediating between high-level moral theory and low-level common morality, and they became very influential in bioethics.[8] As mentioned earlier, for many authors respect for the autonomy of the patient has been the core of this four-element ethical account, but we contend that there is a serious problem in the common understanding of the notion of autonomy as a right, rather than as a capacity that enables physical, psychological and social interactions.

We worry that the "four principles" account, the most salient representative of contemporary bioethics, may sometimes operate with a notion of disease that is simplistic and one-dimensional in comparison with the richness of perspectives opened up by the triad, and by contemporary philosophy of medicine. Thus it is useful to review Beauchamp and Childress's book (hereafter B&C) in light of the account proposed by the triad, in order to consider how to link discussions in the philosophy of medicine with critical bioethical debates, and thus clarify current controversies over the meaning of basic principles, particularly in relation to the principle of autonomy and the obligations that arise from it.

Although the multidimensionality of the notion of disease offered by the triad is absent in B&C, there is a sense in which something equivalent appears in the four-principle scheme,[9] and in fact it is possible to establish some parallels that show why similar concerns appear in both conceptualizations. Thus, we may say that the principles of bioethics reflect (to some extent at least) the triad: the principle of non-maleficence may be associated with the perspective of disease, respect for autonomy with that of illness, and the principle of justice with sickness, whereas the principle of beneficence may be linked to all three of them (at least according to some authors, as we mention later). However it is more usual to see this principle being linked to how the medical profession sees the patient's good, something that is often criticized as introducing paternalism. Let us now examine these principles one by one.

The principle of non-maleficence asserts an obligation not to inflict harm on others (B&C: 113). The authors confine their analysis of this principle to the prevention of harm, which is itself a contested concept. It is true that they do not deny "the importance of mental harms and setbacks to other interests", but they concentrate on physical harm, which in their view can be *objectively* measured (117). Their idea of non-maleficence is to avoid pain, disability and death as much as possible, and to do so by appealing to objective, shared professional standards. They find a specification of the principle in the standards that determine due care in a given set of circumstances: "Due care is taking sufficient and appropriate care to avoid causing harm, as the circumstances demand of a reasonable and prudent person.

This standard requires that the goals pursued justify the risks that must be imposed to achieve those goals" (118). Professional standards are set by health care professionals, and are therefore associated with disease in the sense of negative bodily occurrences identified by the medical profession. So, when non-maleficence is invoked, it could be said that it is underlain by the notion of disease.

In what concerns the principle of *justice*, B&C maintain that no single theory can account for the conflicting demands associated to it. Justice fosters questions about "what the people of a nation should expect from their health care system and how the nation can address citizens' needs for increased insurance, long-term care, and the like" (B&C: 272). Every society, they add, should recognize "an enforceable right to a decent minimum of health care within a framework for allocation that incorporates both utilitarian and egalitarian standards" (272). Those standards, again, are not set by patients alone, but by a number of social agents who identify which negative bodily occurrences are entitled to (or require) health care benefits. B&C specify and balance several principles of justice in particular contexts (227ff.), but in all of them the notion of justice is underlain by this notion of sickness.

When illness is defined as "negative bodily occurrences as conceived of by the ill person", this definition clearly has more to do with conceptions of the good held by patients, and therefore with their *autonomy*, defined by B&C (63) as a "person's right to hold views, to make choices, and to take actions based on their personal values and beliefs". It is true that the principle is still directed at health care professionals, in the sense that it requires action from them, in the form of respectful treatment in disclosing information to the patient and fostering free decision-making. Still, from the perspective of autonomy, illness is the most salient notion.

So far we have argued that non-maleficence is underpinned by the notion of disease, autonomy by illness and justice by sickness. But, what about the principle of *beneficence*? We now turn to this question.

B&C propose a framework of *prima facie* principles, denying the priority of one over the others (B&C: 57). The authors justify the obligation to follow these principles, but acknowledge that their precise demands cannot be precisely settled, but are open to interpretation and specification. Morality, they say, is "rooted no less deeply" in autonomy than in non-maleficence, beneficence or justice (104). "Neither the patient nor the physician has premier and overriding authority, and no pre-eminent principle exists in biomedical ethics, not even the obligation to act in the patient's best interest" (177). This fits well with the triad, according to which absence of health needs to be analysed in three dimensions – medical, personal and social – with none being more important than the other two.

This absence of priority is especially clear when considering beneficence, which requires that agents take positive steps to help others (rather than merely refrain from harmful acts), balancing an action's possible goods against its costs and possible harm. Here lies another reason why the triadic approach looks promising when trying to capture the complexity inherent in the health care relationship: it helps us understand the debates over beneficence, a principle that was initially subject to harsh criticism within bioethics, but which has been recovered by authors such as Tauber (1999) or Pellegrino and Thomasma (1988) as the guiding principle or moral core of the medical profession, provided it is rendered compatible with respect for the patient's autonomy.[10]

DIMENSIONS OF AUTONOMY

We have suggested that, to some extent, a relationship may exist between the principles of bioethics and the triadic notions of disease, illness and sickness. The relationship is not a direct match between the triad and the "four principles" account of bioethics, but similar concerns may underlie both theoretical accounts, in the ethical and in the epistemological domain. Rather than to assume that there needs to be something like a one-to-one link or a many-to-one link, our aim is to see how an epistemological investigation of the triad may help inform an ethical discussion of the principles. In the following section we argue that such a relationship is not adequately emphasized, both in theory and in practice. The four principles of medical ethics are not sufficiently informed by the concerns present in the triad, and in particular the principle of respect for autonomy needs to be reformulated so that it connects better with the illness dimension of the triad and provides an account of the phenomena related to autonomy-within-illness and the associated problems.

On the practical side, our point is that mainstream medical ethics was developed to assist decision-making within a context of acute care, which focuses on decisions that need to be taken in order to restore health. Within this theory, decision-making is conceived to occur related to, and requiring, the kind of autonomy that healthy people may exercise. Thus, ill individuals, who may be thought to be in a categorically different situation from healthy people, are endowed by mainstream bioethics with this idealized form of autonomy.

So, the question is: how is autonomy affected by illness? Patients' experience of illness is shaped by a sense of vulnerability that is both subjective (how patients may perceive themselves) and objective (their susceptibility to external threats, pressures and harm). Yet, as Carel (2009) argues, there is a diverse range of patient responses to illness, and their needs are correspondingly different (for a similar conclusion concerning the diversity of patients' experience of dignity, see Chochinov 2004). Patients' responses to illness are often very personal in nature; they might even be considered as ways of asserting their identity. In this sense, more basic than the capacity to self-rule, and underlying it, autonomy can be observed in how agents manage to maintain a precarious identity with the ability to act so as to ensure the persistence of their agency (Moreno & Casado 2011). In this way, a patient's response to illness, his or her behaviour, is ultimately related to what he or she *is* as an agent.

Patients may be more autonomous and less subjectively vulnerable than we believe them to be, although in ways different from those assumed by the standard model and that need to be better characterized. Conversely, nurses (and other health professionals) may be more vulnerable than is generally believed, since they are continually exposed to existential suffering in stressful environments (Carel 2009: 217–18). As a result, bioethics needs to readdress what it means to be autonomous-within-illness; not to deny that ill people can be autonomous – that would be tantamount to advocating an unacceptable return to paternalism – but to take into account that there are different ways of striving to maintain a precarious identity. Many of those might not easily accommodate standard accounts of bioethics; as we will see in what follows, there are alternative ways of looking at autonomy.

Autonomy in illness

In 1988, the Hastings Center published a special report on the ethical dimensions of chronic illness and chronic care, topics which had hitherto been relatively neglected in bioethics (Jennings *et al.* 1988). A common theme in the ensuing literature is that judgements about quality of life change dramatically when one becomes chronically ill (Carel 2008). Reports show that healthy people judge the life of some ill people to be more "unliveable" than the ill people themselves experience it (Menzel 1992; see also Wasserman *et al.* 2011). Philosophers writing on the challenges of disability have similarly complained that "physicians in particular estimate the quality of the lives of their disabled patients to be much lower than do the patients themselves" (Amundson 2000: 46). In other words, the very idea of a *self*, of the agent's identity, acquires different meanings depending on the perspective of the healthy or the ill. Ethics must take into account how being ill alters our selfhood (Tauber 1999). Related to this, we must ask whether our views on the relevance of the principle of respect for autonomy may change in illness, in comparison with how it is conceived in health, just as the capacity to exercise autonomy may vary between health and illness, at least in some ways.

During the last quarter of the twentieth century, the principles of bioethics were conceived to help with fast life-or-death decision-making. However, longer life expectancy and other social and cultural factors have turned the attention of institutionalized bioethics to chronic disease, shifting the focus from emergency medicine to primary, long-term care. The management of chronic disease requires a more comprehensive account of autonomy than that offered by the standard accounts based on acute disease. When the focus shifts from acute cure to chronic care, it becomes clear that bioethics needs an understanding of autonomy-within-illness, rather than relying on a general account of autonomy-within-health. Moreover, the concept of autonomy includes at least three different aspects or dimensions – decisional, executive and informational – which we will discuss in the following section.

Because the concept of patient autonomy was developed in the context of acute care, it has been identified with the *decisional* autonomy of patients or their proxies: whether to accept or reject a proposed treatment. In contrast, primary care, with its focus on chronic disease and palliative care, is an area of medicine where practice must go beyond the disease-laden idea of "fixing bodies" and move towards viewing patients as people, individuals with stories of their own who live in social networks of relatives, friends and fellow citizens. It must move towards illness and sickness.

A perspective like this forces the notion of autonomy to move beyond respect for the autonomy of patients as respecting their freedom of choice. As Eric Cassell (2010: 43) points out, in practice, the principle of respect for autonomy has been translated into something like this: "present the patients with the current and correct information about their clinical situation and offer them the options from which they must choose". Indeed, B&C refer to *"substantial autonomy"*, expressing a confidence that "Patients and research subjects can achieve substantial autonomy in their decisions, just as substantially autonomous choice occurs in other areas of life, such as buying a house or choosing a university to attend" (B&C: 60). However, the examples chosen in this quote support our previous criticism of this way of understanding autonomy: buying a house and choosing a university are typical choices for the relatively healthy.

Thus, at least in medical practice, the prevailing notion of autonomy identifies it with the freedom of choice of someone who is rational and able to make such choices. Leaving aside the fact that some people cannot make free choices even if they are not ill (for instance, in cases where the stronger party uses his or her influence to control, manipulate or exploit the other), if a theory of medical ethics does not take into account the very fact that creates the health care relationship, that is, that patients need some form of care that may contribute to sustain their autonomous living, then the theory has a problem. In Cassell's words:

> This discussion of autonomy in medicine must seem a little bit strange and unreal. What happened to sickness? It is as if no one is sick. What we know about sickness – not as doctors ... but merely the everyday knowledge of sickness. Because if people are really sick, with everything that goes with sickness, can they really make the best decisions about their care the way we have described? (Cassell 2010: 44)

We believe that B&C's "substantial autonomy" does not fully consider the particular situation of ill people, because this concept does not come from the "kingdom of the sick", but rather from the "kingdom of the well" (Sontag 1978). In particular, it comes from philosophical and legal conceptions of autonomy, such as those proposed by Harry Frankfurt (1971) or Ronald Dworkin (1988). Although they work in different fields of philosophy, what these authors have in common is that they did not develop their definitions of autonomy for patients, but rather for healthy, "normal" agents or citizens.

To paraphrase Carel (2008: 77ff.), what is needed here is a model of "autonomy within illness" that gives more weight to the subjective, first-person experience. To the extent that chronically ill people report experiencing episodes of well-being or happiness, it is possible to talk about autonomy within illness, but it will not be the kind of autonomy that healthy people are presumed to have. As a matter of fact, autonomy-within-health is also under scrutiny, as recent work in neurosciences (Felsen & Reiner 2011) adds new criticisms to the "standard model" of autonomy based on Frankfurt or Dworkin. This research suggests that human brains are indeed capable of the hierarchical control required for reflective thought, but that decisions conventionally perceived as autonomous may not be rational with respect to the deliberative process itself, and are rarely free from covert external influences. If the capacity for autonomy needs to be redefined in order to align our moral values with neuroscientific naturalism, this is especially relevant for our discussion because patients' autonomy is even more complex and precarious than the one assumed by the standard model (Moreno & Casado 2011).

Three-dimensional autonomy

In bioethics, respect for the principle of autonomy is intrinsically linked to the notion of informed consent for therapeutic actions, with the emphasis usually placed on consent. This suggests that respect for autonomy is mainly understood with an epistemological bias towards disease, towards taking into account the available therapeutic options, and fails to give due consideration to illness and sickness. Here we claim that an adequate account of patient autonomy should include other dimensions in addition to the medical decision-making. As Hofmann notes:

> If the medical profession is the only one identifying negative bodily occurrences, their sensitivity to the interests of the person and society will determine whether they act paternalistic or violate patient autonomy. Additionally, one can question how well a person without illness understands information about diseases that he or she cannot experience. Is there a real informed consent?
> (Hofmann 2002: 670n12)

As evident in the above quote, Hofmann doubts that a health professional could really *inform* a patient adequately about something he or she does not experience. He is warning us against using a notion of autonomy that is mainly related to the disease angle of the triad. Our understanding of autonomy would improve if we could situate our concern in a more comprehensive perspective that included illness, the more personal subjective dimension, and sickness, the more social dimension. In other words, *patient autonomy is more than decision-making*.

Indeed, some studies have argued that, especially in chronic disease, autonomy extends beyond "punctuate decisions" (R. Kukla 2005: 35). Patient autonomy cannot be reduced to decisional autonomy: it is not so much a matter of what patients or proxies freely and knowledgeably decide at any given point, but rather an essentially conversational, dialogical *process* (Árnason 2000) in which patients, professionals, relatives and others engage in assuming, assigning and deflecting responsibility within a specific practice. In this process the crucial aspect is not the particular content of the decision, but the *agency* involved – who is accountable in the practice, to whom, and for what. This is an important perspective because it reminds us that society and the state are always present in the patient–professional relationship. Health care is indeed a triangular affair.

In an article published in the *American Journal of Bioethics*, Naik *et al.* (2009) warn that the perspective of mainstream bioethics might be neglecting some important features of what it means for people to be ill. They argue that patient non-compliance (behaviour incongruent with the treatment plan) is interpreted by clinicians as either an autonomous refusal of the physician's recommendations or the result of significant impairments in decisional autonomy that need to be assessed and managed. But some patients with chronic conditions may articulate understanding of the management plan and appear non-compliant when in fact they are unable to implement the steps necessary to meet the treatment objectives. Thus Naik *et al.* argue for an expansion of the concept of patient autonomy to include not only decisional autonomy, but also the patient's capacity to execute complex self-management tasks – what they call *executive autonomy*.

This reconceptualization of the concept of autonomy should be further expanded in order to supplement its decisional and executive components with a particular approach to other aspects of patient autonomy. For instance, what we call *informational autonomy*: the personal management of health-related information, the right to give or withhold it freely and without pressure, the necessary know-how to communicate with others about illness. This component of respect for autonomy has been traditionally associated more with research or information technology ethics than with health care. However, it has been increasingly addressed by European law and bioethics (Casado 2009b) and deserves further consideration.

The informational and executive dimensions of autonomy presuppose an understanding of human agency as intrinsically temporal and social, embedded in culturally elaborated norms, habits and conversations. There is nothing unnatural about autonomy, but it does require a certain form of self-consciousness, which does not arise without the cognitive and communicative abilities required to enable the attribution of some kind of responsibility, which is assigned (or deflected) by discursive, although not necessarily verbal, social interaction. This emphasis on the relationship between autonomy and human communication is shared by other authors. For instance, Philip Pettit (2001: 177) sees human autonomy or freedom as something depending on persons having "the ratiocinative and relational capacity required for being authorized as a discursive partner: their being conversable, in at once a psychological and a social sense." In this sense, to be an autonomous agent (be it patient or doctor) is simply to be the type of self that can live up to the commitments generated in discursive relationships. Performing an autonomous action means performing it as the type of agent who can be held responsible for reasons. After all, we are not born autonomous: we are *made* autonomous, and therefore responsible, by interacting with other agents, including, of course, the professionals who take care of us.

DISCUSSION: WHAT PHILOSOPHY OF MEDICINE OFFERS TO BIOETHICS

Health care is a complex affair. No single concept of disease is capable of capturing, on its own, the complexity inherent in this kind of human relationship. The immanent triadic character of the definition of health by the World Health Organization (WHO) remains a helpful integrative approach to health and disease but, as we have shown, mainstream bioethics, as represented by the "four principles" approach used by B&C, is not sufficiently informed by the triadic concept of disease. This is primarily because the perspective of the ill patient is not adequately present in the principle of respect for autonomy, both in theory and in practice.

Respect for autonomy requires taking illness, the subjectively lived experience of requiring care, into account. But throughout the world, bioethics is mostly being institutionalized by creating ethics committees in every major hospital, and these committees are mostly made up of health care professionals. In our experience, narratives and complaints put forth by patients themselves do not, for the most part, become "cases" and are not often addressed as such by these committees. In Spain, the involvement of lay participants in such committees is generally seen as something that is desirable but hard to put into practice (this absence of social and patient participation in institutional review boards is identified as a problem by comprehensive studies such as Nicolás & Romeo 2009). There may be other examples of how the perspective pursued by the triad might be useful, but in this chapter we have argued that adopting something like it helps us understand why this is happening: by using a concept of autonomy which is modelled on certain presuppositions about the autonomy of healthy, "normal" people, mainstream bioethics prioritizes the health care professionals' point of view to the detriment of the other dimensions appearing from the perspective of people in need of care. This is problematic because in bioethics, there is no such thing as "normal" people: what we have here is autonomy-within-illness, not autonomy-within-health.

This bias towards disease is visible in practice, in the heuristics of how bioethics is practised today. In this chapter we have explored a basic hypothesis about the historical sources of this phenomenon: bioethics was born in a technologically mediated medical culture in which the main focus was on cure, not care. The emphasis was on decision-making, and the decisional autonomy of patients. Other dimensions of autonomy were relatively neglected (how to cope in time – executive autonomy; how to manage communicative exchanges concerning one's health – informational autonomy). This created a bias towards autonomy understood simply as the capacity to decide given certain therapeutic options, which again is more related to the epistemological perspective associated with disease.

Reflecting on the triad of notions disease/illness/sickness can help illuminate and critique the "four principles" account of bioethics. In particular, we have argued that the concept of autonomy should be expanded towards a notion better able to account for the kind of autonomy that ill people could sustain if the appropriate care is provided. This implies a multidimensional stance that takes into account not only the quasi-legal or juridical elements related to decision-making, but also different aspects linked to the executive and informational dimensions of autonomy, in order not to neglect the particularities of what it means for people to be ill. In this chapter we have tried to move beyond decisional autonomy, on the path connecting bioethics and the philosophy of medicine. Much is yet to be done regarding reconceptualizing patient autonomy along these lines, but the resulting model will undoubtedly be more egalitarian and inclusive than the mainstream one. A consideration of the most neglected aspects of the triad supplements our understanding of what it is like to require health care, and what we should focus on in order to provide it and to advance the autonomy debate in bioethics.

Furthermore, this debate on autonomy in bioethics is related to various other issues that affect the way we conceive of medicine. Canguilhem saw medicine as an *art at the crossroads of many sciences* (1978: 34). However, the characterization of medicine as an art, rather than a science, responds in part to an extremely narrow positivist conception of the nature of science (i.e. as the elaboration of theories that explain phenomena), which does not correspond to the conceptions present in contemporary philosophy of science, for which science is not so much involved in the task of constructing theories, but rather consists of a set of practices (experiments, simulations, classificatory practices, data collection and retrieval, etc.) informed by theories. Thus, many would say that science itself can be conceived as an art, because of the importance of its practical or productive function.[11]

The knowledge style of medicine does not coincide with that of a positivistic science, but that does not mean it cannot be scientific. In this sense, a valid way of characterizing medicine's style of scientific knowledge could be to appeal to the triad of disease, illness and sickness as a means of expressing the need to take the personal, social and biological aspects into account. This broader understanding of ailment based on this triad acknowledges the medical perspective of the phenomenon and aims to encompass the naturalist aspiration to objectivity, while at the same time taking into account the perspectives of both patients and society.

CONCLUSION

An exploration of how the triad of notions disease/illness/sickness fits in with the "four principles" account of bioethics should not simply result in a negative indictment that emphasizes certain deficiencies in the way autonomy has been understood in bioethics. Rather, and to put it in more positive terms, we advocate an alliance between bioethics and the philosophy of medicine through a reconceptualization of patient autonomy, in terms of the actions – personal, medical and social – that need to be taken to sustain the form of living of those in need of care. This implies a multidimensional stance that takes into account not only the quasi-legal or juridical elements related to decision-making, but also different aspects linked to the executive and communicative dimensions of autonomy, in order not to neglect the particularities of what it means for people to be ill. We have argued that the concept of autonomy should be expanded from the capacity to rule one's life through independent decisions towards an epistemological and ethical account of how people can interactively enhance their ability to sustain a life through appropriate care. By understanding autonomy this way the gap is narrowed between the ethical and the scientific goals of medicine.

ACKNOWLEDGEMENTS

The authors wish to thank Cristian Saborido (UNED, Madrid) for providing help with some quotations, discussing several versions of the manuscript and participating in the initial presentation of this work in the "Concepts of Health and Illness" Conference in Bristol (1–3 September 2010). We also thank the editors of this volume, Havi Carel and Rachel Cooper, for their comments and questions on the first draft, as they triggered significant improvements. This work was funded by the Basque Government (IT 505-10 research group) and the Spanish Government (FFI2008-06348-C02-02/FISO and FFI2008-06348-C02-01/FISO research projects).

NOTES

1. Unless otherwise stated, in this chapter we will be using these terms in this sense.
2. We are grateful to our editors, who raised some of these problems.
3. Karl E. Rothschuh, whom Thomasma and Pelegrino quote, had written about disease in similar terms considering three axes: *aegritudo* or illness, *nosos* (*pathos*) or disease, and *insalubritas* or sickness (see Mergenthaler 2004).
4. Since the 1970s, the study of medicine in the philosophy of science has highlighted how different the philosophy of science would be if it had developed by taking other disciplines such as medicine as a scientific model, instead of physics (Grene 1977). One of the effects of considering medicine as a science is that the need arises to take into account many factors previously excluded from the consideration of science in more classical developments in philosophy of science (Aronova 2009), such as the sociological context.
5. Hofmann (2002: 653), inspired by Twaddle (1994), represents the three concepts of the triad as three partly overlapping spheres, so that there is one intersection of the three, and three intersections of two of them: disease and illness, disease and sickness, and illness and sickness.
6. Havi Carel recovers Merleau-Ponty's distinction between the biological and the lived body in order to make a point that is similar to that of the triad, as it has to

do with the difference between the scientific understanding of the biological body and lived experience, corresponding roughly to the difference between disease and illness. In this sense, the body plays a central role in our understanding of illness, which is now seen as a rift between the biological and the lived body, a change that is not local but global: "being ill is not just an objective constraint imposed on a biological body part, but a systematic shift in the way the body experiences, reacts and performs tasks as a whole" (Carel 2008: 28–9).

7. Thus, Thomasma (2000: 255) writes: "[P]sychiatry remains wedded to the body precisely because the body and one's self-image created by corporeal possibilities are intrinsically linked."

8. The book is now in its sixth edition, and remains a classic, standard text in the field.

9. We should make it clear that B&C and the mainstream literature in bioethics do not use the terms disease, illness and sickness as in the triad. In B&C's book, "disease" is used seventy-one times, more than twice as often as "illness" (thirty-three times), whereas "sickness" is not used at all (although "sick" appears nineteen times). Some authors prefer to use "illness" in order to stress the phenomenological account of disease as experienced by the ill person (e.g. Carel 2008). If this was the case with B&C, it could be that the pre-eminence of "disease" in their book points to a pre-eminence of the medical perspective in their doctrine. Even when they do not explicitly cite the triadic approach or other conceptual distinctions between "disease" and notions such as "sickness" or "illness", its professional character is reinforced by the fact that in the book this term is used specifically to refer to a particular disease (as in Huntington's or Alzheimer's disease, "chronic renal disease" or "extensive coronary artery disease"), while "sickness" is missing and "illness" is used in a more generic way, as in "terminal illness" or "severe illness".

10. For instance, Pellegrino and Thomasma (1988) reinterpreted the principle as beneficence-in-trust, maintaining that to be guided by beneficence, a physician must perform a right and good healing action that is consonant with the individual patient's values. In order to act in the patient's best interests, the physician must discern together with them what their good is in every particular case.

11. That is what Marjorie Grene said as early as 1976. Solomon (2008: 408) disagrees with the characterization of medicine as an art for precisely the same reasons: "We certainly have a puzzle. Forty years of Science Studies have told us repeatedly that science is not a science. And if physics and biology are not science – in the sense that they do not follow a precisely stated method, do depend on practical skills and on contextual factors, produce local rather than general claims, involve much fallibility and so forth – why bother to point out that medicine is not a science?"

4. THE CONCEPT OF "MENTAL DISORDER"

Valérie Aucouturier and Steeves Demazeux

In the last forty years there have been many attempts to provide a general and useful definition of the concept of "mental disorder".[1] Most of these attempts have in common some general methodological precept: they rely on conceptual analysis, which aims at clarifying the uses of a concept – whether in ordinary language or a scientific vocabulary – in order to get to a clearer understanding of it. In this chapter we question the appropriateness and relevance of this method in its application to the domain of mental health.

In the first part of the chapter, we draw attention to the philosophical presuppositions that underlie some applications of conceptual analysis. As we shall see, certain authors have sought to use conceptual analysis in diverse ways; we argue that some uses have been misguided. This philosophical enquiry has proved to be important in the psychiatric context, since the main issue regarding classifications of mental disorders revolves around what should be included as a mental disorder (one of the most striking historical examples, discussed below, is homosexuality). How are such decisions taken and how should they be made? Who has the authority to decide what should fall under the concept of mental disorder, and based on what criteria? To what extent can the philosophy of language help solve such issues?

The second part of this chapter examines the history of attempts to apply conceptual analysis to the notion of mental disorder. We show how the use of conceptual analysis (understood as a method that claims to objectively analyse the ultimate components of a concept) leads to different results depending on the historical, economic and political context.

CONCEPTUAL ANALYSIS

In philosophy, the method of conceptual analysis can be understood in many different ways. Much confusion has resulted from the fact that those practising "conceptual analysis" have actually been engaged in very different tasks. We argue that the misuses of this method rely on an erroneous understanding of the way language works and that there are (at least) two ways of misusing conceptual analysis: one that relies on a naturalistic fallacy and the other on a false conception of meaning and ordinary language. Before examining them, however, we need briefly to reflect on the relations between language and the world.

Language and the world

Wittgenstein claimed that the meaning of words depends on their uses (Wittgenstein 1953: §43). What he meant is that, depending on what one may call their *function* (which includes an infinite variety of uses, e.g. denoting an object or speaking one's mind) and their *context* of use (which can be scientific, poetic, colloquial, etc.), words may work entirely differently. Thus, meaning cannot be philosophically determined in the same way for each instance of the use of a word. For example, the word "apple" normally denotes an object of a certain shape, colour and taste. Of course the meaning of "apple" is sensitive to the context of its use: "the big apple" is also the name of a big American city, when used in a context not related to food. However, the words "intention" or "disorder" – which are nouns just as the word "apple" is – do not ordinarily refer to any kind of physical or natural object in the way the word "apple" does. One may change the meaning of these words so that they would, but then they would not correspond to the same concept any more.

This occasion-sensitivity of meaning (Travis 2009) does not preclude the existence of rules for the uses of language and words. Hence, what the words "apple", "intention" or "disorder" mean is not entirely up to any individual. If it were, we would simply never know what we were talking about, and would not be able to use language to talk to one another. There are overarching conventions that we learn (implicitly or explicitly) when learning to speak, and which somehow ensure that when we speak to one another in a given circumstance we understand one another. So there is some truth in the idea that, despite the tremendous variety of contexts of uses and the infinity of possible uses, there must be some kind of objective ground of meaning on which we rely. It would be beyond the scope of this chapter to try to discuss exactly where this objectivity of the rules of the uses of language lies and how it modulates with the variety and singularity of these uses. What we have argued so far is that for a language to perform its function it requires both objectivity and context-sensitivity.

So we are left with the following set of questions. Can the term "mental disorder" be treated in exactly the same way as the word "apple"? Do mental disorders form a "natural kind" in the way that apples do in a certain context, such that necessary and sufficient conditions for something being a "mental disorder", or an "apple" can be given? Are there some context-sensitive rules to dig out, which can tell us exactly when this phrase is used correctly (say, in a medical context)? Or are *we* to set these rules – as the authors of the successive editions of the *Diagnostic and Statistical Manual of Mental Disorders* (DSM), the classification of mental disorders published by the American Psychiatric Association, seem to assume – and, if so, how? Let us now see why the two mistaken understandings of conceptual analysis are erroneous.

The naturalistic fallacy

On one understanding the term "mental disorder" refers to a natural kind. This understanding assumes that this phrase must mirror (or aspire to mirror) reality. If that is so, then the conceptual analyst has to find out what kind of natural object a mental disorder is, and to list its natural properties in order to determine what falls under the concept. Conceptual analysis conceived of as the analysis of the concept of mental disorder as a natural kind term is inspired by the causal theory of meaning (Kripke 1972; Putnam 1975). Broadly speaking, according to the causal theory of meaning, the reference of a name is normally fixed by an original act of naming and then that name becomes a rigid designator of that object; it is a name for that object (with its essential properties) in all possible worlds. This theory generally applies to proper names and natural kind terms: in any possible world Barack Obama will remain Barack Obama (whatever changes may have occurred in his physical appearance or biography); in any possible world, water is H_2O (i.e. any liquid looking like water but which is not H_2O is not water). Thus, to consider mental disorder as a natural kind term would imply that some kind has been picked out by our use of the term "mental disorder", even if the essential properties of a mental disorder remain to be determined.

The advantage of this theory of meaning is that it seems to rely on some sort of scientific investigation. One circumscribes an object of investigation – say "water" – and, by investigating its nature, determines some of its properties, for example, that it is H_2O. Although this method may appear legitimate in theory since it aims at building a genuinely scientific vocabulary, it can be problematic when applied to the term "mental disorder" since it assumes that this term is unified and clearly identified within the discourse of psychiatry, just as the concept of "water" is in chemistry and in ordinary language. Wakefield's definition of "(mental) disorder" as a harmful dysfunction (HD) may illustrate such an enterprise:

> I proposed that *disorder* means *harmful dysfunction,* where dysfunctions are failures of internal mechanisms to perform naturally selected functions ... The HD analysis proposes that a disorder attribution requires both a scientific judgment that there exists a failure of designed function and a value judgment that the design failure harms the individual.
> (Wakefield 1992a: 374)

In his analysis, Wakefield treats "function" and "dysfunction" as natural kind terms, thereby assuming that, just as in the case of "water", there are natural kinds that we are naming. But what could these be? Not only does Wakefield assume that there is a "normal" natural function of any organ in the human body, including the mental apparatus (an issue that we shall not discuss here[2]), he also takes the authority to claim *what* ought to be a mental "dysfunction" on the basis of some naturalistic account of mental functions.

Without making any claim about what "mental disorder" is, let us try to see where the analogy with "water" fails. Pointing at this difference can justify our treating mental disorder differently to the way we treat water as an object of enquiry. The fact that these words do not behave in the same way is a sufficient reason for treating them differently. The fact that "water" names a clearly identified reality allows some investigations that cannot take place with mental disorder as an object of enquiry. We will not discover anything about mental disorders before we explicitly decide what sort of object of enquiry this is. And contrary to the study of water, it seems that our conception of mental disorder is essential to the further investigations we may consider of such a phenomenon. Indeed, the issue here does not start from a clearly defined object of enquiry (like water), the nature of which remains to be discovered. What we are trying to do *is* to define our object of enquiry.

The naturalist simply *assumes* that there is some unified object of enquiry in the world called a mental disorder and that scientists ought to discover its natural properties. But if the concept of mental disorder did pick out some bundle of natural properties like "water" does, then there would not be any practical or philosophical problem: we would already have an agreement on what our object of investigation is. Since that is not the case, then we cannot suppose that *because* we have a concept of mental disorder in our language, then there *ought* to be some unified object in the world corresponding to it waiting to be discovered. If we already have this concept, it already has meaning (as unscientific as it might be) and this meaning influences our conception of the specific phenomena to which we are ready to apply that concept. So it seems that conceptual analysis on that understanding is not of much help when it comes to working out a scientific concept of mental disorder. Twin-Earth-type philosophical thought experiments regarding "mental disorder" will not help to clarify our concept here because, unlike Putnam's (1975) experiment with "water", there is no primary consensus on what we are referring to (some kind of substrata) when talking about mental disorder. As a result we may not appeal to some empirical discovery (similar to the discovery that water is H_2O^3) to specify what we *mean* by "mental disorder". It is not as if we had *labelled* something with this term and were now able to study this thing. We are actually trying to do the labelling.

In short, to treat or be willing to treat "mental disorder" as a natural kind is to ignore something Wittgenstein noticed: that far from being clearly disconnected from one another, our various uses of concepts are intertwined and linked by what he called "family resemblances". Instead of trying to propose a unique or core use of a word, one should try to see how the different uses of a notion may be distinct and akin at the same time — how we can see them relate to one another and at the same time be utterly different:

> And the result of this examination is: we see a complicated network of similarities overlapping and criss-crossing: sometimes overall similarities, sometimes similarities of detail. I can think of no better expression to characterise these similarities than "family resemblances"; for the various resemblances between members of a family: build, features, colour of eyes, gait, temperament, etc. etc. overlap and criss-cross in the same way.
> (Wittgenstein 1953: §66–7)

There is no point in trying to look for *the* meaning or *the* reference of the term "mental disorder", whatever direction this search might take.

Asking people

Granted that the causal theory of meaning appears to be irrelevant when it comes to defining "mental disorder", perhaps the so-called "ordinary" understanding of conceptual analysis could be of some interest. Haslam *et al.*

(2007), for instance, have tried to ground the theoretical understanding of "mental disorder" in "laypeople's conceptions". However, if "folk psychiatry" is to be a sort of psychological, anthropological or sociological investigation, then psychologists and sociologists are methodologically best equipped to untie the intricate, sometimes equivocal or polymorphic uses of "mental disorder". The wish to grasp the core representations of the term "mental disorder" within ordinary uses of language understood as a supposed common core of shared (but vague) intuitions seems delusive: at best it arbitrarily reduces the variety of uses to some very indeterminate widely shared intuitions, like "something is wrong with this person", which does not teach us much theoretically; and it condemns us to the idea that either there are universal shared intuitions about what a mental disorder is, or that the scientific concept we supposedly built based on these "folk psychology" intuitions is bound to be historically, culturally and contextually relative, which probably means that it is not a scientific concept at all.

To understand conceptual analysis as some sort of collection of the variety of uses of a word or phrase is also to misunderstand the actual functioning of language and the concept of a family resemblance. Indeed, the point of conceptual analysis should not be to present some kind of pluralistic definition of words based on statistically analysing people's uses and intuitions about the meaning of these words. Rather, it is to disentangle the uses of words while being careful with resemblances so as not to mix one meaning with another. If its point is conceptual clarification then conceptual analysis should not aim at a general all-embracing definition. The aim of conceptual analysis is to point at *differences* of meaning and context variations, which, had they remained unseen, could have led to philosophical confusion – like that of treating mental disorder as the same kind of scientific object of enquiry as water.

So it seems that the core issue and common weakness of the two approaches of conceptual analysis we have been discussing is what Wittgenstein would have called their "craving for generality" (Wittgenstein 1958: 18), which makes us blind to the variety and complexity of uses that is so broad in the case of "mental disorder" that there will always be a context of use working as a counter example to the proposed "scientific use".

The constraints of meaning: what conceptual analysis genuinely is

The variety of uses does not, however, prevent us from reaching some level of generality, which has nothing to do with the search for a core meaning or reference. This sort of generality is to be found in the (explicit and implicit) rules that govern our meaningful use of language. It captures the fact that our use of words (their "grammar") must follow some sort of rules. These rules stipulate, for instance, that when I go to the bakery and ask for a *baguette*, I cannot mean that I want a *croissant* or a *bottle of wine*, unless I am not a competent speaker of French; that is, unless I am mistaken about what *"baguette"* means. And if the baker hands me a *baguette* when I wanted a *croissant* and I am disappointed, *I* am the one who has made a mistake. The same sort of specific rules of meaningful use should apply to the concept of mental disorder. Of course, any one of us might call some of our relatives "crazy", "obsessive" or "neurotic"; this is one possible colloquial use of the concept of mental disorder. But when it is for the practitioner to decide, through a specific technical act, namely the diagnosis, whether her patient has a mental disorder, she herself relies on specific rules that must instantiate a correct use of that term. She then needs to rely on a very specialized use of this concept, by which she cannot either mean the thing you meant when calling your relative crazy (though, the two uses might overlap in the end) or else set the rules herself (and, for example, call a fever "mental disorder").

Hence, although Wittgenstein in his later philosophy sometimes conceives of concepts as a logical class, he does not believe that the meaning of concepts could be reduced to a finite set of necessary and sufficient conditions. As we shall see, this mistake has led psychiatry to think, based on the elaboration of the DSM-III (1980), that a diagnosis ought to rely on necessary and sufficient conditions, as if "mental disorder" referred to a logical class (cf. Hempel 1965). However, even if there are rules of grammar (proper use of language) to be made explicit, these rules should not be rigidly applied (as the DSMs try to do), since they are highly sensitive to a context of discourse. Therefore, instead of trying to erase differences and attain artificial generality, conceptual analysis must point to the differences where they had not been seen earlier. On this ground, one of the main strengths of the "prototype" approach favoured by Lilienfeld and Marino (1995) is to link Wittgenstein's notion of family resemblance and a special theory of diagnosis. Instead of searching for instantiations of concepts with rigid necessary and sufficient conditions of use, they approach mental disorders through the features that lead us to choose one category over another. A mechanical bird, a penguin and a parrot can all be called "birds", although one is not an animal, the other does not fly and the third one can sometimes speak: there is no such thing as a set of necessary and sufficient conditions to be called "a bird". Of course, in an ornithological context, some candidates for the name "bird" may be eliminated for epistemological reasons. Likewise, in psychiatry, specialists do get together to ratify or sanction some uses of "mental disorder". Just like the ornithologists, to do so they can neither entirely rely on folk intuitions, nor completely ignore the fact that many concepts they employ have their root in ordinary uses. As we shall see in the second part of this chapter, history can demonstrate that this holds for "mental disorder". It can be somewhat counterproductive, if not harmful, to try to build a very general notion of "mental disorder", which is meant to grasp and categorize a group of people corresponding to some set of necessary and sufficient conditions.

The limits of conceptual analysis

The rather weak conclusion to be drawn from this is that conceptual analysis, properly conceived, should prevent researchers from succumbing to the temptation of naturalizing mental disorder just by looking for *the* true definition of this notion. When searching for a definition, mental health professionals ought to take some decisions in order to reach a minimal consensus on which to ground further research. But this is a *practical* issue, as Nordenfelt remarks: "We can have good reasons for changing concepts or even creating completely new ones which are clearer and more efficient for our purposes. However, in such a case, we must explain what we are doing and why" (Nordenfelt 1997: 19).

There is a practical issue regarding the decision one makes when one decides to categorize or characterize a given mental disorder, or to characterize the category of mental disorders. And, as Foucault has shown (1961), to be able to do this is to have great power in one's hands (perhaps dangerously so). But this can only be done for practical purposes (scientific research, therapy, etc.). This is not to deny that there are historical, cultural, social and contextual conditions to such an enterprise; on the contrary, they are fundamental. However, conceptual analysis remains silent on that topic: it may prevent confusion, but it rarely leads to the elaboration of new more synthetic, general and scientific concepts since it is itself an attempt to disentangle the different uses of concepts and leave everything as it is.

AN ARCHAEOLOGY OF THE PROBLEM

In the last fifty years, conceptual analysis has been far from silent about the concept of mental disorder. There is a large philosophical literature relying on this method, and the debate between two factions, the pro-fact on the one hand, and the pro-value on the other (Fulford 2002), continues. The aim of this section is not to claim that all philosophical attempts to clarify the concept of mental disorder are in vain, but to highlight the fact that, attractive though it may be, conceptual analysis as a philosophical method often leads to the neglect of important contextual aspects surrounding debate on the use of a concept. Our analysis will be limited to a rough description of the recent history of the debate in the context of American psychiatry from the 1960s onwards.

The seminal project of finding a non-equivocal definition of the concept of "mental disorder" was initiated by psychiatrists and medical doctors (e.g. Spitzer and Endicott) before it began to interest philosophers. The aim was to argue against several objections from anti-psychiatrists (notably Szasz 1960) or sociologists (notably Scheff 1966), who claimed that the concept of "mental disorder" mainly aimed at stigmatizing socially disapproved behaviours. The idea was to provide an *operational definition* of mental disorder, which would serve as a rule for including specific conditions in, or excluding them from, the official classification, the DSM.

The problem took a slightly different turn when it came into the hands of philosophers. The fact/value distinction, which is sharp in the analytical tradition, has unfortunately tended to polarize the debate in a direction that did not necessarily help to shed light on the genuine controversies with which psychiatry is actually confronted.

Szasz's "coup de Jarnac" in 1960

The first step was taken in 1960 by Thomas Szasz, a psychiatrist and professor at the State University of New York Health Science Centre in Syracuse. In the USA, Szasz represents one of the most virulent opponents to the psychiatric institution, the abolition of which he has argued for since the early 1960s. While the anti-psychiatric movement in Europe, at the same time, was mainly supported by radical left-wing thinkers, mostly from the Marxist tradition (like Basaglia *et al.* 1987; D. G. Cooper 1967; Deleuze & Guattari [1972] 2004; Foucault 1961; Laing 1960), Szasz can be described as an individualist anarchist or, as he prefers to call himself, a "libertarian humanist". His main philosophical position, throughout his work, resembles Max Stirner's *The Ego and Its Own* ([1844] 1995): the absolute freedom of the individual must always be protected against the tyranny of social order, religion and political power.

In a short paper, "The myth of mental illness", Szasz (1960) gave what we may call here a *coup de Jarnac* directed against the psychiatric discourse; that is, an unexpected but convincing argument (this old French expression denotes a surprising and successful, but not unfair, strike in fencing).[4] According to Szasz, there is a deep gap between the use of the concept of illness in somatic medicine and its use in psychiatry. He defends a positivist and objectivist view of physical disease, but contrasts it with the case of mental illness. Whereas a lesion can usually be shown in most somatic diseases, the attribution of mental illness typically lacks any identifiable lesion in the body. Thus, the concept of illness applied to mental conditions is merely a metaphor.

Szasz's argument has mostly been seen as a challenge for conceptual analysis. Since his argument seems to directly address "the nature of disorder" (Wakefield 1992a: 374), it somehow appears to be "more to the point" as a critique of the concept of mental disorder than the kind of historical or sociological analysis supported by scholars like Foucault (1961) or Scheff (1966). By bringing the debate more directly onto epistemological ground, Szasz appears to spar with psychiatrists by challenging the meaning of their central concept. From this perspective, if you want to reply to Szasz, conceptual analysis may be employed to demonstrate that he has made a mistake and that a lesion is not a fundamental component of the concept of a disease.[5]

However, we suggest that such responses miss the main point of Szasz's critique. His main attack is clearly directed against the *social use* of the concept of mental illness, rather than its "nature". This important point is illustrated by these two quotes:

> Since the notion of mental illness is extremely widely used nowadays, inquiry *into the ways in which this term is employed* would seem to be especially indicated.
> (Szasz 1960: 113, emphasis added)

> *In actual contemporary social usage*, the finding of a mental illness is made by establishing a deviance in behaviour from certain psychosocial, ethical, or legal norms.
> (Szasz 1960: 115, emphasis added)

If mental illness is a myth, this is mainly due to the ways in which the concept has been used rather than the intrinsic nature of what should constitute a genuine disease. In other words, the main challenge is to demonstrate that the "actual contemporary social use" of the concept of mental disorder is not just a metaphor.

The Round Table: 1973

The second important episode of the debate can be called "the Round Table". In 1973, Robert Spitzer – a young psychiatrist who was to become a key figure in the construction of the DSM-III during the 1970s – congregated around a table with other knights of the psychiatric institution to discuss the issue of homosexuality. Debates following from this discussion led to the withdrawal of homosexuality from the then-current classification, the DSM-II (American Psychiatric Association 1973). This withdrawal was done in the hope that this gesture would bring some peace to the kingdom of psychiatry (see Bayer 1981). The dispute over homosexuality probably played a decisive role in the way American psychiatrists tackled the issue of clarifying their concept of mental illness. Two observations can be made concerning this episode. First, the debate over homosexuality introduced the idea that psychiatrists needed to rely on a general definition of what constitutes a mental illness. The attempt to justify the exclusion of homosexuality by referring to an overarching definition of mental disorder can chiefly be attributed to Spitzer. His main goal was not to circumscribe the meaning of a term, mental disorder, but simply to put forward some clear criteria which would be accepted by most physicians and would constitute a regulatory framework for justifying the inclusion of any mental disorder in the next version of the DSM, the DSM-III. Second, although the idea that disorders are necessarily dysfunctions became crucial later, it is impossible to find in 1973, a clear intuition that the idea of biological dysfunction is an important component. Spitzer contended that the two main criteria for a mental condition to be considered a psychiatric disorder were: (a) that the condition must "regularly cause subjective distress"; or (b) that the condition must "regularly be associated with some generalised impairment in social effectiveness or functioning" (American Psychiatric Association 1973; Stoller *et al.* 1973). In 1975, Spitzer and Wilson gave a more elaborate definition of mental disorder, but one that again failed to provide any hint that the idea of biological dysfunction could be important. The authors went further by saying that it was unlikely that a standard definition accepted by most psychiatrists could be reached. Instead, they promoted what they called a "narrow approach" to diagnosis, focused on mental conditions clearly associated with suffering and disability, in contrast with a "broad approach" that tended to consider every "significant departure from an ideal state of positive mental health" as pathological (Spitzer & Wilson 1975). This distinction between a narrow and a broad approach, which underlines the theoretical position of the authors, had political motivation. Indeed, it was justified by public health considerations: the narrow approach was said to reflect the European approach, presented as successful, while the broad approach was said to reflect the American approach, considered until then as a failure.[6]

The good fellas: 1975

In 1975 two philosophers wrote seminal papers on the concept of disease and illness. Christopher Boorse gave an objectivist account of the concept of disease, based on a value-free understanding of biological functions (Boorse 1975). Tristram Engelhardt claimed that the concept of disease is a normative concept, "freighted with important ambiguities" (Engelhardt 1981). There is much to say about these two papers and their significance. We shall limit ourselves to a few remarks:

(a) These two papers pinpoint the time when a much more specific interest in the *meaning* of the term "disease" arose. Whereas the topic was the general use of the term disease, it is clear that mental disorder was the central issue (Demazeux 2010).
(b) From then on, the definition of mental disorder became a truly philosophical problem, which can be investigated at a conceptual level. This shift brought more complexity and sophistication into the issue. For example, the fact/value distinction from the analytical tradition, with theoretical commitments and its technical subtleties, became a much more explicit dimension of the problem.
(c) Boorse and Engelhardt used two different analytic strategies to fill in the gap between mental and somatic disorders that Szasz exaggerated. Boorse tried to resolve the difficulty of applying medical vocabulary to mental diseases by advancing an objectivist position in both mental and physical pathology. Engelhardt advocated a weak normativist position for both mental and physical disorders. Note, however, that neither philosopher tackled the problem raised by Szasz, which was the actual use of the term "mental disorder" by psychiatrists. On this specific point, the two philosophers did not take a stand. In parts of their essays they even appear suspicious about the general application of the term "mental illness" in psychiatry (Boorse 1975: 66; Engelhardt 1981: 32–3).

The Great Wall of China: 1978

A milestone in the debate surrounding the concept of mental disorder was the publication in 1978 of *Critical Issues in Psychiatric Diagnosis*, edited by Spitzer and Donald Klein. Since they are not very theoretically innovative, philosophers rarely discuss the papers in this volume. Its most quoted section is the long operational definition of mental disorder proposed by Spitzer and Endicott, which is seen as the original version of the definition that was later included (in a much shorter version) in the introduction of the DSM-III (Spitzer & Endicott 1978). But here again, we need to pay attention to some contextual details, notably the practical purposes of the definition. The 1978 definition was the final outcome of the work initiated in 1973 by

Spitzer. And again, the aim was to spell out as clearly as possible the criteria that were to be taken into account when physicians (and psychiatrists in particular) tried to justify the pathological nature of a condition. These criteria were the result of a lengthy process of moving between a high level of generality and the specific definitions of disorders. It can best be seen as a kind of Great Wall intended to delimit "the area of prime responsibility of psychiatry" (Spitzer & Endicott 1978: 16) by fixing "explicit guiding principles that would help to determine which conditions should be included in the nomenclature, which excluded" (Spitzer & Endicott 1978: 37). One new feature of this definition is the clear assumption that an organismic dysfunction is an important part of the concept of mental illness: "The following forms of disadvantage, even when not associated with distress or disability, are *now considered, in our culture, as suggestive of some type of organismic dysfunction warranting the designation of medical disorder*" (Spitzer & Endicott 1978: 20–21, emphasis added). This minimal and cautious theoretical commitment was obviously the result of the growing influence in the literature of the idea of dysfunction.[7] But actually it was mostly due to the debate between Spitzer, Endicott and Donald Klein in the volume.[8] Contrary to Klein, who asserted that "all legitimate usages [of the term 'illness'] imply actual dysfunction" (Klein 1978: 48), Spitzer and Endicott were still reluctant to see dysfunction as a necessary condition for disorder. They merely described dysfunction as a condition that "tends to be attributed" by psychiatrists (Spitzer & Endicott 1978: 20–21). It is clear that, for them, the key criterion of illness was suffering and distress.

The middleman: Jerome Wakefield and the definition of the DSM-III

Wakefield, following Boorse, has proposed an influential analysis of the concept of mental disorder. The reason for calling him "the middleman" is that in 1992–3 he published three papers that need to be read together and which appear to give an ecumenical solution likely to gain approval by both philosophers and psychiatrists. In the first paper (Wakefield 1992a) Wakefield relies on conceptual analysis to conclude that mental disorder is best defined as a harmful dysfunction. In the other two papers (Wakefield 1992b, 1993) he offers a detailed criticism of the operational definition defended by Spitzer and Endicott, but also of the definition of mental disorder provided in the DSM-III (which is a short version of the 1978 definition). His intention is to show that whereas these two definitions are ambiguous and somehow misleading, they implicitly assume the same two fundamental components his analysis has revealed. Thus, he proves that his own definition embraces both the professional and the lay intuition of what mental disease is. However accurate his analysis may appear to be in many respects, Wakefield makes a series of inexact statements.

He first claims that "Spitzer arrived at the definition through the method of conceptual analysis, which is also used here" (Wakefield 1992b: 233). This claim, as we have seen, should be nuanced. It is true that Spitzer aimed to "account for a large number of relatively uncontroversial judgments" about disorder and non-disorder, but there is no assumption in Spitzer's work that there would be a consistent set of beliefs, a natural type or a common conceptual structure behind the term "mental disorder". Wakefield also emphasizes that there is a "widely shared dysfunction conception of disorder" and that "the centrality of dysfunction is repeatedly cited in secondary literature" (Wakefield 1992b: 235). However, the references he gives all date between 1975 and 1978, and he neglects the fact that Spitzer and Endicott, still in 1978, did not think that the dysfunction assumption was central in their definition. The intuition of an organismic dysfunction is more context-relative than Wakefield has claimed. Finally, Wakefield analyses the long definition proposed by Spitzer and Endicott. He concludes that the majority of criteria are redundant or ambiguous, and that they can be reformulated by insisting on the two essential features of the concept: a dysfunction and harmful consequences (Wakefield 1993: 164). But in doing so, he overemphasizes the significance of a common intuition about the concept that we all share (the idea of mental disorder implies that "something has gone wrong in the person"). He also overemphasizes its importance in the psychiatric discourse (as we have seen, the intuition about the centrality of dysfunction is not so apparent in the attempts to define the concept of mental disorder before 1975).[9]

As a matter of fact, Spitzer himself recognized that the definition of a mental disorder as a harmful dysfunction constitutes a sound and balanced solution (Spitzer 1997, 1999). But does this late recognition by Spitzer really mean that Wakefield made clearer some fundamental intuitions already present in his early attempts to define the concept of mental disorder? Or does it just mean that Wakefield's definition fulfils, in a more efficient manner, the several purposes that Spitzer attached to the aim of gaining a general definition of mental disorder? We think this second interpretation is more persuasive with regard to the history of the debate.

Although Wakefield's harmful dysfunction analysis presents many advantages, there has been much criticism of this definition in the last two decades (e.g. Bolton 2008; R. Cooper 2007; Murphy 2006). Critics have mostly dealt with conceptual considerations, particularly in relation to the dysfunction part of the definition. Our position here is quite different. We do not claim that the harmful dysfunction analysis is wrong or flawed. Our point is not conceptual, but rather historical: the harmful dysfunction analysis does not accord with some of the several understandings of mental disorder that have been in use in even the recent history of psychiatry. Indeed, it is far from obvious, in light of recent history of American psychiatry, that there has been a clear intuition among psychiatrists that the concept of mental disorder implies a particular conception of a mental dysfunction.

After 1992, psychiatrists' interest in the discussion surrounding the concept of mental disorder tended to wane. Rachel Cooper rightly pointed out in *Classifying Madness* that, as the political point of the debate about anti-psychiatry and homosexuality had disappeared, psychiatrists progressively lost interest in defining mental disorder (R. Cooper 2005: 41–2). Nowadays, if any general consensus has been reached on the concept of mental disorder, it is clearly in the sense of a general recognition that it is a value-laden concept (R. Cooper 2007: 42).

CONCLUSION

In the history of psychiatry, the concept of mental illness appeared relatively late (and the concept of mental disorder even later; see Pickering 2006), without clear definition and unified use. This general concept was originally aimed at bundling together many different conditions calling for psychiatrists' attention. Today, the concept of mental disorder may appear as a more unified concept than it was several decades ago. But the fact that we can progressively impose more constraints on the use of a concept does not mean that we have discovered its basic elements. Nor does it mean that its current use relies on some clearly shared intuitions. Intuitions, like concepts, are often context-relative. The debate around the concept of mental disorder emerged in a very particular context, about which there would still be much to say. The role played by conceptual analysis, in this debate, has been pre-eminent but is inclined to neglect the specificity and historical originality of the concept of mental disorder. Furthermore, we have suggested that the results of conceptual analysis have depended on the historical, economic and political context in which they were carried out. It is certain that conceptual arguments do count, together with the weight of the numerous institutional, socio-political or ideological influences. But the concept of mental disorder, like the project of reaching a definitive definition of it through conceptual analysis, also has a history, which requires further investigation.

ACKNOWLEDGEMENTS

Supported by the PHS2M (Philosophy, History and Sociology of Mental Health) project through the French National Research Agency (ANR). The authors would like to thank Havi Carel and Rachel Cooper for their helpful feedback on an earlier draft of this chapter.

NOTES

1. See for example Caplan *et al.* (1981); Culver and Gert (1982); Kendell (1975); Lilienfeld and Marino (1995); Murphy and Woolfolk (2000a, b); Wakefield (1992a, b, 2000, 2007).
2. Fulford (1999), Murphy (2006) and Bolton (2008), among others, have shown that this is problematic.
3. Moreover, the discovery that water is H_2O has never eliminated ordinary (non-scientific) uses of the word water and, when it comes to quenching my thirst, the chemist will not have the last word if he suggests that I find pure H_2O. I would rather have a glass of San Pellegrino.
4. In *The Metaphor of Mental Illness*, Neil Pickering (2006) has highlighted how much Szasz's radical claim has impacted on the debate over the concept of mental disorder.
5. Boorse (1976) convincingly replied to Szasz from this particular perspective. And yet, we have to draw attention to the fact that Boorse, in his paper entitled "What a Theory of Mental Health Should Be", does not look at the current uses of the concept of illness or disorder in the psychiatric discourse. Boorse appears consistently cautious on this issue.
6. From a general point of view, we believe that it was no coincidence that proponents of an objective account of mental disorder are mainly American scholars, whereas proponents of value-laden accounts are mostly European scholars. This rough division reflects political as well as sociological and scientific differences in clinical traditions (operationalism is typical of an American style in psychiatry), in philosophical traditions (e.g. see the major influence of Hempel in America, of Hare in the UK and of Canguilhem in France) and, most of all, in public health policy. It is striking that a holistic approach, as in philosopher Nordenfelt's account of disease, has aroused much interest in France and perhaps in Europe, but is still largely ignored in the USA. It is linked to a certain understanding of welfare, when American scholars have shown to be progressively inclined to propose a definition of health as the mere absence of disease.
7. See Boorse (1975), as well as Scadding (1967) and Kendell (1975), and their idea of biological disadvantage.
8. There was deep theoretical disagreement between Spitzer and Klein, which had to do with their respective positions on homosexuality. For Klein, homosexuality, even when it was not associated with subjective distress, was a disease since it "demonstrates operationally an intrinsic involuntary incapacity", that is a natural dysfunction (Klein 1978: 65). But Spitzer's intuition of what constitutes a dysfunction was not as clear, and it was only partly biologically oriented (see for example Spitzer 1974: 17, Spitzer *et al.* 1978: 32).
9. Wakefield also fails to comment on an important concession of the 1978 definition, which indicates that Spitzer and Endicott had a relativistic conception of

what constitutes a disadvantage (and so a dysfunction): "It should be noted that if criterion A is met only by virtue of A.3, disadvantage, the designation of the condition as a disorder is heavily dependent on social definitions of the degree of disadvantage or undesirableness, as well as other considerations, as to the consequences of considering the condition as a medical disorder" (Spitzer & Endicott 1978: 21).

PART II
THE EXPERIENCE OF ILLNESS

5. WHAT IS PHENOMENOLOGY OF MEDICINE? EMBODIMENT, ILLNESS AND BEING-IN-THE-WORLD

Fredrik Svenaeus

The question of my chapter's title involves two issues that have to be settled before moving on to the main topic, the phenomenology of medicine: the issue of what phenomenology itself might be, certainly, and I will return to that shortly; but no less important, the issue of what medicine is.

MEDICINE

So, what is medicine? What is its essence and how are its borders with other human activities to be delineated? As everyone who has pursued the field of philosophy of medicine knows, the exact nature and border of medicine is itself a constant topic of debate. I myself would defend a concept of medicine that stresses the *meeting* of health care professional and patient in an interpretative attempt to help and treat the ill and suffering one, whereas others would look rather for the essence of medicine in the *application* of medical knowledge in attempts to understand and alter the biological organism (Svenaeus 2000b). These two answers to the question of what medicine is do not necessarily exclude each other; they could be brought into dialogue, and the first answer could be made to include the second, just as the second answer could be complemented by the first. The interpretative practice of understanding and helping the patient could, and, indeed, should, include biological knowledge, while the applied biology paradigm would need to address, in some way, that the doctor sees a person and not only the person's body.

Despite the possibility of combining the two alternatives, where one puts the major stress will be important, not only in answering the question of whether or not a particular activity is to be counted as a medical activity, but also in addressing ethical and political questions concerning the mission of medicine today and in the future. If medicine is an interpretative, helping meeting between persons aiming to restore or protect health and alleviate the suffering of illness, the practice *itself* will have ethical roots, whereas if medicine is the application of medical knowledge in a clinical context, medicine will have to be encouraged to grow ethical branches on its morally neutral tree, so to speak. Towards the end of this paper, I will return briefly to the issue of what medicine is in itself, but first I will focus on the second issue mentioned above, that of phenomenology. What is phenomenology?

PHENOMENOLOGY

A preliminary answer to this question can be provided by stating that phenomenology can be considered a kind of *first philosophy* seeking the *foundations* of ontological and epistemological questions by returning to *lived experience* (Spiegelberg 1982). Phenomenology has branched out into many additional disciplines from its inception about 100 years ago with Edmund Husserl, and continued through the work of philosophers like Martin Heidegger, Maurice Merleau-Ponty and Jean-Paul Sartre. Scholars and researchers of art, literature, psychology, sociology, anthropology and history, and recently also nursing and medicine, have tried to make use of the methodology of "going back to the phenomena themselves and abstaining from any taken for granted views in studying them", as it was put by Husserl (Toombs 2001a).

The expression "the phenomena themselves" is understood by Husserl and his followers as that which shows itself in the experiences we are all having all the time. The starting point is not the world of science but the meaning structures of the everyday world, what the phenomenologist calls the "life world". The phenomenologist shows experience itself to be meaningful in the sense that experience is always had by someone, a subject, and that it displays a content for the one who is having the experience (that which I am conscious of: the object). The apple tree in Husserl's back garden has a shape and a colour, a "treeness", or even an "appletreeness", that stands out and shows itself against the horizon of the whole garden: on the lawn, beside the bushes, under the sky. The things that show up to us are thus embedded in horizons of meaning that allow them to show themselves as such-and-such things (Zahavi 2003).

Husserl was not particularly interested in botany but used the tree found in his garden to describe how all things in the life world show up in a spatially organized manner, having front and back sides, having colours, and so on. Phenomena show up to us as meaningful for us; they show up as things with different meaning contents. Surely there was a time for the newborn baby when everything was chaos, but experience soon takes on shape in being had by someone (the baby) and being about something (the breast). The baby is then, step-by-step, invited to the life world we all live in together with its rich meaning structures (for a good introduction to contemporary phenomenology acknowledging the developmental perspective, see Gallagher 2005).

This does not mean that experience does not sometimes have to be interpreted (what do I really see here?) or even re-evaluated (we make mistakes), or that the life world contours of some people are not richer than those of others (I can identify perhaps thirty birds, a skilled ornithologist can identify three hundred), but these nuances of the finely woven web of life world meanings should not fool us into assuming that the world is basically some kind of senseless raw matter out of which humans can construct any contents they want. Nor should it fool us into assuming that the only real structure of the world that there is, is the one we find (or construct) when we dive into the world of science. The life world comes first, the phenomenologist will claim, and this insight protects us from the exaggerations and mistakes of idealism and dualism as well as materialism and naturalism.

PHENOMENOLOGY OF MEDICINE

A phenomenologist can direct her attention to any phenomenon found worthy of study, and this is also the way phenomenology branches out into different disciplines beyond the very basic philosophical themes of being and knowledge *per se*. What experiences, then, are particularly relevant for the phenomenologist of medicine to explore? I will offer some examples of phenomena that I think are central to a phenomenology of medicine, and, indeed, to medicine itself, and although I do not intend my list to be exhaustive, I hope it is relevant to the way the phenomenology of medicine has developed so far. The most important contemporary studies to be mentioned in this relatively young field of study are, I think, the ones by Richard Zaner (1981), Drew Leder (1990), Kay Toombs (1992), Hans-Georg Gadamer ([1993] 1996), Fredrik Svenaeus (2000b) and Havi Carel (2008).

In the strict sense, the phenomenology of medicine is certainly a young field of study, but the issue of how old the field is depends on what topics you take to be medical topics. We find this paper's first example of a topic central to the phenomenology of medicine, namely the ways of the body, dating back to the middle period of Husserl's phenomenology, the 1910s. The phenomenology of the body is analysed in more detail by Maurice Merleau-Ponty in the 1930s and 1940s ([1945] 1962), and it is brought up in connection with medical matters by phenomenologists such as F. J. J.

Buytendijk, Hans Jonas, Herbert Plügge and Erwin Straus in the 1950s and 1960s (Spiegelberg 1972).

EMBODIMENT

It is very important to medicine that we are *embodied* creatures – medicine explores the body and tries to understand how it functions in order to be able to fix it when it breaks, to put it very crudely. This is not all there is to medicine, but the knowledge of bodily processes is surely central to the medical project. Everybody has a body – a body that can be of great joy, but also of great suffering and pain to its bearer. The fundamental point that the phenomenologist would emphasize here is that not only does everybody *have* a body, everybody *is* a body. What is the difference?

When we say that every experience is embodied, this means that the body is my point of view, and my way of experiencing and understanding the world. Not only can I experience my own body as an *object* of my experience – when I feel it or touch it or look at it in the mirror – but the body also harbours, on the subjective side of experience, the proprioceptive and kinaesthetic schemas that make a person's experiences possible in the first place. The body is my place in the world – the place where I am which moves with me – which is also the zero-point that makes space and the place of things that I encounter possible at all. The body, as a rule, does not show itself to us in our experiences; it *withdraws* and so opens up a focus in which it is possible for things in the world to show up to us in different meaningful ways. When I speak to another person I am not attending to the way my body feels and moves, I am focused upon *her* and the things I am trying to communicate to her; this is made possible, however, by the way my body silently performs in the background. The body already organizes my experiences on a subconscious level. Proprioceptively it makes me present in the world, and kinaesthetically it allows me to experience the things that are not me – the things of the world that show up to my moving, sensing body in different activities through which they attain their place and significance.

Thus phenomenology can be understood as transgressing any dualistic picture of a soul living in and directing the ways of the body like some ghost in a machine. The body is me. But phenomenology is also – and this is even more important – fundamentally and from its beginning an anti-naturalistic project; that is, the phenomenologist would also contest any attempt to reduce experience to material processes only. Experience, to the phenomenologist, must be studied by acknowledging its meaning and content for the one who is *having* the experience. It is certainly possible to study experience from the third-person perspective of science also – we could study the ways light rays trigger nerve firings in my brain by way of the retina when I look at a person right now (if we hook me up to a technological device), but this picture of my brain in action would not be the experience of "me looking at her right now". The picture could catch neither the "me-ness" nor the content of the experience that I am having – this is the first-person perspective, which the phenomenologist takes as the starting point of the analysis. The phenomenologist would not contest that the scientific explanations of experiences made by way of scientific third-person-perspective investigations could be important in informing us about the workings of the world and ourselves, but she would deny that such scientific explanations could compensate for, or replace, first-person-perspective explorations of the experiences in question. In order to see this more clearly, let us now move on to my next example of a topic central to the phenomenology of medicine: illness.

ILLNESS

As mentioned above, normally, when we move around in the world, acting, speaking, thinking and feeling, we do not pay any attention to our bodies. They perform their duties silently in the background, not only proprioceptively and kinaesthetically, but also as regards all the autonomic functions of our visceral life – breathing, our hearts beating, stomachs and bowels working, and so on. Sometimes, however, the body *shows up* in resisting and disturbing our efforts. It plagues us and demands our attention. A paradigm example is pain. If I have a headache it becomes hard to concentrate and think. Even before my attention is directed towards the headache itself, the whole world and all my projects become tinted by pain. When I read, the letters become fuzzy, the text itself hurts in me trying to understand it. This is Jean-Paul Sartre's example from *Being and Nothingness* (1956), published originally in 1943 – so the phenomenology of illness, like the phenomenology of embodiment, actually goes back further than the contemporary studies mentioned above. Illness is never Sartre's main object of study, however; it is used mainly as an example to address questions of being and human nature in general (Svenaeus 2009).

Illness, as the headache example of Sartre already shows, displays a "mooded" aspect tied to activities one is performing. Other examples of illness moods are nausea, unmotivated tiredness or the way the body resists my attempts to do different things – like when I try to climb the stairs and my chest hurts. Of course, there are distinctions to be made here. For most people, the chest starts to hurt after five flights of fast climbing, but when it does so more or less immediately or unexpectedly, it is a paradigm example of illness. According to another very influential phenomenologist, Martin Heidegger, every experience we have is, as a matter of fact, attuned – "mooded" – but this attunement of our being-in-the-world normally, just like the embodied character of experience, stays in the subconscious background, not making itself known to us. In illness, however, the mood we are in makes itself known in penetrating our entire experience, finally, when it becomes unbearable, bringing us back to our plagued embodiment, which now resists our attempts to act and carry out things, instead of supporting them in the silent, enigmatic manner of healthy being-in-the-world (Gadamer 1996).

I have tried in earlier works to characterize and to a certain extent delineate the borders of such illness experiences by way of the concept of "unhomelike being-in-the-world" (Svenaeus 2000b). The life world is usually my home territory, but in illness this homelikeness gives in and takes on a rather *unhomelike* character, rooted in thwarted ways of being embodied. It is the mission of health care professionals to try to understand such unhomelike being-in-the-world and bring it back to homelikeness again, or at least closer to a home-being. This involves, but cannot be reduced to, ways of understanding and altering the physiological organism of the person who is ill. Health care professionals must also address everyday life matters of patients with a phenomenological eye, addressing and trying to understand the being-in-the-world of the person's life, which has turned unhomelike in illness.

UNHOMELIKE BEING-IN-THE-WORLD

I should like to add a few words on the phenomenological concept of "being-in-the-world", which I have now used a couple of times in trying to outline the phenomenon of illness. The concept is introduced by Heidegger in his first major work, *Being and Time* (1996), originally published in 1927, and it was quickly picked up by other phenomenologists. By analogy with the way I *am* a body rather than merely having a body, in the phenomenological understanding I *am* my world, rather than just being placed in it as a thing among other things. I am immersed in the life world in a meaningful way, which connects its meaning patterns – and particularly the ones I am relying on in my most vital life projects – to my identity. The world is not merely a physically extended geography in which I happen to have a place among other things; being-in-the-world, in Heidegger's phenomenology, refers to the way human beings *inhabit* the world as a pattern of significance, a set of connecting relations between different "tools", as Heidegger puts it. This way of being-in always has a mood aspect, a tune to it, even though this attunement might rest in the background of our activities, not being noticed by us until we turn to the mood explicitly. In illness, however, the mood in question has a tendency to call for our attention since it is unhomelike in character. The homelikeness of health, in contrast to this, dwells in the background and is rarely paid attention to – we most often take the transparent, homelike being-in of health for granted until illness strikes us.

Being-in-the-world is a process of understanding in which things show up in totalities of relevance as meaningful. In these understanding activities we most often do not pay explicit attention to any of the tools we use – the same way we do not pay attention to our bodies, which, in a way, could be considered the most basic of tools – body-tools like hands, legs, lungs, and so on. Instead we are focused on the things we *do* through the tool use in question — like building a house with a hammer, in Heidegger's famous example in *Being and Time* (1996).

In my study *The Hermeneutics of Medicine and the Phenomenology of Health* I tried to show how healthy versus ill life can be explicated as homelike versus unhomelike being-in-the-world (2000b). This analysis is not something you find in Heidegger's philosophy; his main interest was rather the question of human being, or perhaps, even more demanding, Being – *Dasein* – itself. Homelikeness and unhomelikeness in my phenomenological analysis, inspired by, but not identical to, Heidegger's analysis, refer to two opposed dimensions of the attuned being-in-the-world of human beings. To be ill means to be not at home in one's being-in-the-world, to find oneself in a pattern of disorientedness, resistance, helplessness and perhaps even despair, instead of in the homelike transparency of healthy life. Homelike being-in-the-world does not mean that the person in question is necessarily happy. The phenomenology of homelikeness is supposed to capture the character of the normal, unapparent, things-as-usual ways of everyday life.

Unhomelike being-in-the-world is a wider conception than illness, since external circumstances may render our being-in-the-world unhomelike in ways which we would not refer to as cases of illness in themselves, even though they could, of course, lead to illness in the long run. To be locked up in prison and exposed to harsh conditions for years is such an example. To experience the suffering of a war is another. Existential crisis suffered, for instance, after the loss of a loved one, a third. Remember, however, that it is the being-*in*-the-world of the person that counts as homelike or unhomelike in the phenomenological theory. To live in an environment means to experience it and assign it meaning through feelings, thoughts and actions. Thus the life world of phenomenology is not identical to *physical* surroundings, but is a meaning pattern of human understanding. Whether being locked up in prison results in unhomelike being-in-the-world or not depends partly on the world that the person is thrown into (its physical and cultural characteristics) and partly on the way she projects this given world of necessities and possibilities in her life. The prisoner might in some cases be able to adjust to a homelike existence behind the bars, although the conditions of imprisonment in most cases would offer too much resistance to allow this homelike reinterpretation of the person's life project. The same goes for persons exposed to war or loss of loved ones.

What I would like to stress here is that the unhomelike being-in-the-world of illness, in contrast to other forms of unhomelike being-in-the-world, is characterized by a fatal change in the meaning structures, not only of the world, but of the *self* (that is, the person). Although self and world are always interconnected in a synthetic way through the being-*in*-the-world of the self, it is still possible to make a distinction between the person and the world she inhabits. In this way it is possible to distinguish between a more general homelessness of being-in-the-world, and the unhomelikeness of illness, since the latter is always accompanied by a fatal change in the meaning structure of the self. This unhomelike-making change in the openness of the self to the world is furthermore, in the case of illness, at least typically, a change in embodiment. The lived body forms the core of the self, and the "body-tools" are most fundamental for our being-in. The self, however, is not identical with the lived body, but stretches out into dimensions of emotions, thoughts and language that go beyond bodily being in a narrow sense. In cases of mental illness, the deformation of the self, leading to difficulties in the person's being-in-the-world, is harder to track down to its bodily roots, even though promising attempts have been made by phenomenologists of psychiatry such as Thomas Fuchs (2000).

To sum up: illness is an unhomelike being-in-the-world in which the embodied ways of being-in of the self (person) have been thwarted. In illness the body shows up as an alien being (being me, yet not me) and this obstruction attunes the entire being-in-the-world of the ill person in an unhomelike way.

This distinction between breakdowns in the meaning patterns of embodied self versus the world should be sufficient to counter the argument that the characterization of illness as unhomelike being-in-the-world threatens to encompass too many conditions that we would normally refer to as unhappiness rather than illness, although I admit there are many more qualifications to be made on this point. This is important, since a phenomenology of illness should not, in my view, lead to a medicalization of all our life world predicaments, as modern medicine itself might do by way of new therapies and diagnostics it introduces. Actually, as we will see, phenomenological theory might instead face the opposite problem, of deeming healthy, in some cases, persons whom we refer to today as diseased or disabled. I will bite the bullet on this, however, and see where it might lead us.

ILLNESS, DISEASE AND DISABILITY

It is important to understand the fundamental difference between a phenomenological illness concept and the concept of disease as it is usually understood. A disease is a disturbance of the biological functions of the body (or something that causes such a disturbance), which can only be detected and understood from the third-person perspective of the doctor investigating the body with the aid of her hands or medical technologies. The patient can also, by way of the doctor, or by way of medical theory, or, as often happens nowadays, by way of a webpage on the internet, adopt such a third-person perspective towards her own body and speculate about diseases responsible for her suffering. But the suffering itself is an illness experience of the person who is in a world, embodied and connected to other people around her. Illness has meaning, or, perhaps we should say instead, *disturbs* the meaning processes of being-in-the-world in which one is leading one's life on an everyday level.

Typically, when I experience illness, my biological organism will be diseased, but there are possibilities of being ill without any detectable diseases, or of leading a homelike life, when suddenly the doctor finds a disease (e.g. by way of a cancer screening). The phenomenologist would stress that the full importance and content of illness can be attained only if the doctor, in addition to being skilled in diagnosing diseases, also affords attention to the experience, the being-in-the-world, of the patient. The life of the person (and not only the life of her biological organism) is, as a matter of fact, the reason why diseases *matter* to us as human beings – because they can make our lives miserable and even make us perish. If this were not the case, we would not *care* so much about them. It is because we want to be at home in the world that we study disease agents and try to find remedies for them, even though I suspect we will never succeed completely in this project, since unhomelikeness in its different forms seems to be a necessary part of human life. In a sense our vulnerability and finitude is exactly what makes us human (Heidegger talks about "being-towards-death" as constitutive for our being-in-the-world) so if medical science succeeds in making us invulnerable the creatures in question would not be human, but rather post-human beings.

The distinction between the embodied self and the world it is living in can also help us to understand the possibility of chronic maladies (not only diseases, but also injuries or congenital defects) without illness – that is, the cases of chronically afflicted persons who nevertheless enjoy a homelike being-in-the-world. In the phenomenological sense, these persons, most often referred to as chronically ill or disabled, would not, indeed, be unhealthy. These persons have managed to make adjustments in the meaning patterns of their selves and environments, sometimes assisted by medical professionals and medical therapies, or by other helpers, in ways that compensate for the maladies that they are suffering from. In other words, they have managed to make their being-in-the-world homelike again by way of changing not only the outer circumstances, but also their understanding of themselves in this altered situation. In the case of congenital defect, this possible adjustment to homelike being-in-the-world would take place through a process similar to how every normal child makes itself at home in the world, but needing more help and sometimes medical assistance (Svenaeus 2003).

The prospects of adjusting to a homelike being-in-the-world through a reinterpretation of the self and its situation in life depend partly on the person afflicted by the malady and partly on how severe the malady in question is. Some congenital defects, injuries or diseases might be so severe that a homelike being-in-the-world is not possible, while some maladies might be mild enough to allow for a homelike existence. The point of the phenomenological theory is, indeed, to find the starting point in the person and her life world circumstances, not in her biology, when it comes to questions of health and illness. This approach is not meant to exclude biology, however. The physiology of the body certainly afflicts and sets limits to the different ways we are able to experience and interpret our being-in-the-world. To develop a phenomenological theory of illness and health is therefore not meant as an attempt to replace biomedical research. In light of the successful history of modern medicine, this would certainly be an absurd project. Phenomenology is meant to enrich our understanding of health and illness in adding a level that addresses the questions of how the physiological processes and states are lived as meaningful in a culture.

That homelike being-in-the-world – and this, in the phenomenological theory, means health – is a possibility for some chronically diseased and disabled persons, helps us to discern different ways of promoting homelikeness for the ill. Biological therapy forms one very important way, since the curing of diseases tends to eradicate the unhomelikeness of illness more or less directly in many cases – think of an appendectomy, for instance. Medical rehabilitation – focusing on changing the self-understanding of patients, improving their mental and physical abilities and making adjustments in their life environments – forms the next step in the treatment of, for instance, a stroke. But the possibility of homelikeness for the disabled also has a social and political dimension. This is indeed why we have officially chosen the term *disabled* instead of *handicapped* when it comes to maladies other than diseases, such as congenital defects and injuries. To establish homelikeness requires resources for building environments in which the disabled can make adjustments for their functional disabilities. But it also takes *respect* for forms of life that differ from the normal one, which can be just as homelike but nevertheless very different from ours –

think of Deaf culture, for instance. The being at home or not being at home with one's own body depends not only on life world patterns that make it easier or harder to move and perceive (e.g. using a wheelchair, being deaf or blind), but also on attitudes: that is, how the disabled are met, looked upon and assigned a worth or non-worth by others.

Does it make sense to say that every form of obtrusive embodiment could be compensated for, in terms of homelikeness or unhomelikeness, by changing the meaning patterns of the world that the disabled (like all other persons) rely on in their being-in? Can we always compensate for a non-standard embodiment by creating a non-standard world to be in? This seems to be an empirical question, but allow me to say that I think the words "normal" and "standard" make sense not only in discussing embodiment but also in discussing the meaning patterns of the world from a phenomenological point of view. There are overlapping patterns of cultural consistency in life world patterns, and these seem to be tied, among other things, to our shared ways of embodiment. But there are also great variances in cultural patterns that make different forms of diseases and disabilities easier or harder to live with. Studies by social anthropologists such as Arthur Kleinman bear clear evidence of this (e.g. Kleinman 1995).

To sum up: health consists of a homelike being-in-the-world. Homelikeness is supposed to capture the character of the normal, unapparent, transparency of everyday activities, *not* of feeling happy. Health in phenomenology is meant as a first-person concept, in contrast to a third-person concept of health, which would offer the definition of health rather as simply the absence of all diseases and other maladies. It is possible to be healthy – to enjoy a homelike being-in-the-world – even if the person in question suffers from some kind of malady. This means that being phenomenologically healthy might include being abnormal, either in the physiological sense or in the sense of demanding a non-standard world to be in.

That a diseased or disabled person can, in some cases, with the help of medical assistance, political efforts or hard work on her part enjoy a homelike being-in-the-world, points towards the importance of including a consideration of the ill person's life world in the activities and abilities of health care professionals. But it also illustrates that homelike and unhomelike being-in-the-world are not mutually exclusive phenomena, but rather dimensionally opposed tendencies that characterize our entire being-in. Even healthy life is unhomelike to some extent, though not in ways that are tied to plagued embodiment. Ill life is unhomelike to different *extents* and in different *ways*, depending on diagnosis, person and opportunities to make adaptations in being-in, but in all these embodied forms of not being at home, the ill life always retains some elements of homelikeness if it did not, it is doubtful it could be considered a being-in-the-world at all.

What has struck me as more and more important in my attempts to understand illness from the phenomenological point of view is the importance to health of being able to *adapt* to an altered embodiment and environment in order to stay healthy or become healthy again, when life is obstructed by diseases or other threatening events. This might be the true health, the great health that Nietzsche was talking about and claimed to be enjoying despite his dreadful physiology (Krell 1996). To become homelike in the face of unhomelikeness: this would be the health in illness. The illness in health would be the tendency to fall into unhomelikeness very easily, and to have great difficulties in regaining the homelike state again.

MEDICAL TECHNOLOGIES

The development of modern medical science in the last two hundred years or so has made it possible for us to intervene in our own biology in new and stunning ways. Not only is it now possible for us to cure and prevent many diseases from which people previously died *en masse* or were crippled for life, it is also increasingly possible to enhance our biology beyond the boundaries of restoring normality. Medical technology (gene technology and psychopharmacology, for instance) is now stepping onto the stage of self-transformation, making us become "better than well", to quote the title of a book by Carl Elliott (2003). This process is problematic and has given rise to high expectations as well as worries about the future of humankind. What contributions could phenomenology offer to this bioethical debate?

In its stress on encouraging doctors to focus on the ill person – the being-in-the-world of the patient – and not only on diseases, one can already sense a certain critique from the perspective of the phenomenologist towards a medicine in the hands of techno-science. The patient is, indeed, a subject, not only an object, and health care professionals must never forget this if they are to be successful in doing their job: helping ill people. This does not mean that a phenomenologist would recommend that doctors be less scientific in the sense of less knowledgeable in the field of diseases, only that the doctor must be able to establish contact between this medical, scientific gaze and the meeting with the patient as an ill person. This goes for nearly all kinds of health professionals: even surgeons need an eye for the life world dimension of the patient, as Oliver Sacks shows in his autobiographical story *A Leg to Stand On* (1984).

Technology development and application has a tendency to live a life of its own: it takes over the scene, sets its own goals, and by these means alters the scope of normality. It is very hard to resist new technology, since as soon as a technology has been introduced, the situation of choice has already been altered. If we say no to a technology – for example, an early ultrasound test to detect the risk that a foetus might suffer from Down's syndrome – we must do so from an analysis of what the technology in question *could* lead to. It could lead to a world with less tolerance for abnormalities and weaknesses and a more hostile attitude towards people who choose to have babies who will be a burden to society. But, as the proponents of the technology will say, the technology does not *have to* have these feared consequences, maybe many parents will choose not to have an abortion and will welcome the child – suffering from Down's syndrome or not. Let the individuals make their own informed choices, the technology proponent will say. The answer to this from the technology sceptic will be that the individuals are not really able to make any informed choice, lacking relevant experience in the issue, and also that in reality, the risk assessment will lead to a lot of foetuses being aborted without actually having Down's syndrome. Yes, the technology proponent will admit, the test *could* have these consequences, but in order to avoid them let us work to improve the technology and the information for patients about the risk assessment. This is the only thing we can do, since who are *you* to refuse to let other people make their own choices? We live in a liberal, democratic society, don't we?

At this point, I think the phenomenologist could enter the scene with some valuable contributions to make to the rather polarized and unfruitful debate. The evaluation of medical technologies must be supplemented by a different type of analysis than the consequentialist–libertarian one I have just mapped out, if we are to be able to understand what technological development does to us. This analysis must focus on technologies as a part of our *mindset*; it must explore how the life world of people is altered by the technologies and the driving forces putting them to work. One such force is the market economy, but this is not all there is to the impact of new medical technologies in transforming our understanding of the world and ourselves. We are increasingly becoming objects of a technological gaze that we are making our own. Heidegger in the 1950s called this *"Gestell"* – a framing of our world by science through which everything consequently shows up as calculable and usable (Heidegger [1954] 1977). Heidegger, in his essays on technology, talked about forests, rivers and nuclear technology subjecting us to the *Gestell*, but the true extension of his analysis is the recent developments of gene technology, in which humankind itself is becoming the manipulated, not only the manipulator (Svenaeus 2007).

In my view, the most important thing in a contemporary phenomenological analysis of medical technology is to not fall into the trap of fear and hostility towards technology, something that is very visible, if not in Heidegger himself, then in many of his followers. It is obvious that many medical technologies, if kept within the bounds of sound judgement and application, are too valuable to our lives to be abstained from, although they do force people to take a stand on and possibly change their attitudes towards themselves and their own bodies. Organ transplantation is a good example. It harbours a tendency to resourcify and maybe even commodify our bodies – or at least parts of them, the organs – but the possibilities it offers in saving and healing lives are too valuable to say no to (Svenaeus 2010). The important thing in every case must be to make visible the mindset-transforming aspect of the technologies in question and relate this to the ethics and politics of technology use. "Control" appears to be a central concept in this phenomenological analysis. Who is in control of the technology? And how does the technology change our need to increasingly *be in control* of everything in our life? Can this urge for control also make our lives less worth living in the sense that we no longer have a place for the unexpected and unplanned? Or is it merely like making our roads safer by means of wider lanes, better fences and speed limits, protecting ourselves from unwanted dangers, making our lives longer?

DEATH

A final obvious theme to point towards as essential to a phenomenology of medicine is death. Or rather, since death itself can never be experienced, our "being-towards-death", human finitude, which is a key point for both Heidegger and Sartre in forming their phenomenologies (Heidegger [1927] 1996; Sartre [1943] 1956). Things matters to us because we will die, and death is the ultimate thing we cannot control or postpone forever, even though medicine today, to some people at least, might harbour the promise of such post-human lives (Gordijn & Chadwick 2008).

What is to be said about death from a phenomenological perspective? The phenomenologist will point out that death is an existential concept, and not only a biological one (just as life is, for that matter). Most of us will have no problem accepting that the bodies we live as are dependent on a biology that makes them vulnerable, and, ultimately, finite, but even so, we might have a problem accepting that this will happen to *us*. I can learn everything there is to know about the biological processes of the cancer I have recently been struck by, but this will not stop me from asking "Why me?" and "Why now?" It might sometimes be possible to accept that one is going to die, but I doubt that in most cases this has anything to do with the dying person's being educated in and understanding more about the processes of nature. If so, this education must have taken on some type of philosophical bent.

Persons, and not only their bodies, die – and they do so in relationship with other human beings. Nowadays, and for good reasons, this dying together and yet alone is a process that is assisted by doctors and nurses in or outside a hospital, and medicine therefore needs a phenomenological take on death and dying if it is not to fail in this difficult endeavour of helping those who are beyond hope in the medical sense. Being-towards-death is characterized by Heidegger as an experience that is fundamentally unhomelike in character ([1927] 1996). This refers not to the final moments of life, to dying, but to the *acknowledging* that one is going to die. Being-towards-death is a death within life that we feel and discover at the very heart of our own being. Heidegger himself stresses existential anxiety as the ultimate unhomelike experience in his analysis, but our whole embodiment is a kind of existential mark of our finitude, making itself known to us through obstructions that plague us and which will finally bring us to death. To our final homecoming, one is tempted to say.

CONCLUSION

I have surveyed some of the themes that I think are central to a phenomenology of medicine. These phenomena – embodiment, illness, disability, medical technology, dying – are target points where I think phenomenology could be of great value not only to a philosophy of medicine, but also to medicine itself. Phenomenology can shed light on some of the blind spots of modern medicine and thus help it to better understand itself as a human activity and practice. Finally, I think that phenomenology and its extension, hermeneutics, can also be a tool in understanding medical practice itself as an interpretative meeting. I have touched upon this already in investigating the concept of illness in relation to disease, but it deserves to be pointed out again that medicine rests on a meeting between persons. Persons are indeed embodied, vulnerable, suffering and mortal, and that is why we need something like medicine in the first place.

6. BEYOND THE WOUNDED STORYTELLER: RETHINKING NARRATIVITY, ILLNESS AND EMBODIED SELF-EXPERIENCE

Angela Woods

All of us participate in the making of narratives, but none of us can live wholly in narrative; none of us can even live very thoroughly in narrative. The lack of narrative is a kind of madness, but too much narrative is also a kind of madness. Perfect presence in the present is not recognizable as a *human* life, but perfect continual comprehensibility of the present in relation to the future is not recognizable as a human *life*.   (Sartwell 2000: 67)

NARRATIVE IN THE FIELD OF MEDICINE

All disciplines tell stories of their emergence. These stories serve multiple functions: they assert disciplinary identity, lay claim to specific modes of scholarship and objects of scholarly inquiry, position the discipline within a broader field and provide a rationale for the on-going relevance of particular kinds of work. The medical humanities are no exception.[1] If it were to be distilled into only a few sentences, the foundation story of the medical humanities would go something like this: *During the twentieth century, biomedicine lost its way: the art and humanity of medical practice were lost to rapid scientific advances and new technologies. The medical humanities arose to demonstrate the value and relevance of the arts and humanities in making medicine and health care more humane.*

The concept of narrative plays a central part in this story.[2] Narrative has been seen as pivotal to (re)humanizing medicine because it is held to give us insight into the subjective experience of illness, to enhance physicians' communication skills, to provide new qualitative methodologies for research into all aspects of health care, and to facilitate the ill person's exploration and articulation of changes in her sense of self (Charon 2006, 2007,

2008; Frank 1995; Greenhalgh & Hurwitz 1998; Hawkins 1999; Hurwitz *et al.* 2004; Kleinman 1988). A focus on narrative helps health care practitioners to grasp the complexity of the illness experience and understand its relationship to and impact upon other aspects of a person's life. Narrative helps recognize and legitimize the first-person perspective as another form of knowledge about illness, and emphasizes the ill person's agency as she becomes the empowered author–narrator of her own story.

As well as fulfilling these practical, therapeutic and professional aims, narrative serves the purposes of the medical humanities as an interdisciplinary scholarly inquiry. The concept of narrative traverses disciplines (Hyvärinen 2006), eludes definition (Hutto 2007a: 1) and fulfils a range of conflicting aims and agendas (Atkinson 2010; Bochner 2010; Frank 2010; Thomas 2010). The fact that even minimal definitions, such as Abbott's "narrative is *the representation of an event or a series of events*", are controversial (Abbott 2008: 13) should in theory allow for a diversity of perspectives on the question of what constitutes narrative and separates it from other modes of framing experience. However, as has been repeatedly noted (Hyvärinen *et al.* 2010), there is a "lopsided privileging of the 'natural,' quotidian, realistic type of narrative: the type resting staunchly on sequence, succession, causality, or closure" (Tammi 2006: 26) and a tendency to identify narrative with "meaning or culture or identity" *per se* (Sartwell 2006: 156). These general tendencies are, if anything, even more sharply pronounced in the medical humanities, where a person's narrative is often held to be coextensive with their subjective experience, their psychological health and indeed their very humanity.

My aim in this chapter is to challenge two dogmas of narrative: in the medical humanities, and in the field of medicine more broadly.[3] The first is the claim that we are narrative selves. The second, related dogma is that the best or most healthy way to respond to illness is through narrative. Extending my recent work on "the limits of narrative" (Woods 2011a, b), this chapter focuses on the problem of the "narrative self" through a close reading of Galen Strawson's polemical article "Against Narrativity". Strawson's incisive critique of what he calls the psychological and ethical narrativity theses is helpful in challenging the first dogma of narrative in the field of medicine. At the same time, I will argue that medical humanities work on the embodied experience of illness highlights some of the limitations of Strawson's position. In the final section of this chapter, I will briefly consider alternatives to narrative.

"AGAINST NARRATIVITY"

"Against Narrativity" begins by identifying two major currents in the tide of interdisciplinary interest in narrative:[4] the *psychological Narrativity thesis*, which holds "that human beings typically see or live or experience their lives as a narrative or story of some sort", and the *ethical Narrativity thesis*, which "states that experiencing or conceiving one's life as a narrative is a good thing; a richly Narrative outlook is essential to a well-lived life, to true or full personhood" (Strawson 2004: 428).[5] Strawson rejects both theses as false:

> It's just not true that there is only one good way for human beings to experience their being in time. There are deeply non-Narrative people and there are good ways to live that are deeply non-Narrative. [Views which subscribe to the ethical Narrativity thesis] hinder human self-understanding, close down important avenues of thought, impoverish our grasp of ethical possibilities, needlessly and wrongly distress those who do not fit their model, and are potentially destructive in psychotherapeutic contexts.
> (Strawson 2004: 429)

To develop his account of Narrative and non-Narrative people, Strawson distinguishes between two forms of self-experience – one of the self as a whole person, and one of the *self as an inner mental entity (identified through the use of the asterisk). This could also be described as a distinction between "objective" or "third-person" accounts of a person's characteristics and behaviour, and the "subjective" or "first-person" perspective, a sense of me-ness that is ultimately knowable only by me. People's *self-experience in this second sense is in one of two modes: a Diachronic mode, in which "one naturally figures oneself, considered as a *self, as something that was there in the (further) past and will be there in the (further) future", and an Episodic mode, in which "one does not figure oneself, considered as a *self, as something that was there in the (further) past and will be there in the (further) future" (Strawson: 2004: 429).[6] Using himself as an example, Strawson defines the Episodic *self-experience as follows:

> I have a past, like any human being, and I know perfectly well that I have a past. I have a respectable amount of factual knowledge about it, and I also remember some of my past experiences "from the inside", as philosophers say. And yet I have absolutely no sense of my life as a narrative with form, or indeed as a narrative without form. Absolutely none. Nor do I have any great or special interest in my past. Nor do I have a great deal of concern for my future. (Strawson 2004: 432)

So, according to Strawson, we can map the 'time-style' of our *self-experience across two axes as depicted in Figure 1:

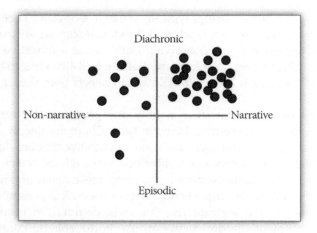

Figure 6.1 Illustration of "Episodic/Diachronic/Narrative/non-Narrative state-space", Galen Strawson's account of time-style modes of *self-experience. Strawson claims that people's distribution on the "time-style" axes is both genetically determined and cross-culturally invariant (Strawson 2004: 431). He acknowledges that people's *self-experience can change over time and circumstance, but suggests that Episodics are on the whole consistently outnumbered by Diachronics. Note that it is not possible, on this account, to be Episodic and Narrative.

Strawson maintains that being Diachronic is necessary but not sufficient for being (naturally) Narrative, as "one can be Diachronic without actively conceiving of one's life, consciously or unconsciously, as some sort of ethical–historical–characterological developmental unity, or in terms of a story, a *Bildung* or 'quest'" (Strawson 2004: 441).[7] Narrativity, then, requires not just that we have a diachronic [D] or temporally enduring sense of *self, but an active drive or tendency towards form-finding [F], story-telling [S] and, on this account, revision [R]. Narrativity [N] can therefore be represented formulaically as [+D] [+F] [+S] [+R]; Strawson, being a paradigmatic Episodic and so "Against Narrativity", describes himself as being [−D] [−F] [−S] [−R]. Although the article acknowledges scope for variation in the degree and combination of the specific tendencies people possess (so, for example, it is possible to be diachronic and form-finding, but not particularly oriented towards storytelling), its fundamental claim is that people lacking in Narrativity can, contra the psychological and ethical Narrativity theses, lead a flourishing life.

It will be important for what follows to highlight the fact that Strawson is concerned not with a capacity for narrative but a propensity for Narrativity. Whether or not a person is able to tell convincing stories about themselves in ways that respect socially agreed conventions is for Strawson neither here nor there. What is important is whether such stories speak to or reveal a sense of *self, which tells us something about whether the person in question has a "natural orientation" to Narrativity. Strawson moves swiftly from seeing Narrativity as something sometimes useful to condemning it as almost always harmful:

> The aspiration to explicit Narrative self-articulation is natural for some – for some, perhaps, it may even be helpful – but in others it is highly unnatural and ruinous. My guess is that it almost always does more harm than good – that the Narrative tendency to look for story or narrative coherence in one's life is, in general, a gross hindrance to self-understanding: to a just, general, practically real sense, implicit or explicit, of one's nature.
> (Strawson 2004: 447)[8]

Although it is only a "guess", the idea that an orientation towards Narrativity is in fact "almost always" harmful seems at face value somewhat melodramatic and even contradictory. If people have a "natural" orientation towards Narrativity, then how would articulating their experience through Narrative *obstruct* *self-understanding? A more plausible suggestion is that a social injunction towards Narrativity – a culturally contextualized demand to tell (particular kinds of) stories about the *self – can be experienced as "highly unnatural and ruinous" for people who, like Strawson, find themselves to be Episodic and non-Narrative. The harm of Narrativity, then, would be experienced principally by "Episodics" who presumably feel themselves to be excluded from what the majority of Diachronics view as legitimate and desirable forms of *self-understanding, or, worse, who are corralled or even forced to view them*selves in these terms and perform accordingly, or else come to be seen as faulty, deficient or as non-persons. Especially, it seems, in the late twentieth and early twenty-first centuries, Episodics face the predicament of being square pegs in a sea of round Narrative holes.[9]

The Episodic–Diachronic distinction has generated considerable debate among philosophers and narrative researchers, especially with regard to questions of ethics and personhood (Battersby 2006; Mackenzie & Poltera 2010; Phelan 2005; Schechtman 2007; Strawson 2007; Tammi 2006). Although, as I have tried to show, there is more nuance in this distinction than its presentation as dichotomy would suggest, it runs a very real risk of being taken for a reductionist account. The unsubstantiated assertion that differences in the time-style of *self-experience are genetically determined and consistent across cultures seems very difficult to defend, particularly from critics who argue that narrative psychology mistakes "a Western, arguably middle and upper class, concept as a universal mode of shaping and articulating subjective experience" (Schiff 2006: 21). Strawson further offers no insight into the way in which different modes of *self-experience are *valued*, legitimized and endorsed in different (historical, social, cultural, familial, professional) contexts. Interlocutors, audiences, co-authors and communities of meaning are worryingly absent from his discussion of Narrativity: identity and narrative are both viewed as essentially private, interior affairs. Yet, at the same time, there is little exploration of what Dan Zahavi describes as a "more primitive and fundamental notion of self; a notion of self that cannot be captured in terms of narrative structures" (2007: 179). But perhaps the most serious problem with "Against Narrativity" is Strawson's neglect of the lived body in his account of *self-experience and of Narrativity. As we shall see, when it comes to matters medical, the centrality of our fleshy materiality will be impossible to ignore.

By virtue of its promise and its flaws, Strawson's work raises important issues for the use and study of narrative right across the field of medicine. It will in turn be complicated and even challenged through that engagement. To accept, even provisionally, his claim that there are "good ways to live that are deeply non-Narrative" does not commit us to a life *without* narrative; rather, it prompts us to identify the *limits* of narrative and to explore alternative ways of understanding, representing and researching health, illness and medical practice. Continuing to focus on Narrativity and models of the self, the rest of this chapter will address in turn the question of limits and of alternatives. In the next section, I will bring "Against Narrativity" into dialogue with one of the most influential studies of illness narrative, Arthur Frank's *The Wounded Storyteller: Bodies, Illness, and Ethics* (1995). I ask: how does Frank's account of the importance of specific kinds of embodied narrative in articulating and transforming the experience of illness force a reconsideration of Strawson's occasionally cavalier dismissal of form-finding, storytelling, diachronic *self-experience? At the same time, does Strawson's work provide the impetus and the tools to challenge *The Wounded Storyteller*'s normative, indeed prescriptive, injunction to narrate?

NARRATIVITY AND THE EXPERIENCE OF ILLNESS

A classic of medical sociology, *The Wounded Storyteller* has also become one of the most celebrated and highly cited works in the medical humanities corpus. It is in many ways a call to arms, urging us to bear witness to the stories of illness, to support the ill person, as "narrative wreck" (Frank 1995: 53–5), in the task of making and sharing their story. Frank suggests that stories of illness tend to take a finite number of narrative forms and argues that the formal properties of each narrative type are intimately connected to a particular mode of embodiment, a "self-story", and a capacity to effect change in the life of the ill person (Frank 1995: 76). For Frank, there are three major types of illness narrative (the third an ideal to which we should aspire):

> Restitution stories attempt to outdistance mortality by rendering illness transitory. Chaos stories are sucked into the undertow of illness and the disasters that attend it. Quest stories meet suffering head on; they accept illness and seek to *use* it. Illness is the occasion of a journey that becomes a quest. (Frank 1995: 115)

"Quest narratives" – in the shape of memoirs, manifestos, or automythologies – empower the ill person to become, effectively, the hero of her own story; they are viewed by Frank as a form of testimony through which the ill person reclaims and reorients the self.

Before exploring in more detail Frank's discussion of the relationship between narrative, illness and embodiment, I want to pause briefly to reflect on what is meant by "illness" in Frank's work and indeed in much of the field of narrative in medicine. Illness is conceptualized by Frank as a wound sustained by the "body-self": it is a devastation of the physical body (wrought partly by the disease itself and partly by the medical treatment of that disease) that is simultaneously an assault on the ill person's capacity for (narrative) self-expression (Frank 1995: xii). The wounded storytellers of Frank's book are people who, like him, have suffered and survived illness,[10] but "could never be considered cured". Members of what he calls the "remission society" are:

> those who had almost any cancer, those living in cardiac recovery programs, diabetics, those whose allergies and environmental sensitivities require dietary and other self-monitoring, those with prostheses and mechanical body regulators, the chronically ill, the disabled, those "recovering" from abuses and addictions, and for all these people, the families that share the worries and daily triumph of staying well. (Frank 1995: 8)

The question of whether a continuity between these kinds of experience is welcome or justified is an important one. Are all wounds fundamentally alike? For Frank, differences in the origin and even nature of the injuries sustained by the body-self, or, for that matter, very real material and cultural differences between bodies, are irrelevant because self-expression through narrative is fundamentally healthy, desirable and even necessary, *for everyone*. Overplaying similarities between the experiences of homeless teenage drug addicts, middle-class medically insured cancer victims, prosthesis-dependent war veterans and people who have suffered from institutionalized racism, sexism, homophobia and other forms of sustained discrimination, is, I would suggest, politically and sociologically suspect. But what is perhaps most striking about the membership list of Frank's "remission society" is that it makes no mention of people diagnosed with mental illness. The implications of this omission merit a more extended discussion than space here allows.[11] Frank's failure to count psychiatric survivors among the members of the remission society highlights a tendency shared by many working in the field of narrative in medicine to treat mental and physical illnesses as resolutely distinct. "Illness", in the work of Arthur Frank, means somatic illness; cancer is the example to which he continually returns.[12] The literature on narrative in medicine is so frequently separated into studies of psyche *or* soma that it is rare indeed to find models of illness that explicitly address what we might think of as the full range of suffering experiences (but see Kleinman 1988). Uneasy though I am to continue this tradition by writing in what follows about non-specific cases of general physical illness, an exploration of the hitherto unacknowledged limitations of this approach is a larger project for another time.

If, for Frank, illness is a wound to the body-self, then stories similarly demand to be conceptualized in corporeal terms:

> The stories that ill people tell come out of their bodies. The body sets in motion the need for new stories when its disease disrupts the old stories. The body, whether still diseased or recovered, is simultaneously cause, topic, and instrument of whatever new stories are told.   (Frank 1995: 2)

He continues: "My thesis is that different bodies have 'elective affinities' to different illness narratives. These elective affinities are not deterministic. Bodies are realized – not just represented but created – in the stories they tell" (Frank 1995: 52).

Narratives are the "self's medium of being" (Frank 1995: 53), they have the power to shape and, it is implied, to heal bodies.[13] But if narratives are a performative revelation of the self, as a form of testimony they are also an ethical way of being for others: "Storytelling is *for* an other just as much as it is for oneself" (Frank 1995: 17). The ill person's sense of *self, her ill body, her illness narrative and her social being in the world are all mutually developed and dependent.

The psychological and ethical narrativity theses here are inseparable, and the full force of their operation in *The Wounded Storyteller* is best observed in the distinction between Frank's three types of narrative. As mentioned above, Frank views quest stories – the so-called monomyth described by Joseph Campbell (1969) – as the idealized form of illness narrative. The plot is, as the name suggests, the arduous but ultimately triumphant "journey through illness"; the body revealed and produced in quest narratives is communicative ("associated with itself, open to contingency, dyadic towards others, and desiring for itself in relation to others"); the self-story is one of heroism, but also one of perseverance, solidarity and inspiration (Frank 1995: 115–36). Despite claiming, somewhat disingenuously, that he was "completely surprised" to realize that the communicative body of the idealized quest narrative is exemplified by the crucified Christ (Frank 1995: 193), the themes of noble suffering, communion with others, the transformative and even redemptive power of physical anguish, testimony and witness all have strongly Christian connotations. Telling of one's *self-transformation as a journey through illness is not only simply desirable, it is positively virtuous.

By now it will not be necessary to rehearse a Strawsonian critique of Frank's valorization of the quest narrative. Stories, according to Strawson, do not positively transform the self but actively propel us away from self-understanding:

> the more you recall, retell, narrate yourself, the further you risk moving away from accurate self-understanding, from the truth of your being. Some are constantly telling their daily experiences to others in a storying way and with great gusto. They are drifting ever further off the truth. (Strawson 2004: 477)

If this danger is courted even in the fairly unremarkable stories of the everyday, then the kind of grand narratives of self that Frank describes – the autobiographies, manifestos and automythologies of the "quest" – must surely present an even greater departure from the "truth of one's being".

In stark contrast to the messianic heroes of the quest narrative are those trapped and mute within the chaos narrative.[14] These are people whose suffering precipitates a breakdown in temporality, language and self-understanding:

> If narrative implies a sequence of events connected to each other through time, chaos stories are not narratives. When I refer below to chaos narratives, I mean an *anti-narrative* of time without sequence, telling without mediation, and speaking about oneself without being fully able to reflect on oneself. Although I will continue to write of chaos stories being told, these stories cannot literally be told but can only be lived. (Frank 1995: 98)

The chaotic narrative is without form and without plot; the chaotic body is contingent in the extreme, monadic and isolated from others, lacking in desire or communion, and experienced as dissociated from the self; the self-story of the chaos narrative is broken, interrupted, distressing and ultimately ineffectual (Frank 1995: 97–114). Although Frank says these non-narratives must in their own way be honoured, and calls for "enhanced tolerance for chaos as a part of a life story" (Frank 1995: 111), it is clear that the narrators of chaos approach a pathological loss of self,[15] a loss that evokes not our condemnation but our compassion.

There is, for Frank, a third mode of illness narrative: the restitution narrative of "Yesterday I was healthy, today I'm sick, but tomorrow I'll be healthy again" (Frank 1995: 77). This story, which emphasizes temporal discontinuity and in which the ill body is dissociated from the *self, is the preferred plot of modern medicine, drug companies and other ideologues beholden to a mechanistic account of the body as machine that medical science can restore to full functioning capacity (Frank 1995: 79–88). It is, on Frank's view, deeply inauthentic and even alienating:

> Is the restitution narrative capable of generating self-stories? No, in the sense that restitution stories bear witness not to the struggles of the self but to the expertise of others: their competence and their caring that effect the cure. In this witness restitution stories reveal themselves to be told *by* a self but not *about* that self.
> (Frank 1995: 92)

Although he acknowledges that the restitution narrative is popular and in fact even sometimes accurate, the fact that it cannot be a *self-narrative means for Frank that it has little moral value. It would seem that illness *must* be experienced as transformative; whether for better (as revealed in the quest narrative) or worse (as registered in the chaos narrative). Stories of restitution are on this view the preserve of those who are in denial, who are out of touch or remain beholden to the dominant narratives of the biomedical establishment.

Perhaps surprisingly, Frank would have no quarrel with Strawson's account of the Diachronic, form-finding, story-telling and revising features of narrativity,[16] even though the two could not be more opposed on the question of its desirability. Narrativity, as linked to embodiment and intersubjectivity, is in Frank's overall schema a natural mode of being that is threatened by illness. The project of telling stories is therefore particularly important for those who are ill and who remain members of the "remission society". There is no room in Frank's account for episodic self-experience, for not being Narrative or for choosing not to narrate. Such a choice would speak only of the silence of chaos or of alienation from the "truth" of self-transformation. The key question raised for Strawson by Frank's work is the extent to which the physical illness that (re)anchors us in the lived body might change our time-style and with it our orientation towards narrative. Strawson, as we have seen, holds that human beings can be "deeply non-Narrative", and although he suggests that "one's exact position in Episodic/Diachronic/Narrative/non-Narrative state-space may vary significantly over time according to what one is doing or thinking about, one's state of health, and so on" (Strawson 2004: 431), he does not discuss in detail the case of illness. Does physical suffering heighten our awareness of and attachment to the passing of time, cleaving us off from a time when health was taken for granted, and forcing us to confront a future that seems now more fraught, more finite? Or is the opposite true – that in illness we become less Diachronic, either because the body commands our present attention, or because the future is no longer a place we can inhabit with the same confidence? These questions open out on to a much larger phenomenological literature on the temporality of illness (see especially Toombs 1990; Fuchs in press), which teaches that we should not seek definitive answers to the question of how illness is experienced in general terms. In many cases, the temporality of illness does seem to disrupt *self-experience, but it does not follow that narrative, particularly the compulsory heroism of the quest narrative, should be the privileged form for the interpretation or restitution of that *self-experience. Nor does it follow that those who live episodically, those who have no orientation to narrative and who, when "obliged to convey facts about their lives ... do it clumsily and uncomfortably and in a way that is somehow essentially narrative-resistant" (Strawson 2004: 447–8), are necessarily living inauthentically or in chaos.

BEYOND NARRATIVE?

Frank's work shows that illness narratives are always embodied, that all stories of the *self are told, and witnessed, by embodied subjects. In the case of illness narratives, the physically ill or broken body is both the subject of the story and the mode of its telling; illness brings the body into the foreground and is a forceful reminder that it must be accounted for. There is no reason to suppose that Strawson's model of diachronic and episodic experience would be incompatible with embodied *self-experience,[17] and so every reason to think that further development of these ideas in the field of narrative in medicine could be highly fruitful. The more fundamental (and in my view irreconcilable) difference between *The Wounded Storyteller* and "Against Narrativity" stems from Frank's adherence to and Strawson's rejection of the psychological and ethical narrativity theses. For Frank, illness is a call to narrative and flourishing is absolutely dependent on narrativity; the schema of quest, chaos and restitution narrative allows for different forms of embodied experience (which can even be experienced in combination, or at different times by the same person), but no possibility of being non-narrative; that is, no possibility of *legitimately choosing* something *other than* narrative. Again, the issue here, as Strawson would argue, is not one of narrative capacity, but rather concerns an orientation towards narrativity, the experience of the *self as diachronic, form-finding, storytelling and revisionist.

If we acknowledge, with Frank, the body's centrality in *self-experience, but agree with Strawson that people, both healthy and ill, can be [−D], [−F], [−S] and [−R], what alternatives do scholars, practitioners and people in the field of medicine have for articulating and conceptualizing the embodied experience of illness? Howard Brody has argued that "suffering is produced, and alleviated, primarily by the meaning that one attaches to one's experience", and that the "primary human mechanism for attaching meaning to particular experiences is to tell stories about them" (Brody 1987: 5). If we accept a weaker version of Brody's claim − that meaning-making and suffering may be linked in certain contexts − what other vehicles for meaning-making beyond the telling of stories could be explored?

Narrative does not have a monopoly on expressivity. Although many people do not believe themselves to be artistically gifted or particularly creative, medical humanities researchers and arts-in-health practitioners have shown that experiences of distress and of physical vulnerability can be brought to life and given shape in a wide variety of media. Deborah Padfield (Padfield *et al.* 2003) and Molly van der Weij (2010) have done powerful work in enabling people to communicate pain through a range of visual media, including photography and drawing; others have explored music-making as a way to express the often-turbulent experiences of illness (Bunt 2010; Lings 2010), or have used novel forms of linguistic expression, such as the strict seventeen-syllable discipline of haiku poetry, to present an alternative to narrative explorations of the *self (Biley & Champney-Smith 2003).

Philosophy, and in particular phenomenology, also has a central role to play in contributing conceptual equipment with which to explore the effects of illness on embodied *self-hood.[18] Phenomenology is not necessarily opposed to or incompatible with narrative explorations of the self, but instead of beginning at the level of language, identity and the life story, phenomenology directs our attention to an exploration of embodied consciousness, perception, and the temporal, spatial, and intersubjective dimensions of our being-in-the-world (see Toombs 2001b). Narrative-based therapies and stories of illness, at least on Frank's model, are fundamentally teleological: they aim towards a self transformed, and a future made psychologically healthier, more coherent, more robust, through the process or journey of narrative. Philosophy, as Havi Carel explains, offers the ill person a "tool with which to analyse, criticize and ultimately improve everyday life", a tool to help rid ourselves of "false beliefs and erroneous judgements", and a way, ultimately, to flourish in the present (Carel 2008: 126–30).[19]

In an era marked by the dominance of naturalistic accounts of disease, any view that takes seriously the subjective experience of illness has an important contribution to make. We are not, thankfully, in a position of having to choose between phenomenological and narrative approaches to illness, or between the *self as captured in photography and the *self as constituted through storytelling. I am not suggesting that narrative does not have important role to play in exploring embodied *self-experience, but we should remember that narrative is simply "one of several cultural forms available to us for conveying, expressing or formulating our experience of illness and suffering" (Hydén 1997: 64). It is on this question of form, of finding a vehicle for "conveying, expressing or formulating" experience, that I would like to conclude. Narrative returns us again and again to structure, coherence and unity (Kraus 2006: 105; Sartwell 2006).[20] In the context of the medical humanities, the creative arts and phenomenological inquiry are also oriented towards understanding the experience of illness – domesticating it, controlling it, giving it form and expression so that its insights can be valued, its transformations grasped, its burden recognized and shared. What place is there for formlessness, for meaninglessness, for silence?

Crispin Sartwell and Sara Maitland are two thinkers whose work challenges us to think not just about the limits of narrative, but the limits of language. Noting that "the centrality or even ubiquity of language in human life is rarely questioned", Sartwell suggests this obsession with language is not fundamental to human experience but "emerges within the era of technology, an era in which our basic relations to the world and to other human beings are conceived technologically" (Sartwell 2000: 3). Maitland, too, argues that contemporary Western culture is fixated on talk, on narrative, on noise, so much so that "too much silence" is seen to be "either 'mad' (depressive, escapist, weird) or 'bad' (selfish, antisocial)" (Maitland 2008: 25). Sartwell's *End of Story: Toward an Annihilation of Language and History* is both a powerful critique of our fixation on narrative and a pursuit of what escapes linguistic representation (in his view, "almost everything"; Sartwell 2000: 5); Maitland's autobiographical *A Book of Silence: A Journey in Search of the Pleasures and Powers of Silence* documents her philosophical, spiritual and phenomenological fascination with silence and her exploration of its many varieties.

Of course, to venture beyond language is to enter risky territory. One of Maitland's friends insists to her that:

> Silence is the place of death, of nothingness ... There is no silence without the act of silencing, some one having been shut up ... gagged, told to hold their tongue, had their tongue cut out, had the cat get their tongue, lost their voice ... All the social movements of oppressed people in the second part of the twentieth century have claimed "coming to language" and "coming to voice" as necessary to their politics ... Silence is oppression. It is "the word" that is the beginning of freedom.
>
> (Janet Batsleer, quoted in Maitland 2008: 28)

As I have argued, the medical humanities' valorization of the narrative self has had particular resonance at a time when twentieth- and twenty-first-century biomedicine is alleged to have silenced patients; to have had ears and eyes only for symptoms, and not for the people whose lives they affect. But like Strawson, Sartwell and Maitland challenge the assumption that narrative, and even speech, is as desirable as it is inevitable. Their work stands as an invitation to attend to what cannot be spoken; to embrace silence as a part of life that is open to contingency and randomness, but also ecstasy and intensity; to resist the impulse to mistake narrative for life. In the case of illness, this is an invitation that I believe scholars and practitioners in the medical humanities must be ready to accept.

NOTES

1. While debate persists as to the nature and purpose of the medical humanities, the prevailing view is that it is not "an autonomous discipline in its own right" (Pattison 2003: 34) but a multidisciplinary (Chambers 2009), interdisciplinary (Evans & Macnaughton 2004) or postdisciplinary (Lewis 1998) field of inquiry that is "beginning maturation" (Ahlzén 2007: 385). Far from obviating the need to tell the story of its establishment as a fledgling field, the plurality of the medical humanities seems to have made this task more urgent.
2. Indeed, the development of the medical humanities from the late 1970s is roughly coextensive with the so-called "narrative turn" across the humanities and social sciences (Bruner 1991).
3. Throughout this chapter, references to "narrative in medicine" or "narrative in the field of medicine" should be understood in the broadest possible terms to include all aspects of health care and the study of health and illness. "Narrative medicine", by contrast, refers to specific forms of narrative-based clinical practice, as in the work of Rita Charon (2008).
4. Although he acknowledges that narrative is an interdisciplinary question or topic, Strawson concentrates his argument on philosophical accounts of narrative identity. Key recent texts in this tradition include those by MacIntyre (1981), C. Taylor (1989), Bruner (1990), Ricoeur (1990), Campbell (1994) and Hutto (2007b, 2008).

5. Narrative, in capitals, refers in Strawson's work to the psychological dimension of narrative, the claim that we are narrative selves. In this chapter, I continue to capitalize Narrative to distinguish between what are elsewhere called "big" stories (stories of and about the self), as distinct from "little" stories (of a more day-to-day variety). For more on this distinction in narrative research see the *Narrative Inquiry* debate (Bamberg 2006; Freeman 2006; Georgakopoulou 2006).
6. I have added the asterisk to "self" in these quotations and throughout the chapter to avoid confusion.
7. Strawson concedes that diachronic and narrative outlooks are intimately linked, but maintains that it is possible to conceive of a "Diachronic person who lives, by force of circumstance, an intensely picaresque and disjointed life, while having absolutely no tendency to seek unity or narrative developmental pattern in it" (Strawson 2004: 442).
8. This somewhat radical position is not unique to Strawson. In his incisive critique of narrative research in medicine, Gabriel (2004: 169) forcefully reminds us that "while stories can be vehicles of contestation, opposition, and self-empowerment, they can also act as vehicles of oppression, self-delusions, and dissimulation".
9. Unfortunately Strawson (2004: 439) does not see it as his responsibility to offer an explanation for the popularity of narrativity today; instead he suggests its prominence is owed to a few leading luminaries: "I ... suspect that those who are drawn to write on the subject of 'narrativity' tend to have strongly Diachronic and Narrative outlooks or personalities, and generalize from their own case with that special, fabulously misplaced confidence that people feel when, considering elements of their own experience that are existentially fundamental for them, they take it that they must also be fundamental for everyone else."
10. Frank writes about his experience of testicular cancer in his 1991 book *At the Will of the Body* (2002). He elsewhere remarks that *The Wounded Storyteller* "is not only *about* narrative recuperation; it also is a narrative in which my own recuperation is performed by aligning myself with the stories I retell. My own recuperation is my stake in these stories" (Frank 2000: 357).
11. As I have argued elsewhere (Woods 2010), excluding people diagnosed as mentally ill from membership of "the remission society" and by implication from the role of "wounded storyteller" has the potential to reinforce the view that severe mental illness shatters a person's narrative capacity, and therefore their very personhood, and that it is something from which it is not possible to recover. Frank would surely not dispute the claim that people who receive a diagnosis of schizophrenia are ill, but are they prevented from being wounded storytellers because their wounds are "mental" rather than "physical", or because their storytelling, incorporating as it might experiences of delusion, depersonalization or hallucination, is itself "ill"?
12. Frank's own experience of surviving cancer, as recounted in *At the Will of the Body*, clearly informs his approach in *The Wounded Storyteller*; indeed, all of the "illness narratives" discussed in the book are published autobiographies of people who are, or have been, chronically physically unwell.
13. Frank does not offer an account of the precise mechanisms by which stories have a positive therapeutic effect, nor does he clarify whether he thinks the development and performance of certain kinds of narrative have physiological benefits as well as a capacity to improve psychological health and well-being. However, his

claim that people's "bodies give their stories their particular shape and direction", and that "stories can heal" (Frank 1995: 27, xii) certainly suggests a relationship of mutual influence between bodies and stories.
14. Or, to continue the religious motif, "For the communicative body, the chaotic body is the traveler whom the Good Samaritan found robbed and beaten by the roadside" (Frank 1995: 104)
15. Although Frank never mentions mental illness specifically, his account of the chaos narrative finds an affinity with interdisciplinary studies of the loss of narrative self in schizophrenia (Gallagher 2003; Gruber & Kring 2008; Mackenzie & Poltera 2010; Phillips 2003; Saavedra *et al.* 2009; see Woods 2011c for a critique of this literature).
16. Indeed, the tendency towards revision is for Frank a virtue rather than a weakness of narrative: "The truth of stories is not only what *was* experienced, but equally what *becomes* experience in the telling and its reception. The stories we tell about our lives are not necessarily those lives as they were lived, but these stories become our experience of those lives ... The social scientific question of reliability – getting the same answer to the same question at different times – does not fit here. Life moves on, stories change with that movement, and experience changes. Stories are true to the flux of experience, and story affects the direction of that flux" (Frank 1995: 22).
17. For example, while our bodies provide an obvious and enduring sense of our continuity in time, it is equally the case that adult episodics may recognize their childhood, adolescent and elderly bodies as theirs without feeling deeply a sense of *self in connection to those bodies.
18. See in particular Toombs (1988, 1990, 2001a); Svenaeus (2009, 2011) and Carel (2010).
19. One of the most engaging publications in recent years is Havi Carel's *Illness* (Carel 2008). Like Frank, Carel's writing integrates a range of perspectives – that of the phenomenologist and the philosopher, the professional academic, the patient, the patient activist and the person who is diagnosed in her mid-thirties with lymphangioleiomyomatosis (LAM), a rare lung disease. Carel's narrative defies Frank's schema and explicitly refuses the triumphal heroism of the quest. What makes Carel's book so compelling in the context of the present discussion is not that it is anti-narrative, but that her story is interwoven with, and indeed becomes the vehicle for, a broader philosophical project. Instead of placing the emphasis on identity and the ill person's storytelling capacity, Carel's exploration of the phenomenology of illness offers a way of grasping the transformations – subtle and profound – to embodiment and "enworldedness".
20. As Shlomith Rimmon-Kenan (2006: 245) reminds us, narratology "gives insightful accounts of order but has no tools for – and no interest in – an analysis of randomness".

7. TRANSITIONS IN HEALTH AND ILLNESS: REALIST AND PHENOMENOLOGICAL ACCOUNTS OF ADJUSTMENT TO CANCER

James Brennan

The Department of Health estimates that 15.4 million (or 30 per cent of) people in England are living with a long-term condition (what used to be called chronic illness), accounting for 70 per cent of the total health and social care spend in England. These statistics demonstrate the astonishing success of biomedicine in keeping people alive but entirely fail to reflect the quality, or lived experience, of these many lives that have been saved. While physical suffering has never been better "controlled", emotional distress remains at high levels. Clinical psychology works with both realist and phenomenological accounts of health and illness, and in this chapter I outline a biopsychosocial and phenomenological model of adjustment, illustrated with quotes from diaries kept by people with cancer and drawn from my clinical work in cancer care. This model accounts for both positive and negative responses to major life transitions such as illness and recovery, and poses questions about the nature of health care.

INTRODUCTION

Cancer is the archetype of protracted or chronic illness, being not only a "long-term condition" but also life-threatening. As old as the dinosaurs, it is a much-dreaded disease that historically has reaped truly abominable suffering. Illnesses like cancer exist within the social world of other people and taken-for-granted meanings. The very word seems to carry a potent existential reminder of our ultimate mortality.

Two million people are currently living with cancer in the UK and it remains a disease associated with fear and profound emotional suffering (e.g. Macmillan Cancer Support 2006). The field of psychological therapy in cancer, or clinical psycho-oncology as it is known, is concerned with the psychological transitions between a person's experience of relative health, often taking it for granted, and their experience of serious illness.

Just as philosophers may wish to understand the relationship between health and illness, psychological clinicians working in the context of cancer need an explanatory model of how human beings negotiate the transition between health and illness. Moreover, psychologists are interested in the transition not only from health to illness, but from illness to health, since increasingly people are recovering from cancer. But even survival has its own psychological difficulties, not least of which is having to re-engage with a changed world and rebuild confidence within it. The life that patients return to is not the one that preceded their illness, yet nor is it the treatment-related world they have recently inhabited and perhaps become used to. The best scientific medical treatments for cancer are usually intensive, distressing to endure, and essentially involve excision, poisons and burns. Managing the side-effects of treatment becomes an over-riding concern, and hospital appointments and (hopefully) reassuring contact with health professionals can (and should) provide patients with a sense of safety and emotional containment. But to leave "active treatment", as it is known, is to leave the security of the medical bunker. And this can be a difficult transition too.

In this chapter I wish to explore the *being* of illness and health, not simply the conceptual meaning of these terms, and I want to consider how people psychologically adjust their minds as they negotiate the transitions between these different positions of health and illness. I shall illustrate some of my arguments with verbatim quotes from the personal diaries of people with cancer as they underwent their treatment. I also wish to point out some links between recent philosophical and psychological investigations into health and illness.

CONSTRUCTIONS OF HEALTH AND ILLNESS

At a common-sense level, throughout our lives most people are aware of feeling ill from time to time, most often in quite trivial ways. We *notice* a change, we may *feel* different physically and mentally, or perhaps we find ourselves *behaving* differently. And, of course, our own sense of being unwell potentially affects the people around us – family members, friends, employers, and so on, who also react to our being ill.

One could argue that our lives exist within a simple continuum of health and illness, albeit what we experience as illness is shaped by our own assumptions about illness, and these are drawn from previous direct experiences as well as our acquired expectations of what health and illness can do. Until faced with illness, people are largely unaware of the unspoken assumptions they hold about their health (and, as it turns out, many other core beliefs they unconsciously hold). I argue that the experience of illness reveals and changes our assumptions about health and illness. Illness therefore has much to teach: many of its lessons may be hard and painful but, movingly, some can turn out to be helpful. This alone is a paradox worthy of interest. How can a threatening and stressful ordeal like cancer lead to profound emotional distress in some instances, and to personal enlightenment and growth in others? I shall address this question later in this chapter.

Health is harder to perceive than illness because for most people health is taken for granted, a more abstract, background almost aspirational ideal. As Svenaeus, quoting Gadamer, puts it:

> Health is not a condition that one introspectively feels in oneself. Rather it is a condition of being there (Da-Sein), of being in the world (In-der-Welt-Sein), of being together with other people (Mit-den-Menschen-Sein), of being taken in by an active and rewarding engagement with the things that matter in life.
> (Svenaeus 2000b)

Like hunger, fear, loss, joy, poverty and other personal experiences, health and illness are sometimes in the foreground of our lives, and sometimes in the background – what Barbara Patterson has described as our "shifting perspectives" (Patterson 2001). This quality of relativity was surely the central point when Aristotle famously said in the *Nicomachean Ethics*:

> With regard to what happiness is, people differ, and the many do not give the same account as the wise. For the former think it is some plain and obvious thing, like pleasure, wealth, or honour; they differ, however, from one another – and often even the same man identifies it with different things, with health when he is ill, with wealth when he is poor. (Aristotle 1984)

In other words, we only become aware of our implicit expectations when the things we may have taken for granted become threatened or taken away. A potentially fatal illness like cancer certainly threatens and takes away a great deal from people's lives, affecting not merely the lived body which may be felt as alien, an object, but also leading to what Svenaeus describes as a more general "unhomelike being-in-the-world", affecting the "meaning patterns" of self and environment (Svenaeus 2011).

This phenomenological view of illness clearly shares its outlook with a more psychological perspective. For example, the psychological therapist, by inferring from the client's words and behaviour, attempts to understand their distress and difficulties through their "meaning-patterns". This client-centred therapy ideal of really *seeing and feeling* from the client's internal point of reference, this identification with another person's inner world is known as empathy. It was one of the core conditions for successful therapy articulated by Carl Rogers (1951).

The phenomenological shift in our patients' meaning-patterns is what psychologists refer to as psychological adjustment. Later in this chapter I will describe a psychological model of adjustment to life transitions, such as the transition from health to illness and beyond.

DISEASE

Illness is not synonymous with disease. Disease is a *medical* state – a physical abnormality of some kind, regardless of whether it can actually be detected; it involves processes that have the potential for, or indeed are damaging the welfare of the system in some way. Thus disease has a more specific meaning than illness and is therefore more easily operationalized.

Disease is an objective, physiological condition that is superimposed on a person's experience of health and illness. The impact of disease on the experience of health and illness is variable and unique to the individual and their meaning patterns. Thus a woman with breast cancer may be entirely without symptoms and feeling healthy until her underlying disease is detected by a mammogram. From her own experiential point of view she is healthy. At the same time, some patients – even those with quite advanced disease, with perhaps only months to live – may *feel* relatively well and be able to engage fully with their lives; they may be creative, productive and happy during their remaining time. Could this be health within illness? Are these terms as mutually exclusive as they sound? Consider this diary entry by a woman mid-way through her treatment for breast cancer:

Cancer diary 1

> *I feel a complete fraud now – perfectly healthy – at peace with myself and the world in general ... Am not angry now about having cancer.*

She presumably feels like a fraud because, having assumed and expected the social identity of an ill person, she now feels "perfectly healthy". She is no longer angry at having illness thrust upon her because she can return to a more familiar or homelike being-in-the-world. Her expectations, her assumptions, are fundamental to her lived experience.

At the other extreme, a person can be racked with despair or fear, to the point where they struggle to get out of bed, but in the *absence* of any definable physical abnormality. In such situations, our emotional responses are not a form of disease, in the sense of the body being dysfunctional. The person may *feel* "ill" in one sense or another: ill-tempered, ill-disposed, ill-at-ease, ill-equipped or ill-supported, but only in this sense ill – they are not diseased. In fact, it may even be functional to stay in bed and take stock of the world outside, before choosing to re-engage with it. Illness, like health, is therefore relative to the individual's homelike being-in-the-world; it is experiential and relative to the individual's meaning patterns.

INTEGRATION

This view of health and illness as extremes along a continuum is therefore too simple. Although disease obviously leads to the experience of illness, nowhere more so than in cancer, it is nonetheless *also* partly dependent on the difference between what the person is *expecting*, their *assumptions* about their well-being, and what they actually experience (e.g. Cancer diary 1 above). In Nordenfelt's view, "health, as assumed by the patient, as well as by the health-care personnel, is a state of affairs over and above the absence of disease" (Nordenfelt 2007: 8). Health and illness are neither mutually exclusive, nor do they depend entirely on the presence or absence of disease.

Nordenfelt has described health as having to do with "the ability of someone to reach their vital goals". When our vital goals are thwarted our health is affected, a definition which neither implies disease nor even illness (in the same way that the experience of illness is not entirely dependent upon underlying disease). On this way of thinking, health is not an end in itself. It merely enables people to get on with their lives, or as Seedhouse said in 1986, "A person's health is equivalent to the set of basic conditions which fulfil or enable a person to work to fulfil his or her realistic, chosen or biological potentials" (Seedhouse 1986: 72). This definition suggests that health may be only loosely related to the experience of illness, but closer to what social scientists call quality of life. An even stronger rendition sees health as personal development in the face of changing circumstances (Mitchell & Cormack 1998).

Reaching vital goals may of course be profoundly impeded by diseases like cancer, but this does not necessarily preclude the fulfilment of a person's potential. One could say that the extent that one *feels* ill, and thus *experiences* illness, is related to how much one is able to achieve health, but this *may* have little to do with underlying disease. It may have more to do with the ability to progress vital goals, or achieve a homelike being-in-the-world, a world that has perhaps regained a sense of familiarity. Consider the following diary entry in which the writer clearly identifies herself as healthy and happy.

Cancer diary 2

Although at times I feel exceptionally frustrated as my energy levels aren't back to normal and I still suffer from some sickness, but to be quite honest I'm very healthy and happy.

So the extent to which people can adapt to the changes, and accommodate the implications brought about by disease and embodied in their illness experience, reflects the extent to which they can reclaim their sense of health, or as Svenaeus puts it, the capacity of patients to "make their being-in-the-world homelike again by way of not only changing their outer circumstances, but also their understanding of themselves in this altered situation" (Svenaeus 2011). Thought about in this way, psychological adjustment is the realignment of expectations and assumptions in light of the implications of new information. The transitions between health and illness, as perspectives shift, involve the adjustment of taken-for-granted assumptions: making sense of recent events and making new meaning and understanding. As described below, illness can reveal many of the core assumptions by which people have lived their lives yet never examined. These revelations can be as distressing as they can be rewarding, but in either case they demand attention, emotions and mental resources.

The term *assumption* can be thought of in exactly its common sense meaning, though in cognitive science assumptions are known as propositional representations (Power & Dalgleish 1997). The assumptions we develop about the world, other people and ourselves are of course shaped by every experience of our own particular lives; in other words, the unique social worlds we each inhabit. At a more subtle level, our assumptions are also wrought by the genetic imperatives that underlie how human beings, as a species, behave and think: things like being especially protective towards one's kin, having emotions in response to threat, from a young age forming attachment bonds with care-givers, and so on.

Most of these assumptions are implicitly learned, without awareness, and therefore not always consciously held or even known to us. A child does not consciously learn how to speak, stand or walk, any more than most adults consciously develop assumptions about their ethical views (philosophers notwithstanding) until they are challenged. In the social world we learn from experience, but the knowledge of what we have learned is not consciously known to us. In other words, what is unconsciously learned usually remains implicit knowledge. One of the aims of therapy is to elucidate these implicit assumptions in order that they may be consciously examined and, if necessary, adjusted.

Assumptions are very much drawn from and exist within a social world.

Cancer diary 3

Have got to adjust my image of myself from being a fit healthy person to (perhaps) being ill, feeling ill, being shunned like a leper by healthy people ... which the world seems full of.

Here we see a cancer diarist feeling the need to alter her assumptions about herself, in other words her identity, from a healthy person to an ill person. Moreover she is aware of the impact this will have on her social status, resulting in what she expects to be stigmatization ("shunned like a leper").

The transition from health to illness is not just about the direct physical effects of disease and its treatment, but the threat they pose and the havoc they cause to people's lives. The lived experience of illness is also not just about what Leventhal describes as *illness representations* – the cognitive assumptions about illness elicited within us when we are ill (Leventhal *et al.* 1980). Our assumptive world of course contains assumptions about what various illnesses represent. Our understanding of cancer, and what it can do to us, largely determines the threat it poses for us. But this is just one part of a larger network of assumptions that we have acquired throughout our lives that are affected by illness. The phenomenological or subjective experience of illness has more to do with what Svenaeus describes as "the ways human beings (what Heidegger calls *Dasein*) inhabit these worldly patterns of meaningfulness (what Husserl and many of his phenomenological successors calls the *life world*)" (Svenaeus 2011).

When our most deep-seated assumptions fail to adequately make sense of a new situation we are left disorientated, afraid and potentially traumatized. The unreal, dreamlike state of shock following a diagnosis of cancer is a powerful example.

Cancer diary 4

It felt like a bad dream. One minute life was chuntering on. The next – well, someone switched the reels ... Somewhere, in some

> *parallel universe, life was continuing to chunter on; here, in this one ... where I was unaccountably stuck after some through-the-looking-glass moment ... mammograms, ultrasound, core biopsies, sitting in a square at Bart's weeping, apologising, on my partner's shoulder in the soft rain, the world suddenly upside down, guilty, I or my body had let us down – him, the kids, me.*

This is literally the dawn of a new reality, the world of illness. To call it a "personal transition" is to coarsely understate its psychosocial impact. One does not have to be a psychologist to appreciate that the experience of illness, particularly when it is cancer, overshadows the symptoms of the disease itself. And you will notice that the woman who wrote this entry in her diary, despite the radical shift of her life into "a parallel universe", is not only concerned about herself. Despite her existential anguish she is equally concerned for the disappointed lives of the people she loves most in the world: "him, the kids, me".

When faced with serious illness many of our most deep-seated assumptions are threatened, violated or even shattered (Janoff-Bulman 1992), and the psychological task is to make sense of what has happened, to understand the implications for our lives and our loved ones, and to confront and re-engage with a world that has irrevocably changed. The task for the clinical psychologist is to help ill people make sense of these implications, so they can recalibrate their assumptions about the world in order to reclaim their vital goals, and in this sense maximize their health, however long or short their lives may be.

A MODEL OF PSYCHOLOGICAL ADJUSTMENT

This social-cognitive transition model of adjustment (Brennan 2001, 2004, 2007) is an attempt to describe how people psychologically negotiate major life transitions, such as that between health and illness, and illness and health.

The model starts from the premise that throughout our lives people develop assumptions and expectations about the world, drawn from the unique social and cultural environments in which we each live. Like kittens and puppies, once babies can crawl around, their biological instinct is to use their bodies and perceptual senses to learn about the physical world around them – looking, touching, smelling, listening and tasting. We are born to explore and interact with the world around us but, unlike puppies, we have the brains and language to do this in much more sophisticated ways. Human cognitive development is the acquisition of information, by which I mean very diverse forms of knowledge: physical embodied *know-how* (skills, habits, behavioural routines – such as walking, writing, bicycling, playing the piano, etc.), *formal knowledge* (facts, social ideas) and, perhaps most important of all, *assumptions* (beliefs, hunches, construct systems, non-verbal reasoning, cognitive maps, internal working models, schema, schematic models; these are some of the many terms psychologists have deployed over the past sixty years).

In short, cognitive development is the acquisition of unconscious or pre-conscious *mental models* (Craik 1948) of the world, based largely on implicit learning. These "preconscious" assumptions are available for scrutiny but otherwise not known. Beneath this is a more unconscious, abstract and less accessible awareness of memory and knowledge. It is sometimes this level that psychologists need to understand. They achieve this understanding through inferring the assumptions that underlie a person's words and behaviour, and then exploring these inferences with the client. Mental models held by the client are hard to perceive and often have to be deduced by things like life patterns, residual emotions and feelings that therapists are able to detect in the client and themselves. It is through such empathic investigation that the therapist and client come to a clearer formulation of the difficulties being experienced and of the mismatch between expectations and experience.

Developing and elaborating mental models is what human brains do best. From an evolutionary point of view, this cognitive skill is highly and uniquely adaptive. The Swiss child psychiatrist Jean Piaget believed that there are two main ways that children learn about the world. The first is *accommodation*, which involves adjusting or elaborating mental models so as to integrate new information, a skill regarded as relatively easy for children, but less so for adults. *Assimilation* is the other main method of learning Piaget identified – the perceptual–cognitive act of fitting what we "see" into the mental models we already possess, a confirmatory bias. It has been argued that ageing brains are susceptible to "hardening of the categories", meaning that we are more susceptible to over-assimilation the older we get. Furthermore, as Carl Rogers observed, "the structure and organization of self appears to become more rigid under threats and to relax its boundaries when completely free from threat" (Rogers 1951). These complementary routes to learning are of course not unique to childhood but characterize all learning that is deeper than associative or operant conditioning. It is what makes the human brain rather different from that of other animals:

> Humans achieve their goals by complex chains of behaviour, assembled on the spot and tailored to the situation. They plan the behaviour using cognitive models of the causal structure of

the world. They learn these models in their lifetimes and communicate them through language, which allows the knowledge to accumulate within a group and over generations.

(Pinker 1997: 186)

It appears to be a natural and adaptive tendency of human beings to learn from their lived experiences and integrate this new information with their mental models of the world. They draw on these mental models to form assumptions with which to make sense of moment-to-moment experience. Experience, in turn, confirms or modifies the mental models that gave rise to the assumption, thus making the mental model more effective in predicting the world and anticipating consequences.

For example, babies are biologically programmed to engage with other people, particularly their primary caregivers. From these early relationships they quickly begin to develop assumptions about how other people can be expected to behave. Our own unique attachment history determines our assumptions about future relationships. Moreover, the assumptions people hold about their relationships with one another are brought into clearer focus when one person develops a serious illness. For example, people quickly realize who depends upon whom within a family. Similarly, assumptions that may have developed over many years about one's partner (e.g. that they will be there to care for me if needed), can be severely tested in the face of adversity. Adjustment to cancer affects a large constellation of people around the patient, all of whose mental models may also be shaken.

Take another core assumption. Between the ages of three and five children mysteriously work out that other people have minds and intentionality of their own, and with this insight comes a brand new sense of self, an existential self as well as a social one. They have developed a new model of other people, a theory of mind. By the time a person is an adult they have a more or less stable self-concept, with less or more self-worth. Faced with the prospect of death, however, people are confronted by themselves; there may be a moral reckoning, a hard look at the assumptions that one has acquired about oneself or by which one has lived one's life. Or perhaps a more kindly life review which simply seeks a feeling of "completion".

Another core assumption has to do with our unconscious relationship with the body, our embodiment. Human consciousness exists within a body, and this existential dependence on our physical selves is naturally also brought into much clearer focus by illness. The body becomes "other", alien, objective, not simply an intrinsic part of consciousness or the lived body. Our homelike relationship with the body is lost; the illness thwarts our capacity to sustain a homelike being-in-the-world. The intimate relationship we have with our bodies, the pains and pleasures it gives us, the changes it undergoes throughout our lives, our sense of our bodies in the social world of appearance, our reliance on it for our agency and power in the world, these are some of the unspoken assumptions we hold about our bodies that, again, may be revealed by the experience of illness.

Cancer diary 5

> *The passage of my life is written on my body, the pockmarks, the little scars of everyday trauma, childbearing, excess weight, sports or lack of them. And now comes a new one, not only surgery but brown veins creeping up my arms from the chemo site. And each hit adds a little ridge to my nails.*

These core assumptions, the unspoken beliefs by which we have lived our lives, are revealed by illness, but even more so when the illness threatens our existence. The assumption of our future existence and the passage of time are basic to consciousness, hope and motivation, so when the future is short, or simply uncertain, this core assumption is starkly revealed. The very act of making plans and maintaining autobiographical goals, what I have termed our *life trajectory* (Brennan 2001), becomes problematic. For example, many people with cancer are reluctant to imagine any sort of future because to do so feels like staring at death, or just tempting fate. However, the risk is that, by failing to make plans, they make themselves vulnerable to loss of hope and purpose, in other words, to despair. I would venture that you would probably not bother to read these words at this moment, if you did not anticipate being alive next month. Again, this may relate to Heidegger's notion of *Dasein* being temporal: "Life matters because the possibilities realised in our being-in-the-world are finite and dependent on a future approached on the basis of our factual past" (Svenaeus 2011).

What we experience in our lives from moment to moment subtly and sometimes dramatically alters these assumptions and expectations. We rely upon this cognitive function to provide us with sophisticated mental models of how the world, indeed how one's life, works. But when a catastrophic experience like cancer comes along there is a mental need to limit the disorientation caused by the implications of the illness. People use defensive strategies like denial, dissociation and avoidance because they psychologically need to. If the assumptive world has no helpful models to account for unfolding events we are likely to find these events traumatic. Therefore, before patients can integrate the new reality of serious disease into their lives, they must first make sense of the implications of what has happened to them and this takes time. Our mental models, what Parkes (1971) called our *assumptive world*, enable each unfolding moment to be experienced as part of a more-or-less continuous and coherent whole. When this is not the case we are at risk of being traumatized.

Human beings depend upon their mental models to accurately predict the social and material world, so consequently any threat to core assumptions is experienced as distressing and may well be initially resisted through defences like denial and avoidance, which serve to protect the integrity of mental models. Such psychological defences are therefore entirely normal, providing a level of continuity and coherence against the threat of mental "fragmentation" (Mollon 2002). They enable new information to be absorbed more gradually, thereby reducing distress. Here's how one cancer diarist put it:

Cancer diary 6

> *My head is swirling with waves of shock as I try to absorb a piece of fact for which there is no appropriate slot in my mind. It'll take a long time to create a slot in my mind that will accept this new and unwelcome statement my body is making about itself.*

Thus we are naturally resistant to changing our previously coherent understanding of the world, since this could require an extensive reorganization of our mental maps. Yet this is what serious illness and other major life changes often entail. Both the individual and those close to them are in transition, in the sense that their core assumptions about the world have been violated or discredited, and over time they will feel compelled to adjust them.

In cancer, people often only become conscious of the core assumptions they have been holding when it is clear that these assumptions have been flawed all along. To summarize, core assumptions revealed by cancer tend to be about one's survival and future (the life trajectory), one's relationships, one's identity, one's body and one's beliefs (Brennan 2004).

TRANSITIONS AND ADJUSTMENT

Adjustment to these sorts of core assumptions does not occur overnight. In fact it is the long demanding treatments and the lingering, even indolent quality of some types of cancer, in other words the time it gives people to think about their mortality, that makes cancer such a feared and distressing disease. By contrast, suddenly dying from a heart attack is seen as easier for the victim, albeit rarely for their survivors.

Paradoxically, while serious illness often forces people to re-evaluate their implicit aspirations and assumptions about the future, causing loss, disillusionment and uncertainty, this process of reflection and re-evaluation can sometimes be helpful to personal development (*health*-enhancing). The assumptions and values people hold may not always be in their best interest, in fact they may be inconsistent with the life they had planned to have and the person they wanted to be. In this sense even illness can be life-enhancing if, for example, it enables people to adjust their aspirations to ones that are more congruent with their values, if it enables them to take charge of their lives, or if they finally feel able to be honest with themselves and others.

Here is how French writer Hervé Guibert described his battle with AIDS, a long-term condition:

> An illness in stages, a very long flight of steps that led assuredly to death, but whose every step represented a unique apprenticeship. It was a disease that gave death time to live and its victims time to die, time to discover time, and in the end to discover life.
> (Guibert 1990)

Those finishing cancer treatment have their own transition to negotiate. They must separate from the secure base of the hospital and its personnel and learn to live with uncertainty (has the treatment worked?), while picking up the pieces of their altered lives. Reclaiming one's own health requires the very energy that one often lacks (i.e. treatment-related fatigue), but this struggle is often not apparent to other people. Nonetheless, in my role as a therapist working in cancer, many people have asked me whether they will retain the valuable lessons they have learned since diagnosis, or whether they will return to what they now see was a state of "blissful ignorance". They yearn for this carefree, taken-for-granted world that they used to know, when they were unaware of mortal danger. At the same time they are reluctant to forfeit the personal wisdom they have gained since their diagnosis. Whether or not one survives, adjusting to cancer, like any life-threatening illness, remains a difficult psychological and emotional path.

CONCLUSIONS

The transition from the world of health to that of illness can of course be tragic and frightening, but, thankfully, most people are extraordinarily adaptable, resilient and motivated to regain whatever health and control they can through re-engaging with their vital goals, sometimes discovering new ones in the process. I have argued that the process of adjusting core mental assumptions is central to regaining the experience of health, even in the face of disease progression. The threat to our assumptive world can paradoxically be both a fertile ground for the development of emotional distress as well as, sometimes, personal growth and positive development. At such times of existential crisis people can discover, perhaps for the first time, what they truly value in their lives:

Cancer diary 7

> *Just something about the word makes you think of the end. I'm thinking of all the things I have done, I really do appreciate what I've got from life, but I also want a lot more, not material things, just ordinary things like enjoying my garden, the birds, playing hide and seek with Harry in the garden ... I really appreciate the simple things in life now, things we normally take for granted. It's a pity we have to go through something as awful as this to bring you back down to earth and start life – looking through different glasses – almost like a child, learning all over again.*

Finally, as I have tried to show, if health care is to live up to its name, it must embrace the biopsychosocial and philosophical meanings of health. Homelike being-in-the-world is much more than the removal of disease; it is also, as Havi Carel (2008) has eloquently argued, learning how to live well in the present.

ACKNOWLEDGEMENTS

The cancer diary quotes used in this chapter are drawn from the *Cancer Diaries Project*, a qualitative research project conducted in 2001 by J. Brennan and C. Moynihan in which people who had kept a diary during the course of their treatment for cancer were invited to share their diaries with the authors. These diaries were reported more extensively in Brennan (2004).

8. PAIN AS ILLNESS

Elisa Arnaudo

INTRODUCTION

In 1976, Ivan Illich argued that one of the problems historians of pain have to face is the "profound transformation undergone by the relationship of pain to the other ills man can suffer" (Illich 1975: 97). Illich argues that "pain has changed its position in relation to grief, guilt, sin, anguish, fear, hunger, impairment and discomfort ... it seems as if pain were now only that part of human suffering over which the medical profession can claim competence or control" (Illich 1975: 97).

In Western culture, pain is a medical problem: this means that pain experience cannot be correctly understood without addressing the medical framework in which pain is lived today. My primary aim in this chapter is to analyse the ways in which contemporary biomedicine has tried to handle the complexity of pain, particularly when it becomes a disease.

I will start by introducing the gate control theory of pain – a theory formulated in 1956 that has profoundly changed current neurophysiological conception of pain mechanisms. Gate control theory has superseded the previous specificity theory, allowing a better understanding of pain, elucidating some problematic painful conditions in which the link between injury and pain was not so clear as specificity theory postulated. Gate control indicates instead that there is always a variable relationship between stimulus and pain perception, and highlights the contribution of psychological factors to pain perception.

I then discuss the definition of pain formulated by the International Association for the Study of Pain (IASP), drawing attention to how some controversial issues stemming from the medical conception of chronic pain may derive from an organic/psychological distinction between different kinds of pain already present in the definition. This problematic approach to pain has given rise to a nosological category of painful conditions generally defined as "psychogenic pain" based on the acknowledgement of a predominant psychological aetiology of pain.

I will then turn to chronic pain and its problematic acknowledgement as a disease in itself. Chronic pain, generically defined as pain persisting longer than the expected healing time, challenges the traditional biomedical model mainly because of its blurred aetiology and because of the complex interplay of physiological, psychological and environmental factors in this condition.

I will analyse the theoretical path that has led to chronic pain being construed as a new disease, focusing on an attempt to understand this pathological condition, and pain itself, as a complex phenomenon. I will show how the psychological features of chronic pain have been developed to ensure individual experiential issues are construed as prominent aspects of chronic pain. The reappraisal of psychological issues in chronic pain – pursued in different ways in pain medicine – is troublesome because of the resistance to change of the biomedical disease model, anchored in a reductionist and dualist view of mind and body relations. This approach to pain does not see the psychopathological aspects as always intertwined with other features in a chronic condition but as a cause of pain itself or at least of its continuation. This has led to a much-debated disease classification of pain as "chronic pain syndrome" and entailed a problematic understanding of chronic pain as a disease, particularly in relation to individual accountability in maintaining pain behaviour when psychological factors are judged to play a role in the persistence of pain.

I will further remark on how focusing on meaning – a pivotal issue in chronic pain experience – may challenge the supposed dichotomous view of mind and body and may even offer a common language for the natural sciences and humanities in approaching the phenomenon of pain. Moreover, understanding the meaning of chronic pain experience also entails an analysis of how medical understanding of mind and body relations actually shapes the experience of pain sufferers.

WHAT IS PAIN?

In medicine, pain has always been a valuable symptom, indicating the presence of disease. According to the standard view, the physician's question "Where does it hurt?" is a prologue to a patient–doctor encounter heralding the diagnostic process. Therapeutic action then consists of attempting to discover the pathological entity responsible for the pain, thereby bringing about the healing of the patient and, with this, the cessation of pain. In this framework, pain is viewed as a physiological warning signal, the body's protective response to tissue damage. This paradigm, however, has been criticized in the wake of clinical and other evidence. An exemplary case in this regard is phantom limb pain, which clearly denies a finalistic view of pain as aimed at signalling the presence of a damage in the body, thwarting the traditional biomedical view of pain.

A remarkable contribution in this vein is René Leriche's *The Surgery of Pain*, in which the surgeon refuses to consider pain solely as a physiological sensation, defining it for the first time as a pathological phenomenon. This revolutionary concept is based on an anti-reductionist view of pain: Leriche claims that pain does not have any sense, nor is it a sense, unless it is considered in relation to human individuality. "Physical pain is not a simple question of nerve impulses moving at a fixed speed along a nerve. *It is the result of the conflict between a stimulant and the individual as a whole*" (Leriche 1940: 488, my emphasis).

Leriche's aim was to force physicians to abandon the conception of pain as a natural and therefore somehow acceptable, disease-related fact, emphasizing its inseparableness from the sufferer: pain is "douleur maladie" (pain-disease) because pain is "a monstrous individual phenomenon and not a law of the species. A fact of disease" (Leriche 1940: 490). This criticism of the standard medical view of pain has a broader scope than just a philanthropic memento of the tragedy of individual suffering, for Leriche sees individual pain as something that is somehow created by the sufferer. As epistemologist Georges Canguilhem has remarked, Leriche's conception of pain-disease involves the "total coincidence of disease and the diseased person" (Canguilhem 1978: 51). Pain is not something that happens to the individual but an event that involves and is always shaped by the sufferer in her complexity: indeed, physiological, psychological and socio-cultural factors are always interrelated in pain perception. Pain, especially when persistent, has to be conceived as the outcome of painful perception echoing in an individual with prior experiences, future expectations and present existential conditions.

In 1965, psychologist Ronald Melzack and neuroscientist Patrick D. Wall introduced the gate control theory of pain mechanisms; this theory has superseded the previous neurophysiological conception of pain mechanisms, the specificity theory, according to which pain was viewed as a specific sensation (such as hearing) transmitted through its own receptors and transmission pathways, which projected "painful sensation to a pain center in the brain" (Melzack & Wall 1965: 971). The main problem with this conception was the idea of direct communication from skin to brain, entailing an invariant relationship between stimulus and pain perception. In this framework, pain was nothing but the perception of a noxious stimulus transmitted from the body to a passive recipient, the brain. Clinical evidence against this theory came mainly from pathological painful conditions such as phantom limb pain (the pain felt in a limb that has been amputated), causalgia (a severe burning pain resulting from the lesion of a peripheral nerve) and peripheral neuralgia (the pain resulting from peripheral nerve infection or a degenerative disease). Traditional therapies such as surgical lesions to the peripheral and central nervous system aimed at interrupting the painful sensation were often unsuccessful. Sometimes pain spread "unpredictably to unrelated parts of the body where no pathology exists" (Melzack & Wall 1965: 971), occurred after long delays, and persisted even after stimulus removal, showing the inconsistency of a conception of a "fixed, direct-line nervous system" (Melzack & Wall 1965: 971) Furthermore, the specificity theory could not account for many peculiar but not rare pain conditions such as the different locations of perceived pain and the damage site, persisting pain in the absence of detectable injuries or a change in location and intensity of pain with time.

The gate control theory of pain postulates the existence of a barrier in the system transmitting a painful sensation that can be modulated by different factors and may thus modify the perception of pain. This theory conceives pain as an on-going process in which the whole central nervous system acts as "an active system that filters, selects and modulates inputs" (Melzack 1999: S123), integrating afferent upstream processes with downstream modulation from the brain. The perception of pain is therefore the outcome of a complex system of modulation of the original stimulus composed of different factors, both physiological (i.e. fibre activity) and psychological (anxiety, attention, prior experience).

The gate control theory's renewed conception of pain underlies the well-known definition of pain formulated in 1979 by the IASP. According to the IASP, pain is:

> an unpleasant sensory and emotional experience associated with actual or potential tissue damage or described in the terms of such a damage ... Pain is always subjective ... Many people report pain in the absence of tissue damage or any likely pathophysiological cause; usually this happens for psychological reasons. There is usually no way to distinguish their experience from that due to tissue damage if we take the subjective report. If they regard their experience as pain and if they report it in the same ways as pain caused by tissue damage, it should be accepted as pain.
> (Aydede & Güzeldere 2002: S266).

As many authors (e.g. Morris 1999) have emphasized, the contribution of this definition lies in the statement that there is no one-to-one correlation between tissue damage and pain and that pain may be perceived without a detectable organic cause. Indeed, the IASP definition confers epistemic authority in pain perception on the person in pain. Moreover, following Melzack and Wall's theory, the definition indicates that there is a wide gap between nociception (the detection of tissue damage by special transducers attached to peripheral fibres) and the perception of pain, which is always a psychological state.

An interesting description of pain addressing the variability of pain experience was subsequently given by John D. Loeser and Ronald Melzack. They identify four broad categories in the pain phenomenon: nociception, perception of pain, suffering and pain behaviours, sustained by anatomical, physiological and psychological substrates. Nociception is defined as the neural process of encoding and processing noxious stimuli, and differs from the perception of pain, which "is often [but not always] triggered by a noxious stimulus" (Loeser & Melzack 1999: 1608) or lesions in the peripheral or central nervous system. Acute pain is initially associated with specific autonomous or somatic reflexes, but these disappear in chronic pain. Pain can occur without nociception at all, and in chronic pain the intensity of the pain perceived may have little or no relation to the extent of the injury or disease. Suffering is defined instead as the "negative response induced by pain and also by fear, anxiety, stress ... and other psychological states" (Loeser & Melzack 1999: 1608). Lastly, pain behaviours result from pain and suffering and are conceivable as "the things a person does or does not do that can be ascribed to the presence of tissue damage" (Loeser & Melzack 1999: 1608).

Despite the radical change in perspective brought about by the IASP definition, the claim highlights the difficulty of dealing with the complexity of pain phenomenon by dividing the pain experience into sensory and emotional parts, dividing it into neurophysiological and psychological domains. The sensory aspect of pain correlates this psychological state to one or more specific body parts while the emotional aspect – derived from its unpleasantness – preserves the psychological status of pain perception. The IASP definition continually wavers between these two aspects of pain: on the one hand, sensory pain features correlate it to other sensory modalities that locate the sensation and tend to relay pain to an organic substrate, both in its aetiology (pain perception may be related to actual or potential tissue damage or described as the pain caused by it) and in its perception (localization). On the other hand, there is an on-going attempt to encompass pain as a psychological state, and therefore as a strictly subjective phenomenon. It is obvious how useful this distinction is for a scientific objectivation (a quantitative criterion to measure the phenomenon) that ties pain to an organic substrate utilizing an aetiological criterion that can be traced back to an acute disease model.

The IASP definition has gone farther than any previous attempt to define pain, given the breadth and variety of the phenomenon. Moreover, its aim was to settle on a common language that could be accepted, primarily by health professionals who treat patients in pain. This definition is meant to encompass all that an individual can define as pain, whether the cause is tissue damage or not. Even if it is stated that the sufferer should be given epistemic authority in pain experience (Aydede and Güzeldere 2002: S268), if there is no identifiable tissue damage and the person claims to be in pain, the conclusion is that psychological reasons are involved. The IASP definition therefore acknowledges the reality of all painful experiences, but at the same time tries to fit them into an aetiology-grounded model that dichotomizes mind and body relations, classifying pain without organic detectable cause as "psychogenic".

PSYCHIATRIC CLASSIFICATION OF PAIN

This category of pain commonly defined as "psychogenic" was introduced in the third edition of the *Diagnostic and Statistic Manual of Mental Disorders* (DSM-III) as psychogenic pain disorder, even though in the first and second editions of the manual (DSM-I and DSM-II) there were already present psychogenic painful conditions; in the DSM-I they are classified as psychophysiologic musculoskeletal reaction (002-580) including "musculoskeletal disorders such as "psychogenic rheumatism", backache, muscle cramps, myalgias ... in which emotional factors play a causative role" (American Psychiatric Association 1952: 30), while in the DSM-II the category is psychophysiologic musculoskeletal disorder (305.1).

Psychogenic pain disorder diagnosis was mainly based on a lack of proportionality between the pain perceived by the patient and pathophysiological clinical findings, thereby implicating psychological factors in the production of pain. Subsequently, DSM-III-R (revised) changed the classification to somatoform pain disorder, whose diagnostic criteria were reformulated eliminating the need to prove the existence of aetiological psychological factors. In addition, another aspect, a "preoccupation with pain for at least six months" (Ballantyne *et al.* 2010: 410) was indicated as relevant, placing at the core of this nosological entity the patient's pathological relation to her pain, not the severity of pain itself. Finally, this pathological condition has been classified in the DSM-IV as pain disorder, eliminating causal adjectives such as "psychogenic" and "somatoform". The diagnostic criterion to define pain disorder is severe pain in one or more anatomical sites as the predominant focus of the clinical presentation where "psychological factors are judged to have an important role in the onset, severity, exacerbation or maintenance of pain" (Hardcastle 1999: 19). Two types of pain disorder are recognized: pain disorder associated with psychological factors and pain disorder associated with both psychological factors and a general medical condition. Pain disorder is classified as acute if it lasts less than six months or chronic if it persists more than six months. This new definition acknowledges that there is no need to exclude a medical condition to prove the existence of psychological factors, even though the distinction between the two seems to indicate a discrimination between "'pure' psychosocially mediated pain conditions and 'mixed' psychosomatic pain disorders" (Aigner & Bach 1999: 356), thus implying a return to the concept of psychogenic pain.

This notion has widely been criticized. It has been argued that this is nothing but a label adopted to classify pain when no physical explanation is available (see Hardcastle 1999). Moreover, pain classified as psychogenic tends to be seen as "not real", "all in the patient's mind", assimilated to other somatoform mental disorders (pain disorder, conversion hysteria and hypochondriasis all belong to the category of somatoform disorders), or, even worse, malingering. This point is not so easily dismissed because of the kind of individual accountability for pain – at least for continuous pain – that may arise from a possible overlap of "psychological" and "unreal" pain. As anthropologist Jean Jackson has highlighted, in an oversimplified schema of the commonly used clinical meanings of "real" and "unreal" pain, "any pain with inputs from psychological factors is to some degree unreal because of the nonphysical nature of these causes and the problematic nature of responsibility for them" (Jackson 1992: 143).

The proposed revision of DSM-IV designed to constitute DSM-V suggests subsuming pain disorder into complex somatic symptom disorder with combined somatization disorder, hypochondriasis and undifferentiated somatoform disorder. This change is motivated by the common feature shared by these conditions, that is, the clinical presentation of somatic symptoms and/or concern about medical illness. More interesting is the footnote explaining that these disorders are grouped for the purposes of "clinical utility (these patients are mainly encountered in general medical settings), rather than assumptions of shared aetiology or mechanism" (American Psychiatric Association 2010).

The ICD-10 (WHO's International Classification of Disease) associates pain disorder with persistent somatoform pain disorder, in which:

> the predominant complaint is of persistent, severe and distressing pain, which cannot be explained fully by a physiological process or a physical disorder, and which occurs in association with

emotional conflict or psychosocial problems that are sufficient to allow the conclusion that they are the main causative influences.
(World Health Organization 2010a)

In ICD classification the focus on aetiology is even stronger than in the DSM one: in the American Psychiatric Association's manual, psychological and psychosocial factors are seen as playing a pivotal role in pain onset but also in pain severity, exacerbation or maintenance, leading to a more blurred conception of pain aetiology.

By focusing solely on pain causes, ICD classification entails instead a mutually exclusive evaluation of the disorder so that if a physiopathological process is not detected, the conclusion is that pain is due to psychological factors.

CHRONIC PAIN

In his behavioural analysis of chronic pain, psychologist William Fordyce criticizes the use of the term "psychogenic pain" to designate a painful condition characterized by a discrepancy between physical findings and pain behaviour due to "some emotional, motivational, or personality disturbance problem" (Fordyce 1978: 60). In his view, this classification is a prime example of a questionable approach to chronic pain, which by dismissing the interactions between pain behaviour and environmental factors fatally fails to account for pain behaviour (Fordyce 1978: 70–71).

In his 1974 study on pain patients, psychologist Richard Sternbach claims that the distinction between psychogenic and somatogenic pain is useless, mainly because the related pain experiences do not differ from one other: for practical purposes – that is, for dealing with patients – it is better to avoid classifications such as "psychogenic pain" when speaking about "pain which is better understood in psychological than in physical language" (Sternbach 1974: 21). A similar plea to avoid sharp distinctions exclusively based on a supposed psychological or physiological aetiology is made in the classification of chronic pain syndrome, which shares some problematic features with "psychogenic pain". In this work, Sternbach recalls Thomas Szasz's general psychoanalytical theory of pain, based mainly on a conception of pain as the result of a perceived threat to bodily integrity, whether real or imagined: what is necessary for pain is the perception of such a threat. This means that whether pain is classified as real or imaginary depends on whether an observer finds objective evidence for the threat. Usually, that decision is made by a physician looking for signs of physical injury. However, Szasz argues, the threat may be psychological rather than physical (see Sternbach 1974: 26).

Even though the "psychogenic pain" label has been dismissed, the underlying conception of an aetiological predominance of psychological factors in some painful conditions persists, especially when pain is not associated with a well-defined cause, giving way to a problematic acknowledgment of some chronic pain conditions.

ICD-10 classifies chronic pain and intractable (i.e. treatment resistant) pain as "symptoms, signs and abnormal clinical and laboratory findings, not elsewhere classified": this category collects:

> the less well-defined conditions and symptoms that, without the necessary study of the case to establish a final diagnosis, point perhaps equally to two or more diseases or to two or more systems of the body. Practically all categories in the chapter could be designated "not otherwise specified", "unknown etiology" or "transient". (World Health Organization 2010b)

Medical texts generically define chronic pain as pain that lasts longer than the usual course of an acute injury or disease, although the difference between acute and chronic is not solely temporal but is grounded in major physiological, psychological and behavioural differences. Acute pain is usually associated with a well-defined cause, consisting of changes in autonomic activity roughly proportional to the intensity of the stimulus; common examples of acute pain are postoperative and traumatic pain. Furthermore, acute pain normally vanishes after healing, whereas chronic pain is defined by the fact that the pain persists after healing and may even spread to other body areas. Moreover, "because pain is unrelenting, it is likely that stress, environmental and affective factors may be superimposed on the original damage to tissue and contribute to the intensity and persistence of the pain" (Loeser & Melzack 1999: 1609).

Although chronic pain has now been recognized as a legitimate disease because of clearly observable and measurable factors, like changes in physiological response patterns, psychological and behavioural features (Baszanger 1998: 89) its aetiology remains uncertain. This is because chronic pain can be initially triggered by an injury or a disease but, as the definition states, nociceptive impulses persist after healing often without a known cause.

As Jackson has emphasized, chronic pain transgresses traditional biomedical categories (Jackson 2005), primarily because persistent pain does not fit in a traditional biomedical model in which pain, conceived as the body's biological protective response to injury, does not cease with healing. Besides, chronic pain challenges the biomedical reductionist approach through its liminal position that is problematic both in its aetiology and in symptomatic classification. This gives way to an ambiguous classification of painful conditions like fibromyalgic syndrome characterized by a non-proportional relationship between physiopathological findings and patients' pain behaviour, suggesting that psychopathological factors may play a pivotal role at least in the continuation of pain.

As sociologist of medicine Isabelle Baszanger has pointed out, the acknowledgement of the gap between experimental pain and clinical pain in the history of the chronic pain entity has allowed the inclusion of individual reactions as a central aspect of pain-disease. On this view, pain cannot be understood by measuring the intensity of experimentally provoked pain, but only "by a detailed and careful history and the patient's statement, coupled with observation of the patient's reaction to the pain, and an evaluation of the patient's personality (physiopsychological makeup)" (John J. Bonica quoted in Baszanger 1998: 33). So the constitution of chronic pain as a disease has also been based on an acknowledgement of the devastating consequences of this pathological condition on an individual's life: Bonica, one of pain medicine's pioneers and among the founders of the IASP, described chronic pain as "exclusively malefic because it is powerfully destructive of the physical and psychological well being of the individual and his or her family and associates, and has no redeeming features" (Craig 1984: 838).

Bonica's work has mainly focused on the effort to free chronic pain from acute pain, construing chronic pain as a disease. To reach this goal, chronic pain conditions have to be considered a complex illness consisting of both physiological and psychological features, specifying mutual interactions between these aspects as one of the most prominent features of chronic pain. Acknowledgement of the psychopathological aspects of chronic pain has been pivotal in the constitution of the medical speciality of pain medicine, even though the role played by these factors in chronic pain has been strongly debated within the burgeoning field. This is largely due to the difficulty of stressing the importance of psychological factors, while avoiding the risk of "psychologizing" the condition. In Bonica's view, this would have meant misunderstanding the complex construction of the condition and, in practice, would have driven biomedicine to relinquish the management of chronic pain to psychology. Instead, the aim of pain medicine was to demonstrate the need for a multidisciplinary approach to chronic pain on a par with the complex nature of the condition.

There have been a remarkable number of different approaches to chronic pain in the history of defining chronic pain as a disease entity. This is exemplified by the controversial notion of "chronic pain syndrome". In 1975, Richard G. Black suggested reserving the definition "chronic pain syndrome" for patients who complain of persistent pain often not compounded by physical problems or diseases, attempting to distinguish between a psychological and physiological aetiology. Bonica and other IASP members rejected this approach, claiming that it fundamentally misunderstood the complexity of chronic pain conditions (Baszanger 1998: 90–91). Eventually, the IASP textbook *Classification of Chronic Pain Syndromes* grouped all existing chronic pain conditions together: nociceptive, neuropathic, long-term disease-related, non-life-threatening and psychogenic pain. Nonetheless, controversies remain: the authors claim in the introduction that "it is common in North America to find that patients are described as having Chronic Pain Syndrome" (International Association for the Study of Pain 1994: xiii) who are diagnosed when there is "a persisting pattern of pain that may have arisen from organic causes but which is now compounded by psychological and social problems in behavioural changes" (International Association for the Study of Pain 1994: xiii). In this case the IASP Subcommittee on Taxonomy deems it better to "make both physical and psychiatric diagnosis and to indicate the contribution ... of each diagnosis" (International Association for the Study of Pain 1994: xiii). The definition of chronic pain syndrome is criticized by the IASP because, even if it is recognized that experientially pain is a unitary phenomenon, it is still necessary to identify psychological and physiological contributions and also because "it was noted that the term CPS [chronic pain syndrome] is often, unfortunately, used pejoratively" (International Association for the Study of Pain 1994: xiii).

Chronic pain syndrome – whose diagnostic traits are very similar to those of the DSM pain disorder – has been defined as a psychosocial disorder in which somatic preoccupation consumes the patient's attention, leading her to pursue a maladaptive behaviour that may be incapacitating (National Pharmaceutical Council 2001). This disease conception focuses on the patient's reaction to the painful condition and conceives the sufferer's behaviour as the main issue in chronic pain disease. Different theoretical and practical approaches to chronic pain still coexist in pain medicine, and the peculiar status of chronic pain might account for this. What is interesting to evaluate is how different conceptions in the biomedical framework may influence patients' experience.

As Baszanger has pointed out, strong controversies have arisen in the history of the construction of the "chronic pain entity" because of the psychological, cognitive and behavioural features of chronic pain. The main argument revolves around whether such features are among the causes or rather the consequences of pain (Baszanger 1998: 94). The connection between chronic pain and depression is a case in point, and the debate on whether depression is an aetiological factor of chronic pain or a consequence continues. If depression is judged to be the cause of chronic pain, it would be classified as a mental disorder, whereas if depression is considered a consequence of persisting pain, chronic pain is the disease and depression a symptom. In the meantime, in 2010 the US Food and Drug Administration (FDA) approved the use of the antidepressant Duloxetine for the treatment of chronic pain syndromes such as chronic musculoskeletal pain, arthritis and lower back pain. This is the first non-steroidal anti-inflammatory or opiate analgesic drug to be approved for chronic pain treatment (US Food and Drug Administration 2010). The efficacy of antidepressants in the management of some chronic pain conditions is today widely known, but antidepressant use is not unproblematic. In order to achieve patient compliance, the administration of antidepressants often has to be pursued in conjunction with therapy that addresses the meaning of painful experience.

THE MEANING OF PAIN

Recalling Eric Cassell's definition of suffering as "a state of severe distress associated with events that threaten the integrity of the person" (Cassell 1982: 640), I argue that the biomedical approach to chronic pain should take into account the sufferer's lived experience of pain which is a pivotal aspect of the disease itself. Chronic pain has to be understood as something in which the meaning the sufferer attributes to her condition deeply influences the disease itself, and meaning has to be construed as a personal and intersubjective issue. As David B. Morris has pointed out, "pain is never the sole creation of our anatomy or physiology. It emerges only at the intersection of bodies, minds and cultures" (Morris 1991: 3) and medicine is unquestionably an important meaning-maker in relation to pain and disease. The biomedical framework not only shapes the medical conception of illness, but also the patient's conception; that, in turn, can affect illness itself.

The answer a doctor gives to the patient's question "Why am I in pain?" is hugely important because, as we have seen, psychological and behavioural aspects of the experience modify illness itself. As Sternbach pointed out, one of the main issues of chronic pain experience is the fact that the patient cannot give meaning to chronic pain. Even if the doctor gives the patient an understandable explanation, the pain – which is usually conceived as a warning signal – may still have no meaning for the patient whose main concern is to end her suffering (Sternbach 1974: 6). Moreover, for many pain syndromes it is difficult to recognize a clear, univocal cause and this, in addition to the despair in the seeming endlessness of the suffering, may worsen the patient's perception of her condition. Furthermore, the intrinsic subjectivity of pain may present a problem for the patient's attempt to communicate the intensity, quality and related perceptions of her pain to the physician who may be frustrated by the difficulty in understanding the severity of her condition.

Clinicians who deal with chronic pain patients know that the first and most important step in treating these patients is listening to their accounts of their lived experience. Patients' narratives of dealing with their chronic conditions may give the physician access to a world that Byron Good claimed is "largely unshared and unshareable" (Good 1992: 47). Here, concepts such as space and time, but also mind, body, the self and their mutual relationships, change meaning, or at least lose their common significance.

As Jackson has pointed out in her ethnographic research at a chronic pain centre, in chronic sufferers' experience, pain defeats "a simple subject-object dichotomy because objectification and subjectification stand in a dialectical relationship to each other" (Jackson 1994: 203). Contrary to what can be imagined, subjectification does not always lead to peace of mind for these patients. "Understanding the subjectivity of pain is not simply a matter of establishing the equations 'object = "out-there-and-real"' and 'subject = "not real"', because experientially the pain remains very 'real' for sufferers" (Jackson 1994: 20). Analysing patients' accounts, Jackson called attention to the inconsistency of mind–body and subject–object dualisms because pain changes the meaning of them "by consisting of both sensation and emotion, by being simultaneously thinking and doing" (Jackson 1994: 209). In pain experience, the sensory features of pain are not related to emotional aspects as an addition: they always co-occur. This has been demonstrated by attempts to comprehend chronic pain conditions: in extreme situations, patients live an experience that may be linguistically translated into the expression that "one *is* pain" (Jackson 1994: 209).

Revealing the meaning of pain may be useful to develop theories and practices common to different domains such as neurology, psychology, clinical medicine and the social sciences. This means devising an approach that goes beyond the biomedical model as we know it, while not abandoning it entirely. This can only be done by searching for language that can utilize patient experience that can be shared by the humanities and scientific domains alike. Current research indicates that this goal can mainly be pursued through neurological studies of brain activity (see Coakley & Kaufman 2007) and through phenomenological studies.

Neurologist Howard L. Fields has shown the dialectical relations in pain between the action of meaning on the brain and, conversely, brain influences on meaning production. Although the brain is a bodily organ, "it has the unique property that its operation is completely symbolic. Patterns of neural activity are representational" (Fields 2007: 37), and some of them are devoted to produce sensation, others to producing language and memory, and others the body and the external world. Sharing the same code, these data may interact because "whether conscious or unconscious, bodily or cultural memories, current perceptions and imagined features are written in the same language, that is electrochemical changes in nerve cells" (Fields 2007: 37). This is an aspect of how individual experience, being a continued meaningful production of contents, affects our brain functions, our sensations and perceptions, and hence our pain. On the other hand, the impact of meaning, or the impossibility of ascribing meaning to a painful experience, can modify our neurobiology. Fields suggests we consider placebo analgesic response to comprehend the complexity of the factors involved in pain experience. Even though scientists have yet to identify the neural mechanisms involved in the placebo effect, there is compelling evidence of the mutual transformative power between pain and individual beliefs on brain activity and the activity of "pain-modulating circuitry in mediating and suppressing effects of meaning and expectancy on pain" (Fields 2007: 57).

A wider perspective on pain may also be fruitful to discuss pivotal issues in chronic pain such as mind–body dualism. As Penfield's studies have shown, the mind–body dichotomy can be challenged by considering neurological processes such as projection: electrical activity in nerve cells elicited by electrical stimulation may produce an experience of pain that is projected onto a specific body part. In this framework, mental and physical pain may be reviewed by reshaping the sense of mental and physical terms: pain is both physical and mental because nerve cells and their activity are physical, but it is also mental because pain is always subjectively experienced in what is generally called the mind (Fields 2007: 42–3).

However, if pain sufferers' experience is barely shaped by the biomedical model in which it is lived, work on the meaning issue cannot simply dismiss old biomedical frameworks such as mind and body dualism but has to discuss how they are actually lived by the patients.

As Robert Kugelmann has pointed out (see Kugelmann 1996), the discourse of two pains (organic/mental) has to be regarded as meaningful in the sufferer's lived experience of illness. Kugelmann suggests viewing pain as something that is an "it" but "what I am" too, recalling Buytendijk's conception of pain as an entity that places the body in opposition to individual self-consciousness. The discourse can be widened to include social meanings of the ambiguous condition of chronic pain in patients' perception of their state.

CONCLUSION

In conclusion, it can be argued that the main feature of chronic pain as a disease more than pain perception in itself, is suffering, the individual's dramatic response to the perceived threat of self-disintegration. This condition has somehow to be accounted for and elaborated in order to preserve the self from a total collapse. Since the available framework will disregard the complexity of chronic pain experience, forcing it to fit in an organic/psychological model, the meaning of this experience will always be problematic for the patient and therefore her suffering will be unrelieved. In this perspective, the chronic patient's "somatic preoccupation" in which she uses a physical language to explain her pain against a lacking organic diagnosis may be the individual's attempt to handle her own experience, in an existing meaning framework that is hard to reshape.

As has been suggested, the study of meaning production with respect to pain is the common goal to be pursued in different knowledge domains, and whose primary influences may affect patients' experience. Focusing on *meaning* in pain phenomenon, the commonly accepted boundaries between mind–body, biomedicine–psychology and sensation–emotion become blurred. The remaining question is whether the framework characterizing Western medicine is due to culturally bound habits, and hence subject to change, or whether approaching the lived experience of illness as a whole is an inherently unreachable goal for medicine as we know it.

PART III
ILLNESS AND SOCIETY

9. INTERSEX, MEDICINE AND PATHOLOGIZATION

Melanie Newbould

INTRODUCTION

In this chapter I examine a group of conditions that are included under the general heading of disorders of sex development, but which used to be called intersex conditions and, prior to that, hermaphroditism. Most of these conditions include atypical genital anatomy, frequently described as "ambiguous", because it is not entirely typical of either sex. Much of what I discuss relates to congenital adrenal hyperplasia (CAH), which is the most common form of intersex and which is, therefore, one of the conditions in this group that is most frequently discussed in medical, sociological, psychological and ethical literature. In 2006, the term "disorder of sex development" was introduced into the medical literature, its use suggesting that all such conditions were within the remit of medicine (Spurgas 2009: 102). The new terminology took the place of the former and more neutral term "intersex", a term that could be used outside the medical context (Long 2006). The change in nomenclature has proved a matter of some controversy, since not all of the people included in this category regard themselves as suffering from a medical disorder (see responses to Hughes *et al.* 2006). In this chapter I will use the term intersex.

Though for some writers, such as Boorse, disease is a matter of using statistical methods to identify the subnormal (1977: 543; 1997: 7–8) and, in most circumstances, does not involve value judgement, intersex conditions are important in that they provide an illustration of how, in practice, medicine relies heavily on social norms in deciding what constitutes "normal" or "abnormal" function. All biological characteristics are subject to variation, and this includes entities such as penile or vaginal length. Decisions regarding what is normal are treated as if they were biological facts, but any cut-off point that separates the normal from the abnormal must be defined arbitrarily and frequently relies on social norms regarding appearance. This is also true in other aspects of medicine. To give some examples, there is the perceived need for leg lengthening procedures in the skeletal dysplasia achondroplasia, in which the limbs are short (Sanford 2006), or the need to alter the position of ears that are unusually prominent, so that they lie closer to the head.

Appearance-altering surgery was performed on the genitalia of intersex infants and young children from the 1950s onwards, and continues to be performed, although with less frequency. This procedure is based on the assumption that there is a "normal" appearance to be achieved through surgery. There is a further complication in intersex because genital appearance is usually considered to be straightforwardly tied to an individual's sex. I argue that this premise is false. In biological terms, it can be extremely difficult to identify the "true sex" of an individual because the presence or absence of a Y chromosome is no longer the sole determiner of sex; multiple individual genes located on several different chromosomes are known to be involved. While gender is also complex, it is simplified by the fact that most individuals know which gender they are, and this applies to both intersex and non-intersex individuals. Gender becomes apparent as the child grows and cannot be reliably predicted from anatomical characteristics in infancy. Performing early genital surgery on a child fails to take this into account. Surgical intervention also relies heavily on the assumption that the ability to perform heterosexual intercourse will be of major importance in the future life of the individual. This may or may not turn out to be true.

I argue that, far from achieving its intention of making those with intersex conditions more "normal", medical attention and intervention has the effect of emphasizing the supposed abnormality. In some cases, intersex individuals who have lived their lives under medical observation have written accounts relating how this attention made them feel different. For those who had early surgery, scars and other problems emphasized any perceptions of abnormality. There is also some evidence from medical anthropology studies that involved intersex individuals in other cultures. Here the observations required by the study seem to have had the effect of introducing the notion of pathology to an entity previously considered a rare but normal and accepted phenomenon.

I will start by examining some of the biology of CAH and other intersex conditions. This involves a more general discussion of sex and gender.

SEX AND GENDER

In the mid-nineteenth century, doctors first discovered that some women had testes. At that time the reasons for this were not understood but it is now known that in such individuals the body is unable to respond to testosterone, the major hormone produced by the testes.[1] In most individuals with testes, testosterone leads to the development of characteristics usually recognised as "male", such as male-type genitalia, facial hair, deep voice, and so on. These women had no male characteristics. One of the first such women identified was a celebrated Parisian beauty and fashion model, L.S. (Dreger 1999a: 9). The discovery caused concern to the doctors who made it, because it disturbed their view of what made someone male or female. It was considered vital to be able to identify sex accurately so that there was no risk of same sex marriages taking place and persons of uncertain sex provided considerable disruption to the social order of the time (Dreger 1999a: 9). The women concerned were in no doubt that they were female and had sought medical assistance for infertility, rather than any uncertainty about their sex (Dreger 1998: 1–3). This served as an illustration that it might not be so easy to identify an individual's sex; an organ such as the testis that usually is thought of as straightforwardly male can be found in someone who has an unambiguously female appearance. For some writers this continues to be a problem; for Germaine Greer, for example, no one with testes can be female (2000: 88).

The difficulties can be better appreciated by briefly considering what is generally known about sex and how this relates to intersex. In mammals there are four biological entities normally considered to identify sex: chromosomes, type of gonad (testes or ovaries), anatomy of the internal pelvic structures (the presence of a uterus, for example) and, most easily determined, the anatomy of external genitalia. In intersex individuals, one or more of these four entities is of a different "sex type" to the others. CAH is one of the commonest forms of intersex and also one in which unusual genital anatomy frequently occurs in females. The physiological situation is relatively simple; the chromosomes are of the usual female type (which means that there are forty-six in total, two of which are X-chromosomes), the gonads are ovaries, a uterus and fallopian tubes are present but the external genitalia have a variable degree of masculinization. One of the enzymes needed to manufacture steroid hormones in the adrenal cortex is congenitally absent, resulting in varying degrees of deficiency of steroid hormones. Those with this condition sometimes cannot retain salt in the body so are particularly vulnerable to acute problems manifesting as diarrhoea or vomiting, and they need life-saving hormone replacement (Brain *et al.* 2010). Because the normal hormonal pathway is blocked, side-products are produced in excess and these have a virilizing effect, hence the change in genital anatomy and the enlargement of the clitoris. The hormone deficiency that forms one part of CAH is a genuinely life-threatening disease. However, the unusual genital anatomy is not life-threatening but, rather, something that can make the sex of an infant at birth difficult to determine. Girls with CAH do have a disease, but it is one that is easily treated by hormone replacement. I argue that in itself the unusual anatomy is not a disease. Rather, CAH is a form of intersex that has been medically addressed by an attempt to put the body "right" by surgical intervention, often by clitoridectomy. Male infants can also have CAH. In this situation, the genitalia are also atypical in that these boys have a larger than average penis; interestingly this is not usually considered a major disadvantage and surgery is not usually considered.

In more general terms, the view that there are two distinct and easily distinguished sexes is becoming scientifically problematic. The molecular biology governing human sex differentiation is not straightforwardly binary and this has led Vernon A. Rosario, an American child psychiatrist, to use the term "quantum sex" to describe the way in which the multiple various determinants of physical sex differentiation interact and finally arrive at the sex of an individual human (Rosario 2009: 269). He borrows this term from quantum mechanics, where the simplistic model of nucleus and electrons is now replaced by a more complex one involving statistical probabilities that gives a more accurate picture. In genetics, rather than a simple Mendelian model of "one gene–one trait", it is now known that there are "many genes conferring small statistical odds for different traits under particular environmental and developmental circumstances" (Rosario 2009: 268) and this applies to sex determination as well.

Ultimately no one type of structure and no one form of gene can be said to be "naturally" male or female. In the nineteenth century, mammalian embryologists discovered that the early embryo has the potential to develop into either a male or female form so that it is only at around week eight of gestation that the human embryo shows sex differences (Rosario 2009: 271). From the early twentieth century onwards it had been recognized that in several species, including ours, one of the chromosome pairs differed between male and female, leading to speculation that the material leading to sexual differentiation was located there. It was not until 1990 that a gene governing differentiation into testes was identified and localised to an area of the Y-chromosome – named SRY (sex-determining region of the Y chromosome) – though it is still not understood exactly what this gene does to control testicular development.

It became rapidly clear that this was not the whole story. In humans there are both SRY-negative individuals with testes and SRY-positive individuals without them. In some of the latter cases, it appears that a second gene, DAX-1 (on the X chromosome), if present in a double dose, can override the effect of SRY so that an individual with XY chromosomes and a functioning SRY gene develops ovaries and not testes. It is now clear that the Y chromosome plays only a part in the determination of male sex; many other genes on other chromosomes are also involved, such as SF-1 on chromosome 9, WT-1 on chromosome 11, SOX-9 on chromosome 17 and MIS on chromosome 19. All of these play some role in the development of testes and male sex. Studies of ovarian tissue development are in their infancy, but it does not appear that their growth and differentiation is a passive process resulting from the absence of male hormones, as was believed until recently. Rosario therefore predicts that there will be a shift to "a dozen or more genes each conferring a small percentage likelihood of male or female sex that is still further dependent on micro- and macro-environmental interactions" (2009: 279). Thus there is no single and simple biological parameter that confers a certain sex on an individual.

It is also no longer the case that sex can be determined by the role that an individual plays in reproduction (if they reproduce); new reproductive techniques have potentially blurred the margins between male and female. Both female spermatogenesis and male oogenesis are theoretical possibilities, since mammalian embryonic stem cells can be induced to develop into both sperm and oocytes in controlled conditions (Kehler *et al.* 2005). Ectogenesis and male pregnancy are sometimes topics for ethical and legal discourse (e.g. Alghrani 2007 on the former), though all the techniques mentioned are at present only remote theoretical possibilities. However, this evidence leads to the conclusion that biological sex is not the straightforward binary ontology suggested by the medical approach described below. It is the product of the interaction of many genes and environmental factors. A simple binary model of sex, on which much of intersex treatment is based, is therefore no longer scientifically accurate.

Gender is not necessarily a simpler issue, but by the age of two and a half to three years most children know if they are boys or girls (Siann 1994: 69). During the latter half of the twentieth century there was a search for a physical entity that caused gender; for example, the English courts spent over thirty years arguing over the status of trans-sexual individuals before the Gender Recognition Act, 2004, was passed by Parliament. The Act clarified that gender was not directly tied to any physical entity such as genital anatomy. Perhaps the best way to think of gender is that it is not generated by any individual anatomical or physiological characteristic but is generated by the whole organism and the interaction with the ambient society. As gendered beings we continually attempt to approximate to a set of normative ideals that "live outside of us and were always there before we arrived" (Wilchins 2004: 131). For Judith Butler, gender is always a doing, a performance, rather like a drag act (Butler 2004: 209, 213–14). There is no inner essence of our being that is gendered. The majority of human individuals (though not all) self-identify as male or female. This characterization of gender applies to those with congruent chromosomes, gonads, and internal and external anatomy. It also applies to those individuals classed as intersex, who, in the vast majority of cases, have a clear gender identity as either a male or a female, and only rarely do they self-identify as anything other than this (Spurgas 2009: 104). Therefore, in the majority of cases intersex people are men and women who happen to possess anatomical differences. In other words "it is not necessarily the case that it is any more work or harder work for intersexed persons to do gender than it is for anyone else" (Holmes 2008: 14). So while the biological characteristics identifying sex may be difficult to identify and interpret in some circumstances, identification of gender can be easier. Often by the time a child can speak, he or she will tell you their gender. For most this will be just as predictable from physical parameters, but in some cases it will be a surprise. For example, chromosomally female individuals with CAH identify as female in most cases, but a subset (around 10%, markedly higher than in the general female population) have a male gender identity (Kemp 2006: 12).

So, many people are aware of their gender from their first words and this is not necessarily connected to their sex, which can be, in some situations, difficult or perhaps impossible to identify. Thus, in terms of anatomy, it is not possible to say what makes someone male and what makes someone female. However, in most areas of life, sexual difference is seen as so obvious and natural a matter that it needs no argument or discussion (Holmes 2008: 18).

> That the world is composed of men and women, boys and girls, orders our world and regulates practices ... In fact, sexual difference could be said to be the primary structure that itself structures the social order in which we move and make sense of the world. (Feder 2006: 191)

Indeed, the idea that all beings must have a fixed male or female gender is so entrenched that there is even a recent report of a dog that required surgery for ambiguous genitalia before anyone would adopt it (*The Telegraph* 2010).

I now turn to the nature and effects of the surgical techniques employed in treating intersex people.

A HISTORY OF INTERSEX SURGERY

The story of medical involvement in intersex in the twentieth century has been frequently reported and discussed in the literature (Dreger 1998; Fausto-Sterling 1998; Harper 2007; Karkazis 2008; Kessler 1990; Preves 1999). From the nineteenth century onwards many aspects of medical care for intersex and other conditions have been conducted with what could be termed a scientific approach, dependent on an understanding of the science underlying physiology and psychology that was prevalent at the time. Treatment has been presented as being based on a "naturalistic" or "biomedical" approach to medicine, grounded on what is considered "normal"; anything which deviates from this so that function is subnormal is considered to be diseased (Boorse 1997: 7–8). However, in the area of intersex, medical treatment was based on a simplistic view of sex and gender, in marked contrast to the complexity of the issues discussed above. As I outlined in the previous section, gender was considered to be congruent with physical sex. This, in turn, was taken to govern the nature of the role the individual would occupy in society. Whereas the model used was thought to be a biological one, in fact it was strongly influenced by cultural views regarding sex, gender and social roles.

From the 1950s onwards a treatment protocol based on the identification of sex and gender was developed in Baltimore (Money & Ehrhardt 1972: 151–4) and proved influential throughout the world for forty years or more. It was at this point that surgical fashioning of ambiguous genitalia started. Management was based on the pioneering ideas of paediatric psychoendocrinologist John Money, who led a multi-disciplinary team, composed of surgeons, endocrinologists and others (for his description, see Money 2002). At the time, girls and boys were treated differently by their parents (Money & Ehrhardt 1972: 117–45) and Money believed that this was the most influential factor in the acquisition of a gender identity (Money & Ehrhardt 1972: 145). He believed that children were rewarded for gender-appropriate behaviour by the responses of parents, peers and society (Siann 1994: 65). In turn it was felt that responses were generated by parents and peers in accordance with the perceived gender of the child, based on his or her appearance. Therefore appropriate genital anatomy was considered vital in order for a child to develop a secure gender identity, which had to conform to the anatomical sex. Genital surgery was carried out on neonates and was considered a surgical emergency (Money & Ehrhardt 1972: 152). Next, treatment with appropriate hormones took place to facilitate further gender-appropriate social interaction. Medical developments such as the discovery that synthetic cortisone was an effective treatment for the hormonal deficit of CAH (Money 2002: 1) meant that this was all technically feasible for the first time in medical history.

Medical and surgical intervention in the 1950s to 1990s was based on a strong assumption: people had to be able to have heterosexual relationships. The sex of rearing was often based pragmatically on penis/clitoris size. A baby without a penis was reared as a female, whatever the gonad type or chromosome complement. In the case of a small penis, the structure might be deemed "too small" (meaning that it was not thought likely to function as a "copulatory organ"). If this was the case, then the child was castrated and reared as a girl (Karkhazis 2008: 56–7). The general rule was that the ability to have heterosexual intercourse was of prime importance for boys but fertility was less important. For girls, on the other hand, the ability to orgasm was not given much importance but they had to be able to take part in heterosexual intercourse, so a vagina was constructed where necessary. For females, fertility was deemed very important so that girls with CAH were always raised as girls, despite some of them having very masculinized genitalia and the fact that a proportion of them do develop a male gender identity (Kemp 2006: 12). Often the enlarged clitoris was removed surgically. It was never considered that a girl might have a use for a phallus capable of penetration. The possibility of a future gender change or a desire to take part in non-heterosexual sex in years to come was never considered.

INTERSEX IN THE TWENTY-FIRST CENTURY

Some aspects of medical practice in this area have undergone a marked improvement from the situation in the 1950s. Genital surgery is no longer considered a neonatal emergency and is not performed on young infants without careful thought and planning; but such surgery is not proscribed. This is not an area where there is legislation, case law or formal guidelines from an authority such as the National Institute of Clinical Excellence (NICE). Guidelines from those experienced in managing the medical problems involved were published in 2006 in the form of a consensus statement (Hughes *et al.* 2006). Nevertheless, examination of this important paper reveals that in some respects there has been no change in medical attitudes. The consensus statement continues to assume that the ability to have heterosexual intercourse and to have appropriate genital anatomy to achieve this is very important, as indeed it might be for many individuals – but not, perhaps, for all. Clitoral surgery in CAH also remains a valid option, although only for those children deemed to show severe enlargement and with preservation of the clitoral nerve supply wherever possible (Hughes *et al.* 2006). It had been suggested in the past that early clitoral surgery alleviated parental distress and improved attachment between parent and child, but the consensus statement concedes that good evidence for this is lacking (Hughes *et al.* 2006). As discussed later, such surgery can be seen as mutilating in those with a female gender identity but, perhaps more importantly, it is based on the assumption that gender identity can be accurately predicted in young infants, which, as mentioned previously, is not the case. Girls with CAH and other conditions may have vaginal surgery after puberty where necessary.

There is now no suggestion that boys with a micropenis[2] should be reared as girls; it is well established that these boys are as likely as any other males to possess a secure male gender identity (Reiner 2006: 161). However, specifically discussing the associated problem of hypospadias, in which the urethral opening is abnormally placed (sometimes lying beneath the phallus), the 2006 statement warns that the "magnitude of phalloplasty in adulthood should be taken into account during the initial counselling period if successful gender assignment is dependent on this procedure. At times this may affect the balance of gender assignment" (Hughes et al. 2006: 557). Therefore, even as practised today, surgical treatment may not take into account the complex question of what makes someone a certain sex. Sex continues to be perceived as a simple binary, and this simplistic and inaccurate model directs treatment of intersex.

INTRODUCTION OF THE TERM DISORDER OF SEX DEVELOPMENT

In 2005, fifty or so experts in the management of children with atypical sex development met to discuss intersex, a meeting that was to result in the consensus statement referred to above. They also considered the appropriate terminology. They agreed to banish "to antiquity the term, intersex and instead, introduce an all-embracing Disorders of Sex Development (acronym, DSD) terminology" (Hughes 2010: 159–60). The new guidelines for treatment and terminology were universally welcomed and adopted by European centres involved in the medical care of such children (Hughes 2010). The medical experts involved had no problems with the word "disorder". Hughes refers to one form of CAH associated with a mutation in a specific gene:

> To imply that a mutation in the CYP21 gene resulting in 21-hydroxylase deficiency and leading to a life-threatening cause of ambiguous genitalia (congenital adrenal hyperplasia) is a variant or a difference, not a disorder, is akin to suggesting that atheromatous plaques in the coronary arteries resulting in a myocardial infarct is not a cardiovascular disorder.
> (Hughes 2010: 161)

Hughes implies that it is not possible to separate the different aspects of the problem he is describing. He argues that the unusual genital anatomy is as much a part of the medical state resulting from the enzyme deficiency as the salt loss. However, it might be argued that the consequences of the enzyme deficiency are associated with very different implications for the individual concerned and need to be considered separately. The biochemical defect is, perhaps, straightforwardly a disorder and a genuine medical problem, without treatment of which the people affected would be subject to serious morbidity and death. It is the status of the condition's other aspects, such as the atypical genital anatomy, that is disputed. Some people with intersex conditions, notably those represented by the Intersex Society of North America (ISNA) broadly agreed with Hughes and had no problem with use of the term disorder for all aspects of intersex, including the unusual genitalia (ISNA 2007). This group disbanded in 2007 and later reformed as the Accord Alliance (Holmes 2009a: 1; www.accordalliance.org) with the intention of working with medical experts to implement reforms in a mutually acceptable framework. In contrast some patient groups have continued to argue that a difference in genital anatomy should not be regarded as a disorder (Dreger & Herndon 2009: 212).

MEDICINE AS THE ARBITER OF NORMALITY

The gulf between biology and the normative ideals of the social order has implications for the ethics of medical and surgical treatment of ambiguous genitalia. The aim of the treatment is to try to make the patient conform to a notion of normality based on a simple binary male–female model of sex, whereas the reality is much more complex. In sex there is no simple binary. However, potentially mutilating surgery continues to be carried out "to remake the body in the social image of that gender. Such efforts at 'correction' not only violate the child but lend support to the idea that gender has to be borne out in singular and normative ways at the level of anatomy" (Butler 2004: 63).

In summary, some see a body with ambiguous genitalia as different, but others see something that is "wrong", which needs to be "put right" by medicine and which therefore lies within the broad scope defined by the term disease. Consideration of how and when the different becomes pathological touches on an extensive debate in the philosophy of medicine that can only have the briefest mention here. For three decades or so there have been two major views concerning the concept of disease (Carel 2008: 11). The first of these is the naturalistic concept, in which disease is seen in terms of biological dysfunction (Carel 2008: 11). Boorse is one of the major proponents of this approach. For him the "normal is the natural" (Boorse 1975: 57). In other words, the normal is the statistically typical form or function of a typical member of the species, as represented in a textbook of physiology or anatomy, and disease is a subnormal deviation from this. In Boorse's view, judgements regarding disease are frequently value-neutral (Boorse 1977).

Because diseases are a "deviation from species biological design" (Boorse 1977: 543), their identification relies on science and, sometimes, statistical calculation, not "evaluative decision" (Boorse 1977: 543).

For many other philosophers of medicine, concepts of disease are not free of value judgement and their ideas fall into the second major, normative, approach to disease, illness, disability and medicine. For these writers, disease and disability are more than a biological malfunction. They may be seen as preventing an individual from achieving ordinary human goals in relation to the society given that the external circumstances, such as the political situation, permit this (Nordenfelt 2006: 12–13, 149). The normative approach also involves the way in which the person with the malfunction is perceived by society. For example, Amundson, discussing the disadvantages experienced by people who find themselves in the "abnormal" category, considers that these difficulties "derive not from biology, but from implicit social judgments about the acceptability of certain kinds of biological variation" (Amundson 2000: 33). This statement of Amundson's seems apt in the example of intersex. Standard medical practice continues to be informed by the idea that there are strict norms defined for genital anatomy and that deviation from these provides a reason for medical intervention.

There are of course many other matters in medical practice about which strict definitions of normality are made. Foucault (discussing the concept of mental disease) pointed out the importance of medicine in defining normality:

> We are becoming a society which is essentially defined by the norm ... The norm becomes the criterion for evaluating individuals. As it truly becomes a society of the norm, medicine, par excellence the science of the normal and the pathological, assumes the status of a royal science. (Foucault 1976: 197)

Towards the end of the twentieth century an idea developed that medicine was a tool wielded by a medical hegemony within society in order to control its subjects. For Illich, judgements as to what constitutes ill health are made by doctors but on behalf of society. From the 1970s this process has been subject to criticism and the "medicalization critique" (Lupton 1997: 94) developing from these views has been an influential stance within social sciences. Ivan Illich, a Catholic priest, was one of the important writers in this field. For Illich, a profession is an elite that wields power over those who require its services. Professionals, like priests, supply unique services to those who consult them (Illich et al. 1977: 17). Unlike merchants or craftsmen, who may tailor the goods they supply to your requirement, "professionals tell you what you need" (Illich et al. 1977: 17); "professionals assert secret knowledge about human nature, knowledge which only they have the right to dispense" (Illich *et al.* 1977: 19), and "Medicine now determines what disease society shall not tolerate" (Illich *et al.* 1977: 21). Thus, for Illich, medicine undermined rather than improved health, both because of side-effects of treatments and because it restricted lay autonomy by providing limited choices due to strict enforcement of norms about normality and health.

In the first volume of *The History of Sexuality*, Foucault discussed "the importance assumed by the action of the norm" ([1976] 1998: 144). He pointed out how sex was an important commodity in the political economy from the eighteenth century onwards, because it was so important in the control of population numbers in addition to its importance in regulating individual behaviour. This led to societal controls on how sex could be used. It had become officially limited to the legalized relationship of marriage and all other forms of sex were hidden or repressed. The need for constant control means that there has to be a constant preoccupation with the very subject. For example, schools: although everything was arranged so as to avoid discussing sex, in fact matters such as the layout of the building (separate entrances for boys and girls) illustrated that this was a constant preoccupation. Foucault points out that there was a proliferation of discourses on relevant topics involving law (proscribing certain behaviours) and medicine, defining what might be regarded as perversion and what might be considered normal. As part of this recognition of the abnormal in the medical context, homosexuality came into being as a medical disorder in 1870 (Foucault 1998: 43). The growth of this preoccupation with what was normal so far as sex was concerned also coincided with the development of medical interest in intersex and with the idea that it was a disease, which is to say a special sort of difference – one that was the object of study by physicians and that needed to be medically corrected.

FEAR OF DIFFERENCE

Many of those with unusual genital anatomy also find it difficult to escape the idea that there is such a thing as normal genitalia. Any difference or perceived difference to what is deemed the norm can be problematic for the individual concerned. It is interesting that many adult women with intersex disorders consent to have vaginoplasty and clitoridectomy in order to be made more "normal", as indeed do many women who cannot be regarded as having a disorder by any objective standards (Goodman 2009). In the case of intersex disorder those adults wishing to have surgical alteration of genitalia include those with female partners in addition to those with male partners (Creighton *et al.* 2009: 254). Thus a major goal for at least some adult women is to have an "adequate" vagina. "Inadequate" is the term used in the Consensus Statement (Hughes *et al.* 2006: 557) to imply a structure requiring surgical reconstruction as judged by medical professionals. In the context of intersex the term is used in a functional sense, meaning adequate or not for the purposes of heterosexual intercourse. However it may also have a wider meaning, implying perceived as "normal" or aesthetically pleasing (or otherwise) as judged by the woman concerned. The "key issue facing the intersexed is actually a key issue facing humanity in general: fear of difference" (Del LaGrace Volcano in Creighton *et al.* 2009: 253). It is of course true that this fear applies to many more situations than the relatively rare context described in this paper, hence the growing trend toward appearance-altering surgery. Indeed, there are television shows based around the idea of radical transformation of an individual through cosmetic surgery, such as *10 Years Younger* on Channel 4 in the UK.

> [This] is a particularly obvious example of the homogenizing function of cosmetic surgery: every body appearing on the show must be measured for its deviation from a norm set by heterosexual desirability and youth read through a binary gender system.
> (Heyes 2007: 97)

However, the situation is more complex. As Heyes points out, the narrative used by the shows in question is "less about becoming beautiful, and more about becoming oneself" (2007: 96). Therefore rather than aspiring to external norms, the participants engage in a narrative in which "the makeover enables the recipient to achieve long-standing personal goals presented as intrinsic to her own individual authenticity" (Heyes 2007: 97).

There is a further question concerning surgical intervention carried out with the purpose of making atypical genital anatomy more normal. Does surgery achieve normalization? As will be seen from some of the accounts given below, this is not always so. Rather it is as if medical attention and treatment reinforce the sense of abnormality and inadequacy. This may also apply in uncontested disease. As an example, those with respiratory disease may be subjected to respiratory function tests, the findings of which are expressed in terms of percentage of expected values. A low percentage value has the effect of emphasizing the deviation from normality, heightening a sense of failure (Carel 2008: 37–8).

MEDICALIZATION AS THE CAUSE OF PATHOLOGY

So far we have determined that difference from what is considered normal is perceived as disease according to at least some models of health and disease.

There are two further approaches that I will now discuss, in order to demonstrate that rather than affecting a cure, the medical approach actually pathologizes intersex. First, I will discuss some anthropological evidence. Second, I will look at accounts from individuals subjected to medical treatment in the past forty years to investigate its effects.

In the 1970s and 1980s there was considerable Western anthropological research into intersex in several cultures where a specific condition is frequent. In partial androgen insensitivity, children with XY chromosomes and other male-associated genes and testes may fail to develop virilized genitalia at birth because of a failure to respond to the testicular hormones *in utero* and so can be born with female-type appearance. However, at puberty, the increased androgen production inherent in this state does have some effect so that these individuals do virilize, sometimes to the extent that they appear to change sex. In the ambient culture this meant that they changed gender in some cases. This was recognized for many years in Papua New Guinea and the Dominican Republic, where there were words and phrases in the language to describe such individuals (Eckert 2009: 65). Several Western investigators became interested in this phenomenon. For example, the work of Julianne Imperato-McGinley, an endocrinologist, examined the phenomenon in the Dominican Republic (Imperato-McGinley *et al.* 1979). She was interested in the importance of nature (androgen exposure) rather than nurture (upbringing) in determination of eventual gender identity and role. It has been pointed out that this work was done solely using terms and ideas from Western medical discourse but, perhaps more significantly, there is some evidence that this work has had the effect of changing and pathologizing the phenomenon it was examining. "Through their investigations, Western researchers created a social category of 'sexual deviation' that had not previously existed in the community" (Eckert 2009: 65).

There is evidence that it may also be true that medical intervention and attention are the cause of pathology in Western cases of intersex. To examine this I will look at some of the empirical data concerned with the experience of individuals with intersex conditions in general, and most particularly women with CAH, who are the largest group of intersex individuals included in this literature and who are also particularly likely to have had appearance-changing genital surgery during infancy or childhood. This requires a method of examining the lived experience of the condition that is in contrast to those discussed earlier, for neither Boorse's biostatistical theory nor the normative theories of health include substantial input from the ill person (Carel 2008: 8). So in order to access the patient's experience we need a different, phenomenological, approach in addition to the objective accounts. We have already seen that in sensitive and socially loaded cases, such as those involving intersex, the objective accounts carry with them implicit cultural values, and so are not as objective as practitioners may think. Physicians with their scientific approach to medical care could be said to manage disease, whereas the patient experiences the consequences of the pathology and disease in terms of pain and inability to achieve goals; this could be described as experiencing the illness (Toombs 1993: 39). By giving a voice to the ill person (or the person experiencing medical attention) this "privileges the first-person experience thus challenging the medical world's objective, third-person account of disease" (Carel 2008: 8) and "sees illness as a way of living, experiencing the world and interacting with other people" (Carel 2008: 8). This is a phenomenological approach in which the actual illness experience is important, rather than the biomedical facts of the disease process. One important matter to consider here is that "the body is not an automaton operated by the person but the embodied person herself. We are our bodies; consciousness is not separate from the body" (Carel 2008: 13). It therefore follows that bodily changes, including surgical intervention, actually change perception, subjectivity and the identity of the person (Carel 2008: 13).

In order to access some of the first-person experience of those with intersex conditions, I draw on empirical work carried out from the 1990s onwards (e.g. Harper 2007; Preves 1999; and, most particularly, Karkazis 2008). This research appears to show remarkable consistency in the conclusions reached. Accounts from those who have not experienced medicalization of any sort are very rare in the modern era (Eckert 2009: 41). It is as if the specific medical framework surrounding intersex people is essential for their identification (Eckhart 2009: 41). There is some literature describing the life experience of intersex individuals in a former era; for example, the autobiography of Herculine Barbin is well known. This was published in 1980 with an introduction by Michel Foucault (Foucault 1980), but this account is not entirely relevant to present-day experience.

While there are undoubtedly intersex persons who feel that medical and surgical treatment was right for them (Holmes 2008: 16), not everyone shares this view. Medical attention is a constant part of life for those with intersex from the very first moments of the child's existence. The literature describes the confusion and bewilderment of parents (and indeed midwives and doctors) at the delivery of an intersex infant: "either they called it wrong, or that's a bit different for a girl" (Karkazis 2008: 184, quoting Sara Finney, whose child was eventually declared female). Then there is attention from nurses, doctors and medical students: "who are all these people?" (a quote from Gloria Jackson, who was told by the attending hordes of doctors, nurses and medical students that "We've never seen a baby with CAH"; Karkazis 2008: 185. As pointed out by Karkazis, this has the effect of emphasizing that a medical condition is present rather than a difference in anatomy, albeit an unusual one. It also has the effect of making the child's atypical genitalia the defining feature in the life of that child and that family (Karkazis 2008: 185). Parents commonly feel confusion and shame (Karkazis 2008: 186–8) and may decide not to tell wider family and friends. Whether the newborn is a boy or girl normally plays a fundamental part in their introduction to family, friends and to the social world in general. The process usually commences immediately following birth with the production of pink or blue cot cards in the postnatal ward, so that those with an intersex child are immediately confronted by a major difficulty. Some parents feel that they lack a vocabulary to talk to others; they lack a "phenomenological toolkit" (Carel 2012) to describe their experience. Some parents (though not all) also found it impossible to discuss the diagnosis with their growing intersex child, even if regular medication, such as hormone replacement therapy, was needed (Karkazis 2008: 188–96), partly because they were distressed and embarrassed about the matter and partly because they wished to protect the child.

What about intersex from the point of view of the patient? As noted above, many individuals were not informed of their diagnosis and often spent a childhood under medical surveillance and, in some cases, taking medication without knowing why (Karkazis 2008: 220; Preves 1999: 56). In some cases, girls had clitoridectomy and vaginoplasty in their early teens without being told that the surgery was going to happen (Karkazis 2008: 221). For some children this reinforced their sense of otherness and difference (Karkazis 2008: 220; Preves 1999: 58). The medical attention lavished on these children also resulted in similar feelings (Karkazis 2008: 222), particularly when subjected to repeated genital examinations from doctors and medical students. Some of the children were made to feel that their body was not right or was shameful, and that it was outside their control (Karkazis 2008: 223; Preves 1999: 55). The sense that they were somehow abnormal and freakish was reinforced, whether or not there had been surgery to "normalize" genital anatomy (Karkazis 2008: 224). In the context of intersex it seems that performing surgery emphasizes deviation from the normal in at least some individuals' experience (Greenberg 2006: 89). Also, it is not necessarily true that surgery results in a return to normal; for example, it may result in scarring. Iain Morland (discussing hypospadias repair, another form of childhood genital surgery carried out for a congenital variation of penile anatomy) describes how:

> In the school locker-room (that fabled location on which some surgeons base judgments about the fate of intersexed people who don't receive surgery) I was teased not because of intersex characteristics ... but specifically because of scars caused by surgery.
> (Morland 2009a: 301).

Adolescence could be a particularly stressful time – "I was really isolated, extremely lonely, and couldn't talk to anyone about how I was different, my diagnosis or my body, or the surgeries. I was suicidal for most of my teenage years and a lot of my twenties" (Karkazis 2008: 224, quoting Elissa Ford who has partial androgen insensitivity syndrome). Often it is not until their twenties or later that intersex individuals are able to discuss their diagnosis and other issues with family and others (Karkazis 2008: 226). Involuntary clitoridectomy can be a great source of regret and anger for the women who underwent it and they may direct their resentment towards their parents and also towards the medical team who treated them (Karkazis 2008: 227–8). The complaints usually centre on loss of sexual function and, particularly, clitoral sensation, following surgery (Karkazis 2008: 231); for these girls, the fact that their genitalia had been made to look more womanly was insufficient. Comparison with female genital mutilation for non-medical reasons is obvious here; a person is guilty of an offence if he excises, infibulates or otherwise mutilates the whole or part of a girl's labia majora, labia minor or clitoris (Female Genital Mutilation Act, 2003). This is a comparison that has been made previously on numerous occasions, for example, by Alice Domurat Dreger (2004: 149).

It is notable how different the perceptions of the individuals concerned are when compared with those of the treating physicians. The medical professionals think in terms of a "good cosmetic outcome" as satisfactory, but often the patients feel "a lasting sense of discomfort and shame about their bodies" (Karkazis 2008: 228–9) even when by all objective accounts the surgery is successful. The overwhelming impression is that the patient experience, the first-person view of intersex, is vastly different from that of the biomedical perspective but that this view plays almost no role in medical decision-making. It seems that at least some of the problematic experiences for these individuals arise from the process of medicalization, which leads to feelings of alienation from, and loss of control of, their own bodies.

CONCLUSIONS

There has been much work making a similar argument to that presented here. Suzanne Kessler was one of the first to analyse the understanding of gender among doctors working with intersex children in 1990, revealing the sexist and heterosexist assumptions implicit in the treatment offered (Kessler 1990). In 1993, Anne Fausto-Sterling brought the matter of intersex to a wider audience with a much-cited paper titled "The Five Sexes" (Fausto-Sterling 1998). The point here was to challenge the assumption that sex was a simple binary and the Intersex Society of North America was formed around this time. In 1999, Alice Domurat Dreger (Dreger 1999b) introduced the voice of those with intersex conditions into the literature. Some of the accounts describe adverse experiences following surgery (e.g. Moreno 1999) and some describe a satisfactory life as a woman with a large clitoris (Dreger & Chase 1999) or as a man with a micropenis (Hawbecker 1999). Scholars increasingly challenged the notion of intersex as disease (e.g. Dreger 2004). Around this time many clinicians, certainly in the US and UK, wished to reform the treatment offered, and this culminated in the consensus statement discussed above (Hughes *et al.* 2006). However, there is no doubt that the debate surrounding medicine and intersex has escalated rather than died away. The sociologist Morgan Holmes described her own experience of "normalizing" genital surgery, reiterating that intersex is troubling but that does not mean that those with intersex conditions are "troubled" (Holmes 2008: 13). Over the past few years there have been several multi-author volumes that include contributions from legal scholars, bioethicists and writers in gender studies, which deal with a wide range of topics pertinent to intersex (Holmes 2009b; Morland 2009b; Sytsma 2006).

The argument about the need for early genital surgery in intersex infants (most commonly girls with CAH) continues, despite the work mentioned above. For example, a recent paper from Australia reports a high percentage of "acceptable cosmetic results" for surgery of this type (Crawford *et al.* 2009). As we have seen, from the patients' perspective this is not necessarily the most significant outcome, though this study did include a patient questionnaire looking at general quality of life, assessed as not statistically different from that of peers. This seems to avoid the central problem of intersex. Men and women born with atypical genital anatomy are different. They do not conform to the societal norm. In the case of intersex the abnormality of genitalia results in questioning the strict cultural rules dictating what constitutes male and female, rules that carry with them a set of notions of behaviours and moral judgements. Because the binary division into male and female is so central to our culture, the threat intersex poses is perceived as much greater than it is, particularly since one's gender is not necessarily connected to one's sex.

In theory, at least in England, the Gender Recognition Act, 2004 makes it clear that, in legal terms, sex and gender are separate. We have seen that it is becoming clear that identifying someone's sex can now be extremely difficult; biologically, there is no simple binary anymore. However, even today, infants and children may be subjected to surgery to which they are too young to consent in order that they conform anatomically to what is considered appropriate. From birth onwards they are subjected to the medical gaze. The available evidence seems to suggest that interaction with medicine fails to affect a medical resolution but rather is itself pathologizing. One possible solution is for those responsible for the care of intersex infants to try to form an idea of a possible future (Roen 2009: 34). While it is difficult to do, it is necessary that the child is seen as a person with a future outside infancy. Roen entreats people to think of possibilities other than those dictated by considerations of what is normal. She uses the term "queer embodiment" (Roen 2009: 35) to discuss the possibility that what is normal is not all that can be natural and right. She believes that families should be assisted by all who work with them in supporting their children; without such support "atypically sexed children very soon come to understand that their difference is the problem, rather than having any chance to find out about others who are like them and take up opportunities to celebrate difference" (Roen 2009: 35).

NOTES

1. There are several reasons why this is so. In some cases there is a complete congenital and genetically determined absence of the cellular receptors needed to respond to androgenic (male-type) hormones such as testosterone produced by the testes and other organs in the body. This leads to complete androgen insensitivity and to phenotypic females showing no male characteristics. In other cases there may be a genetic deficiency of some of the enzymes needed for the effects of testosterone in the cells of the organs forming secondary sex characteristics. This leads to a partial androgen insensitivity because there will be some cells that can respond and others than are unable to. See for example Karkazis (2008: 24).
2. The size of a micropenis is usually considered to be less than 2.5 standard deviations below the mean; one recent study (Khan *et al.* 2011) gave a threshold figure of less than 10.1 cm stretched flaccid length, defined as "the distance from the pubic bone to the tip of the glans penis under gentle painless extension" (Khan *et al.* 2011: 2), but in some cases the structure may be much smaller. Many individuals with a micropenis may have no other features of intersex, but infants and children in this group in practice may be managed by the "DSD team", because of their experience in the area of unusual genital anatomy. In at least some (but not all) of the individuals involved heterosexual intercourse is possible. For an example see Van Seters & Slob (1988). Two of the males described in this paper are genotypically female, with CAH, but had been assigned a male identity at birth. They did not receive surgery as infants, perhaps because this was not available. Both were secure in their male identity and each chose to have hysterectomy, oophorectomy and mastectomy as adults.

10. STIGMATIZING DEPRESSION: FOLK THEORIZING AND "THE POLLYANNA BACKLASH"

Charlotte Blease

INTRODUCTION

Depression is a worldwide phenomenon (Blazer *et al.* 1994). Annually, the economic costs of this mental disorder due to loss of work and medical expenses run into tens of billions of dollars globally (Greenberg *et al.* 1993: 5). During the past few decades, diagnostic rates have risen yearly, and in the US (World Health Organization 2010c) and the UK 10 per cent of the adult population is diagnosed with depression each year (Office for National Statistics 2002).

Despite its prevalence, individuals suffering from depression appear to be subject to persistent stigma. In this chapter, following Kurzban and Leary, I understand stigma to be negative evaluations of an individual which can be "discrediting; negative attributions; perceived illegitimacy; or a devalued social identity" (Kurzban & Leary 2001: 188); this conceptualization leaves open the possibility for self-stigmatization as well. Worryingly, recent evidence seems to indicate that public education campaigns have been ineffective in the face of such stigma (Angermeyer & Matschinger 2004; Dumesnil & Verger 2009). This chapter puts forward an explanation for why the public appears to be "depression illiterate". Employing a "folk theory" model of cognition, drawn from philosophy and psychology, I propose that the stigmatization of depression may result from individuals' implicit attempts to uphold a core common-sense set of optimistic beliefs about the world which are important for psychological well-being. This hypothesis – which I dub "the Pollyanna Backlash" – accounts for stigmatization by invoking two claims: (a) individuals adhere to positive, tacit beliefs about the world and themselves; and (b) individuals respond in a "quasi-scientific" manner to threats to their beliefs. The folk theory explanation developed in this paper is that depressed behaviour presents a threat to our putative "Pollyanna-ish" positive beliefs and that stigmatization is tantamount to the conservative upholding of such beliefs in the face of "anomalous" behaviour. I contend that this "Pollyanna Backlash" hypothesis presents a promising possible explanation for the prevalence of depression stigmatization; however, it is one that is not without its problems and requires further study.

The argument put forward in this chapter provides a new model for conceptualizing depression. This is significant because it has implications for understanding: (a) how people with depression view their illness; (b) how healthy individuals respond to the symptoms of depression; and (c) how we might improve "depression literacy". If the framework for this chapter is correct, then it can also be expected to have implications for thinking about our responses to other forms of illness, and even death as these also threaten our conception of ourselves and our worldview.

The chapter is divided into four sections. First I describe the symptoms of depression and survey the evidence for stigmatization of depression despite public education campaigns. I then outline the motivations for a folk theory view of cognition. This section surveys literature from cognitive psychology and philosophy of mind which claims that our common-sense views are tantamount to folk *theories* and that our reasoning with such theories takes a *quasi-scientific* form. The third section forms the nub of the chapter: in this section I apply the folk theoretical considerations of the previous section to the case of depression. I examine the folk theories that are purportedly threatened by depressive behaviour and apply the "folk as scientists" model in order to explain the evidence of stigmatization. In the final section, I outline some outstanding problems with the "Pollyanna Backlash" hypothesis and make suggestions for further research.

DEPRESSION AND EVIDENCE OF STIGMA

At the outset, it is crucial to get a clear understanding of the symptoms presented by patients with episodes of major depression. In this chapter, I have chosen to focus on attitudes to individuals suffering from major depression rather than the milder form of depression known as dysthymia. This is because the available literature overwhelmingly focuses on stigmatization, and attitudes to, major depressive disorder. Thus, for brevity, I will use the term "depression" interchangeably with "major depressive disorder". The DSM-IV of the American Psychiatric Association lists the following criteria for major depressive disorder (American Psychiatric Association 2000: 356):

> A. Five (or more) of the following symptoms have been present during the same 2-week period and represent a change from

previous functioning; at least one of the symptoms is either: (1) depressed mood or (2) loss of interest or pleasure.

Note: Do not include symptoms that are clearly due to a general medical condition, or mood-congruent delusions or hallucinations.

(1) Depressed mood most of the day, nearly every day, as indicated by either subjective report (e.g. feels sad or empty) or observation made by others (e.g. appears tearful). Note: In children and adolescents, can be irritable mood.
(2) Markedly diminished interest or pleasure in all, or almost all, activities most of the day, nearly every day (as indicated either by subjective account or observation made by others).
(3) Significant weight loss when not dieting or weight gain (e.g. a change of more than 5% of body weight in a month), or decrease or increase in appetite nearly every day. Note: In children, consider failure to make expected weight gains.
(4) Insomnia or hypersomnia nearly every day.
(5) Psychomotor agitation or retardation nearly every day (observable by others, not merely subjective feelings of restlessness or being slowed down).
(6) Fatigue or loss of energy nearly every day.
(7) Feelings of worthlessness or excessive or inappropriate guilt (which may be delusional) nearly every day (not merely self-reproach or guilt about being sick).
(8) Diminished ability to think or concentrate, or indecisiveness, nearly every day (either by subjective account or as observed by others).
(9) Recurrent thoughts of death (not just fear of dying), recurrent suicidal ideation without a specific plan, or a suicide attempt or a specific plan for committing suicide.

B. The symptoms do not meet criteria for a Mixed Episode.

C. The symptoms cause clinically significant distress or impairment in social, occupational, or other important areas of functioning.

D. The symptoms are not due to the direct physiological effects of a substance (e.g. a drug of abuse, a medication) or a general medical condition (e.g. hypothyroidism).

E. The symptoms are not better accounted for by Bereavement, i.e. after the loss of a loved one, the symptoms persist for longer than two months or are characterized by a marked functional impairment, morbid preoccupation with worthlessness, suicidal ideation, psychotic symptoms, or psychomotor retardation.

We can note two key points with respect to these symptoms. First, while the criteria for major depressive disorder include physiological as well as mental symptoms, for depression to be present, as criterion A indicates, there must at least be depressed mood (low feelings) or diminished interest in daily activities. These symptoms are suggestive of a negative outlook on oneself and the outside world. Second, we can note that the depressive symptoms often cause observable social dysfunction and withdrawal (criteria C and E): the extensiveness of the social impairment makes depression publicly evincible. It is this latter feature of depression that renders it susceptible to stigmatization.

When considering the stigmatization of depression we need to bear in mind three issues: (a) the particular experiences of stigma perceived by those suffering from depression;[1] (b) how widespread stigmatization of depression is; and (c) the responses of the public to depression following educational campaigns. By considering these issues we will be in a position to gauge whether our folk theory explanation of depression is (to any degree) apposite.

Let us consider the first issue – the experience of stigmatization by those suffering from depression. Research unequivocally reports that the experience of stigma by primary care patients (individuals who have presented with depression to general medical practitioners) is widespread (Dinos *et al.* 2004; Lai *et al.* 2001; Roeloffs *et al.* 2003): as many as 67 per cent of primary care patients with a history of depression reported experiencing stigmatization in the workplace (Dinos *et al.* 2004: 313). But stigma is reported in all social contexts (including among family and friends). Representative testimonies of such experiences included being "blamed for being 'emotionally weak', 'inefficient', 'unproductive', and 'lazy'" (Lai *et al.* 2001: 113). Depressive behaviour is even interpreted moralistically: subjective testimonies include views that displayed fearfulness about admitting to mental health problems:

> I didn't say anything to my family 'cause I thought they would be appalled actually, they're very, very – my mother in particular – very moralistic. The whole idea of not working, not earning a living, being on benefits or anything is appalling as far as she is concerned. (Dinos *et al.* 2004: 196)

Similarly, stigma also appears to be widespread among patients, many of whom, reportedly, do not consider depression to be a "real illness" but, rather, the result of "'weak or 'flawed' personality", and as a "new label for problems of daily living within the range of normal experiences" (Cornford *et al.* 2007: 360; see also Pill *et al.* 2001; Shaw *et al.* 1999).

It should be noted that the stigmatization experienced by those suffering from depression is estimated to be under-reported: many people with depression never seek medical help (and one explanation for this may be self-stigmatization: individuals do not judge themselves as ill but as failed in some way).[2] While we can note that such studies are based on self-reports (a problematic research method; Nisbett & Wilson 1977), here we are interested in the phenomenology of the illness and, as such, depressed people's accounts of responses to their symptoms are of paramount importance. Where we may take issue with such self-reports is over the possibility of negative misperception: given that people with depression embrace deeply negative views of the world and their circumstances (as part of their symptoms) it might be contended that their judgements of third party perceptions are likely to be overly harsh. Fortunately, however, we can go some way towards correcting for this problem by probing the second of our concerns – assessing the attitudes of the public towards people with depression.

While there is need for more research into public attitudes toward people with mental illnesses (and, indeed, more cross-cultural studies), current findings appear to support the pessimistic perceptions experienced by patients with depression: people do seem to display negative views towards depression (Goldney et al. 2001; Peluso & Blay 2009; Perry et al. 2007; Wang & Lai 2008).[3] One recent study in the US revealed that approximately 40 per cent of subjects believed that depressive behaviour arose from "bad character"; 80 per cent believed that specialist treatment for depression was unnecessary (Perry et al. 2007). Moreover, studies show that stigmatization is apparently unaffected by exposure to individuals with depression – including family members and friends – and even by having experienced an episode of depression oneself (Goldney et al. 2001: 282; Wang & Lai 2008: 191).[4]

Given these findings we need to consider the effectiveness of the education campaigns which have been launched in an attempt to overcome the pervasive problem of stigmatization. In the last fifteen years governmental and health agencies in a number of countries have launched campaigns aimed at improving public awareness of depression and eradicating stigma. Such campaigns use a range of television and newspaper advertisements, billboards, and educative leaflets distributed in primary care settings. These include the "Depression Awareness, Recognition and Treatment Programme" (DART) in the USA launched in 1988; "Depression Awareness Day" held annually in the USA; "Defeat Depression Campaign" in the UK (1992–1996); "Changing Minds Campaign" in the UK (1998–2003); "Beyond Blue" launched in Australia in 2006; and "National Depression Initiative" launched in New Zealand in 2006.

Have such campaigns proven effective? Perhaps surprisingly, there have been very few systematic follow-up studies of such campaigns; however, the research that has been undertaken reveals disheartening results. The only study devised to follow-up attitudes over a ten-year period, which employed a vignette technique, was conducted in west Germany by Angermeyer and Matschinger (2004).[5] This study asked the following questions: "Does the German public show more positive and less negative emotional reactions towards people with major depression in 2001 than in 1990?" and "Is the desire of the German public for social distance from people with major depression less pronounced in 2001 than in 1990?" (Angermeyer & Matschinger 2004: 178). The researchers concluded:

> The optimistic view ... that attitudes to people with depression have improved in recent years is not supported by our findings ... The desire to distance oneself from someone with depression was as strong in 2001 as it had been in 1990. Overall, one has to conclude that the attitudes of the public in Western Germany have remained more or less unchanged.
> (Angermeyer & Matschinger 2004: 181)

Interestingly, with regard to the persistence of self-stigmatization, the latest meta-analysis into depression awareness campaigns 1987–2007 concluded that "No study has clearly demonstrated that such campaigns help to increase care seeking or to decrease suicidal behaviour" (Dumesnil & Verger 2009: 1203).

While research into stigmatization of depression and into public education is limited, we can tentatively draw the following conclusions: (a) patients with depression experience stigmatization of their illness; and (b) educational campaigns on depression "literacy" appear to have had negligible impact. Before I present the "Pollyanna Backlash" hypothesis for the persistence of depression stigmatization, I turn to survey the "folk theory" view of common sense in psychology and philosophy.

THE "FOLK AS SCIENTISTS" STANCE

Motivations for the account

The folk theory view is the claim that our common-sense understanding of the world is a thoroughly theoretical account. On this view, our naive (prescientific) views relating to physics, biology, sociology, psychology, and so on are regarded as networks of fallible generalizations, and as such they are subject to vindication or elimination with progress in science (Atran 1999; Churchland 1996; McKloskey 1983).

This stance is not without some criticism in the philosophical and psychological literature. It has been argued, for example, that such conceptual frameworks do not constitute "theories" since we are often not explicitly aware of such views and, moreover, conceptual generalizations are employed for practical purposes rather than for the pursuit of the goals that define science (Wilkes 1984). However, in response to such criticisms, Paul Churchland has argued that such arguments "betray a narrow and cartoonish conception of what theories are and what they do" (1993: 33). Churchland notes that learning and employing a theory amounts to the acquisition of a range of skills – "skills of perception, categorization, extension, physical manipulation, evaluation, construction, analysis, argument, computation, analysis, and so forth" (1993: 34) – and that practices can be overthrown and replaced by better ones. Churchland argues that having a theory amounts to having an admixture of know-how as well as know-that.

The folk theoretical view is given additional credence by a second consideration: the empirically supported claim that people tend to reason in a quasi-scientific manner. There is a sizeable social and cognitive psychological literature devoted to understanding "folk *reasoning*". This research is replete with references to the notion that folk reasoning bears resemblance, in various ways, to scientific reasoning as described by Kuhn in *The Structure of Scientific Revolutions* (1962). However, empirical literature is vague with respect to the ways in which folk reason like scientists, even if we accept Kuhn's views of scientific reasoning (Brewer & Samarapunagavan 1991; Brewer *et al.* 2000; Chinn & Brewer 1994, 1998; Fletcher & Fitness 1993; Fletcher & Thomas 1996; Levin *et al.* 1990; Reif & Larkin 1991; Samarapungavan & Wiers 1994).

This leads us to ask: why should we embrace a broadly Kuhnian model of scientific reasoning, and what does it mean to say that people reason in a quasi-Kuhnian manner? There are at least three reasons for taking Kuhn's model of science seriously. First, the "folk as Kuhnian scientist" claim receives indirect vindication from the cognitive science of science where Kuhn's views on scientific reasoning are consistently regarded as credible (Churchland 1993, 1996; Nersessian 2003). Second, Kuhn's work on scientific reasoning maintains weight in the naturalized, historically sensitive philosophy of science community (Bird 2004; Hoyningen-Huene 1993; Kuukkanen 2008). In short, since the publication of his seminal work in 1962, Kuhn's views on the nature of scientific reasoning have never lost favour within naturalized philosophy, even if they have generated some thorny problems for philosophers; and in cognitive science they have lately been embraced. Third, as noted, the plethora of research by social psychologists that contends that our ordinary reasoning bears resemblance to Kuhn's views on scientific reasoning gives added credibility to Kuhn's broad claims: scientific reasoning is a form of cultural bootstrapping from "naturally endowed" cognitive heuristics: as such we can expect science to share many features with commonsense reasoning.

Kuhn's account of science

How are we to understand the claim that people reason in a Kuhnian manner? Kuhn contends that science is periodically cyclical: all fields in science start off with a period of immaturity when there are a number of different, tentative theories and no consensus about which of these is correct. In essence, for Kuhn, science is a social enterprise and he contends that it is the allegiance of a community of thinkers to a particular "paradigm" that is emblematic of science. The term paradigm refers to a multiplicity of components that include: (a) symbolic generalizations, such as laws (e.g. "force = mass × acceleration"); (b) metaphysical generalizations, which are usually tacitly embraced (e.g. "forces exist"); (c) shared epistemic values among scientists (Kuhn contends that scientists favour five such values: (i) accuracy, (ii) consistency with other theories, (iii) simplicity, (iv) scope – i.e. the possibility of extending the paradigm to new domains – and (v) fruitfulness – i.e. the paradigm should prove successful); and finally, (d) "exemplars" – concrete ways of viewing the world and solving particular problems that arise within some domain of enquiry (Kuhn 1962: 23ff).

It is this final component of "exemplars" that forms the leitmotif of Kuhn's views on scientific reasoning – scientists, he says, engage in "puzzle-solving" where exemplars play a key role (Kuhn 1962: 177–8). Kuhn contends that when we do a crossword puzzle we assume that if we apply the rules correctly we can find the correct answer; equally, he notes, scientists assume that correct application of the paradigm will uncover the answers to particular problems. Just as people approach crossword puzzles, for example, with an understanding of how such puzzles work, Kuhn contends that scientists approach the world mindful of a particular exemplar (a set of explicit and tacitly understood know-how and know-that). By applying this exemplary understanding they can discern answers to particular problems that may arise. For example, by understanding force as the product of an object's mass and its acceleration ("F = MA"), by tacit understanding that there exist such things as "forces", "mass" and "acceleration", and given sufficient schooling in mathematics, the use of relevant instruments to calculate such values, and so on, we can employ this exemplar to solve subsequent puzzles about the force, mass or acceleration of objects. In order for science to progress and, indeed, for any scientific work to ensue, Kuhn contends that scientists must adhere to the paradigm and its rules.

Kuhn views science as a cyclical phenomenon; inevitably, he claims, various problems in this "puzzle-solving" pursuit will arise and prove intractable: he dubs these "anomalies". Kuhn contends that, at first, anomalies are only tacitly perceived and cause scientists to express discomfort with the paradigm (Kuhn 1962: 56, 61). As more anomalies emerge, however, scientists become consciously aware that something has gone wrong with the paradigm. At first, they consciously choose to defend the paradigm and deflect the anomalies via *ad hoc* measures: for example, they may blame the instruments used or declare that some human error has occurred. However, with mounting anomalies, especially ones that recurrently strike at central tenets of the paradigm, and where there is mounting, external social pressure to deal with the paradigm's failings, a period of "scientific crisis" is said to ensue. During crisis periods scientists start to articulate the tacitly held aspects of their paradigm and begin to question every aspect of the paradigm. At this time, scientists are said to be at a complete loss: while they have lost faith in the old paradigm and seek an alternative one, they may still feel a conservative pull toward their former viewpoint. Kuhn calls this "the essential tension", between the conservative defence of normal science and the need to pursue more innovative theories: "the successful scientist must simultaneously display the characteristics of the traditionalist and of the iconoclast" (Kuhn 1977: 227).

Folk as "quasi-Kuhnian" scientists

Needless to say, common-sense reasoning may not exhibit all of the features described by Kuhn; we may not employ paradigm structures in their entirety in everyday life and we may not engage in full-blown puzzle-solving activity in order to solve everyday problems. Nonetheless, findings in social psychology suggest that there are key areas of overlap between science and common sense (Brewer & Samarapunagavan 1991; Brewer *et al.* 2000; Chinn & Brewer 1994, 1998; Fletcher & Fitness 1993; Fletcher & Thomas 1996; Levin *et al.* 1990; Reif & Larkin 1991; Samarapungavan & Wiers 1994). This research indicates the following shared aspects of "folk" or common-sense reasoning with Kuhn's views on scientific reasoning: (a) even when aspects of theories are tacitly known, "folk" (like scientists) exhibit conservatism when it comes to their theories; and (b) in particular, when faced with anomalies people tend to respond by employing *ad hoc* manoeuvres in order to preserve existing theories. In the following section I will employ these two minimal claims to propose an explanation for folk responses to depression.

STIGMATIZATION OF DEPRESSION AS A FOLK THEORETICAL RESPONSE

Assuming this folk theoretical model, we need to ask: what are the theories that appear to operate in our thinking about depression? We can draw on empirical work which proposes that there are three folk beliefs that are pivotal to our psychological well-being and our view of our place in the world.[6] These are:

- The world is benevolent.
- The world is meaningful.
- The self is worthy.
  (Janoff-Bulman 1992: 6; see also Bolton & Hill 1996: 353)

The first belief draws on psychological research that indicates that individuals distinguish between their own fortune and that of others: individuals have a propensity to be optimistic about their own future and to display positive biases about themselves and the past; this well-known tendency has been dubbed "The Pollyanna Principle" (Janoff-Bulman 1992: 6–7; S. E. Taylor 1990; Taylor & Brown 1988). Studies reveal, for example, that people have an overwhelming tendency to view their life experiences as positive rather than negative: it seems that people really do view the world through metaphorical rose-tinted glasses (Matin & Stang 1978 cited in Janoff-Bulman 1992: 7).

The second principle is supported by well-established research which shows that people have strong tendencies to understand events as meaningful (Bering 2011; Janoff-Bulman 1992: 8–9; McAdams 2005; Pennebaker 1997): people view events as "happening for a reason" – something it is incumbent on us to discover. Research shows, for example, that people tend to recover faster from traumatic (random) life events when they interpret them as part of a bigger "life narrative" imbued with significance: for example, a victim of a serious sexual assault who decides to devote her life to helping other victims may feel that her life has taken on a new and important meaning (Pennebaker 1997).

The final folk belief draws on well-replicated studies which show that individuals tend to self-evaluate themselves as above average when it comes to being "good, capable and moral" (Janoff-Bulman 1992: 11–12; S. E. Taylor 1990; Wilson 2002: 198). People tend to endorse more positive comments about themselves than negative ones: "most people, for example think that they are more popular, talented, attractive, and intelligent than the average person, which of course can't be true of everyone" (Wilson 2002: 198).

If we invoke the "folk theory" stance and the "folk as scientists" viewpoints, we can collectively term these three key beliefs "the Pollyanna Proto-Paradigm" (hereafter "PP"). In dubbing these a "proto"-paradigm we can make due reference to the fact that any such employment of these folk beliefs does not constitute a paradigm: while we might contend that such *tacitly* held beliefs constitute a theory of sorts, it is clear that many elements of a paradigm are not in place. There are no symbolic generalizations; even if there are exemplars we may argue that there is no full-blown puzzle-solving activity. However, given what we understand about the attributed folk beliefs we might tentatively contend that the PP does consist of tacitly embraced metaphysical generalizations. So, while the prefix suffices as a rather large caveat to the effect that the PP is certainly not a paradigm, by presenting folk as "quasi-scientific" and thereby presenting their theories on a continuum with scientific paradigms, it seems reasonable to dub this set of beliefs a "*proto*-paradigm".

With this in mind, we can make the following predictions based on the empirical claims that folk act like scientists when it comes to conservative allegiance to any such "paradigm":

(a_1) Any behaviour that undermines aspects of the PP will constitute an anomaly.
(b_1) Individuals will react conservatively with respect to this "paradigm": that is to say, individuals will be dismissive of perceived anomalies of the PP.

Are these predictions borne out in the case of depression? It seems that behaviour such as "loss of interest of pleasure in life", fatigue, "feelings of worthlessness or inappropriate guilt", and recurring suicidal ideation (American Psychiatric Association 2000: 356) can be interpreted as overt examples of anomalies with respect to the PP. The tacit belief that "the world is benevolent" appears to be undermined by the negative behaviour of the person suffering from depression who presents the view that life is, on the contrary, a set of *unpleasant* experiences. While this belief refers to the individual's *own* life experiences, depressive behaviour appears to counsel that life itself – not just his or her life – is not predominantly pleasant. Similarly, the tacit (and, indeed, often explicitly stated) belief that events have "meaning" is apparently rejected by the person suffering from depression whose behaviour shows "markedly diminished interest or pleasure in all, or almost all, activities most of the day, nearly every day" (American Psychiatric Association 2000: 356): the person suffering from depression seems to occupy an existential abyss – daily endeavours, and even life, are deemed to be pointless and insignificant. Finally, the folk belief that "the self is worthy" is clearly rejected by the individual suffering from depression: such individuals suffer from feelings of worthlessness, which are manifested in low self-esteem and excessive guilt. It would appear, thus, that the depressive's conduct is strikingly at odds with the three key tenets of the PP:

the individual suffering from depression does not consider life to be benevolent or meaningful, nor does she consider her life to have any value: in severe depression this leads to suicidal ideation that life is not worth living at all.

However, it should be pointed out that the third folk belief – that the self is worthy – while at odds with depressive behaviour, need not be interpreted as anomalous with respect to that belief for third parties. On the contrary, rather than posing an anomaly to the PP it might be considered that depressive "feelings of worthlessness or excessive guilt" point to some vindication for the non-depressed observer of their higher than average moral self-worth. In short, by embracing self-stigmatization (self-blame, guilt and denial that one is suffering from a *bona fide* illness) the person suffering from depression seems to affirm the tacitly held belief of the non-depressed that the latter are superior. In this case, it seems that the non-depressed individual is vindicated in his or her tacit adherence to the PP.

If we accept these behaviours as anomalies (with regard to the beliefs "the world is benevolent" and "the world is meaningful") and confirmation ("the self is worthy") of the PP, do we find that individuals react in ways analogous to scientific responses? In fact, as the empirical literature suggests, individuals' responses do appear to uphold the predictions of this provisional explanation: individuals (including those suffering from depression) seem to react by engaging in a "Pollyanna Backlash". As we have seen, in the face of anomalies, scientists seem doggedly to adhere to the prevailing paradigm and to blame anything but the paradigm when discrepancies between the paradigm and new evidence are perceived. When scientists reject the existing paradigm too quickly they are regarded as "the carpenter who blames his tools" (Kuhn 1962: 79). It seems that, insofar as we can draw on the "folk as [*Kuhnian*] scientist" viewpoint, when new evidence is at variance with the paradigm, individuals – like scientists – blame the "carpenter" rather than the tool (the paradigm). It certainly seems that, rather than accept depressive views about the unpleasantness of the world and its pointlessness, we find that people suffering from depression are blamed for being weak (Lai *et al.* 2001: 113), their behaviour is regarded as a "personality flaw" (Cornford *et al.* 2007: 360; Perry *et al.* 2007), and so on. As we have seen, individuals overwhelmingly appear to respond to depressive behaviour by declaring – in a manner reminiscent of the conservative scientist – that depression is not a "real illness" and does not require specialist help (Perry *et al.* 2007). There is also evidence that mental health professionals are as likely to stigmatize individuals suffering from depression as the general public: the PP can explain this given its claim that people will respond in a conservative manner when bombarded with anomalies (Nordt *et al.* 2006; Wolff *et al.* 1996). Moreover, the PP predicts that such responses will be typical among *all* individuals: we find that even people suffering from depression engage in self-blame, and friends of depressed individuals, just like many of those who have recovered from major episodes of depression, are just as likely to stigmatize and avoid those exhibiting the illness as anyone else (Angermeyer & Matschinger 2004: 181; Wang & Lai 2008: 191).[7]

Insofar as we can accept the following: (a) the theoretical approach to folk psychology; (b) the empirical research which indicates that we typically embrace the core beliefs of the Pollyanna Paradigm; and (c) the empirical research on stigmatization of depression, the predictions (a_1) and (b_1), above, are supported.

LIMITATIONS AND CONCLUSIONS

The Pollyanna Backlash explanation presents an interesting, *inferential* explanation from some key themes in the philosophical and empirical literature that merits investigation: as it stands there are limitations to the proposal that are in need of further research. First, the issue of the universality of the beliefs comprising the PP needs to be established. Are these beliefs deemed to be tacitly held by *everyone, in every cultural milieu*? This point has been raised by Henrich *et al.* (2010) who contend that behavioural psychologists routinely draw on samples from "Western, Educated, Industrialized, Rich, and Democratic (WEIRD) societies" with the assumption that there is little variation between different cultures and populations. According to Henrich *et al.* (2010: 61), "Western, and more specifically American, undergraduates who form the bulk of the database in the experimental branches of psychology" are "among the least representative populations one could find for generalizing about humans" and "frequent outliers" in existing cross-cultural research.

Promisingly for the PP hypothesis, there are a number of cross-cultural studies on the prevalence of "depression" and responses to it: existing evidence shows that depression is not only universal but stigmatized in other (non-Western) cultures (Furnham & Malik 1994; Horwitz & Wakefield 2007; Kleinman 2004; Parker *et al.* 2001; Raguram *et al.* 1996). The somatization of depression in (for example) China and India indicates that there are moral and cultural sanctions on the patient's symptoms (Kleinman 2004; Raguram *et al.* 1996). Nevertheless, more cross-cultural work needs to be undertaken before we can say assuredly that people respond to depressive behaviour in comparable ways and that both the PP and the "folk as scientist" views hold in different cultures.

Even if it were possible to defend the Pollyanna Backlash explanation as applicable within certain cultures, such a restricted view would still leave us with several outstanding problems. For instance, are there people who are genuinely realistic (who do not appear to embrace the PP) but who are not depressed? How damaging would this finding be to the explanation? In addition, we still need to establish *why* it is that people suffering from depression do not appear to adhere to beliefs about the "benevolence of the world" and its "meaningfulness". Is this as a result of exposure to too many anomalies that have overturned these beliefs (perhaps negative events that have precipitated the illness)? If this were the case, individuals may be responding in a "folk scientific" manner, and this understanding of the causes of depression might yet be explicable within the PP framework. Nonetheless, we also know that many people are born with a predisposition to depression. Do such individuals have a tendency to shed their beliefs quicker, or are they more sensitive to anomalous data? How do these views fit with the "folk as scientist" purview? By the same token, given the analogy with science and our understanding of scientific progress, it would seem that the more one is exposed to anomalous (depressive) behaviour, the more likely that crisis with the prevailing paradigm will ensue: does this occur in the case of exposure to people suffering from depression – do people become depressed when they are exposed to "depressing" events and behaviour?[8]

Granted that we can resolve these issues, and the PP holds, this still leaves the question of scope for educating the public about depression. *Prima facie*, the folk theory view appears to imply serious limitations for public understanding of depression; it may be that overcoming folk theories of depression will be as difficult as overturning "folk physics". If mental disorders are akin to concepts like "gravity" health agencies may require more than advertising campaigns in order to educate the public.

In conclusion, the Pollyanna Backlash awaits further research on the causes of depression and the nature of well-being, as well as closer comparative examination with the "folk as scientists" premise, in order to assess its promise as an explanation for the stigmatization of depression. However, given the tentative retroactive success of the Pollyanna Backlash presented here, the hypothesis is surely worthy of future investigation – improving understanding of the most common mental disorder in the world today is of concern to us all.

ACKNOWLEDGEMENTS

I would like to thank Havi Carel and Rachel Cooper for very helpful comments on an earlier draft of this chapter. Thanks are also due to Bethany Heywood, Robert McCauley, Dominic Murphy, Stephen Stich and delegates at the Concepts of Health Conference held at UWE in September 2010 for helpful remarks during the construction of the chapter.

NOTES

1. It should also be noted that stigmatization (including social exclusion) differs according to symptoms displayed: the stigmatization of schizophrenia differs from depression, for example (Kurzban & Leary 2001).
2. It is estimated that around 50 per cent of people suffering from depression in the UK go untreated and 60 per cent attest that they would be embarrassed to consult their doctor with depression (Sims 1993: 30).
3. The studies on public attitudes to mental illness invariably employ vignette methodologies, which involve short descriptions of individuals with various symptoms, followed by questions about the case, asking subjects how they would respond to such a person and how they would classify or explain any such behaviour.
4. It should be added that individuals suffering from other mental and physical disorders are also subjected to stigmatization; the particular range of symptoms is likely to be relevant to the nature of the stigmatizing response. Individuals suffering from schizophrenia, for example, exhibit a range of cognitive symptoms (including delusions and disorganized speech) and frequently display poor self-care. Responses to schizophrenia include avoidance marked by fear of unpredictability, as well as disgust (Park *et al.* 2003).
5. Investigations into the Defeat Depression campaign (1992–1996) in the UK were seriously flawed for their use of face-to-face interviews (Paykel *et al.* 1998; Priest *et al.* 1996). Questionnaires asked, explicitly, for subjects' views on depression, thereby avoiding, outright, implicit stigmatization. Indeed, the surveys found that "most changes [while positive] were relatively small in magnitude" (Paykel *et al.* 1998: 522).
6. It is likely that there is an evolutionary psychological explanation for the prevalence of these folk beliefs; however, in this chapter I have chosen to avoid the minefield of questions about the origins and emergence of these beliefs: rather, following the empirical literature, I assume that they play a role in normal psychological well-being.
7. Understanding underlying questions of why the violation of PP is *emotionally* threatening (it entails huge amounts of emotional investment, is time-consuming, and so on) takes us into the realm of evolutionary psychology. The question of how the PP hypothesis dovetails with evolutionary psychology is important but takes us beyond the present concern, which is to establish that responses to depression have overtly *Kuhnian* features.
8. Work has already been done to apply, in detail, the "folk as scientists" framework to the case of post-traumatic stress disorder (PTSD). In the case of PTSD, traumatic life events have been interpreted as major anomalies that precipitate this illness; in order to bolster the Pollyanna Backlash explanation, the range of symptoms associated with PTSD need to be compared carefully with major depression (*prima facie*, there does appear to be some room for comparison).

11. DOING HEALTH: A CONSTRUCTIVIST APPROACH TO HEALTH THEORY

Britta Pelters

INTRODUCTION

Health is important to us, but it remains difficult to get a conceptual grip on the term "health". Health still often appears as Gadamer described it: a clandestine (and therefore not configurable) gift and "wonder of absent-mindedness" (Gadamer [1993] 1996: 126, my translation). With the rise of "surveillance medicine"[1] (Armstrong 1995), however, a great deal of effort focuses on health promotion and disease prevention, especially in public health. As a consequence, the "clandestine gift of health" is more often conceived as self-made, not given, and a risk diagnosis frequently replaces one of a manifest disease as a cause for medical attention, although risk reveals vulnerability, not disease. How can this situation be conceptualized?

In the following chapter, the situation of women with a genetic disposition to develop hereditary breast and ovarian cancer is introduced as a starting point for the examination of different health theories, followed by a proposal of a constructivist understanding of health.

BRCA-POSITIVE WOMEN: A CASE STUDY OF RISK AND DANGER

BRCA-positive women: life with chronic risk

BRCA represents the *br*east *ca*ncer genes (BRCA1 and BRCA2) associated with a familial cancer syndrome called hereditary breast and ovarian cancer (HBOC). HBOC includes the accumulated occurrence of different types of breast and ovarian cancers as well as a number of less common cancers (colon, prostate, skin and pancreas), linked to family-specific DNA variations at these two DNA sites. These variations are linked to very high lifetime cancer risk figures in healthy individuals. The risk of developing breast cancer up to the age of 70 is 65 per cent (BRCA1) and 45 per cent (BRCA2), compared with a population risk of around 10 per cent. The risk for ovarian cancer is 39 per cent (BRCA1) and 11 per cent (BRCA2), compared with a population risk of 1–2 per cent. These figures can vary considerably depending on the studied population (Antoniou et al. 2003; Gerhardus et al. 2005). Although reliability is problematic when discussing these figures, they may nonetheless be regarded as "reliable" in a more practical sense: all the women in question have been told that they have a lifetime risk of 80 per cent for breast cancer and 60 per cent for ovarian cancer, and therefore these figures are the ones upon which they construct their health identities.

The situation of BRCA-positive women is characterized by a diffuse combination of different health references (i.e. sources that offer feedback on a woman's health identity). A BRCA-positive woman is a healthy or at least asymptomatic woman who is informed by the predictive breast cancer gene test (BRCA test) that she has a genetic disposition to develop a cancer belonging to the HBOC syndrome. In the course of counselling, the woman learns of her actual increased lifetime risk of 60–80 per cent to develop breast cancer and 40–60 per cent to develop ovarian cancer up to the age of 70. Being labelled "at risk" means therefore being aware of one's own health-related vulnerability. Moreover, because these are familial cancers, the women are reconnected to a family history that is often characterized by death and suffering of other family members because of the cancer which appears as a core illness narrative of the family. Finally, the woman has to decide on medical management options. Those options include a biannual intensified screening scheme and prophylactic surgery (removal of the breasts and/or ovaries). In these medical contexts the woman is often referred to as a patient, whereas in the literature one may find reference to the "healthy sick" (Scholz 1995), the "unpatient" (Jonsen et al. 1996) or the "perpetual patient" (Finkler 2000).

Being aware of the possibility of a cancer that will not necessarily develop and the need to manage that knowledge is also called *living with chronic risk* (Kenen et al. 2003). It is compared to living with chronic disease, differing from it by the absence of a progressive disease and the presence of an even more virtual danger.

Living with chronic risk can be described as a *knowledge-triggered vulnerable state* of being in-between different standpoints concerning the dimensions of time, family relationships and health. On the time axis, the woman has reached a certain stage in her life cycle and developed the conception of an (often cancer-free) imagined future. With the test result, an alternative future that needs to be avoided appears. Simultaneously, she is referred

DOING HEALTH

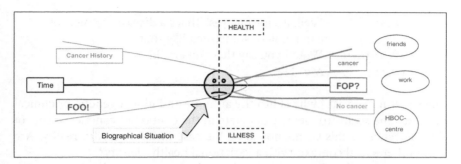

Figure 11.1 The enmeshing of time, family relationships and health-related self-definition.

back in time to a familial health history. In addition to this confusion of different life versions, associated familial relations become important. The woman's family of origin (FOO) suddenly regains significance, whereas a family of procreation (FOP) may provide an alternative approach to living but can also become a difficulty in this context. This mixture of different assignments needs then to be understood against the background of a social shift in notions of health whereby a health–disease dichotomy is being challenged by the increased emphasis on risk (Aronowitz 2009). The enmeshing of time levels, relations, responsibilities and contextual health references may lead to a diffuse health-related self-definition, which may vary from health with or without well-being to illness without disease (see Press et al. 2005). What is called a "health identity" therefore consists of a personal as well as a relational health identification.

Illustrative quotations of BRCA-positive women

The complexity of this health-related self-definition is reflected in the narrations of BRCA-positive women.[2] Gaby, a forty-year-old secretary and single mother of one, says: "I'm healthy, absolutely ... this [genetic disposition] is running on another track." Here it may be asked: on what track is the genetic disposition running? Is it the "illness track"? Is Gaby able to change tracks voluntarily or does this just happen? If so, when does it happen?

Lydia (fifty-one) is the owner of a laundrette and a married mother of three. In the interview with her the following situation turns up:

> INTERVIEWER: Do you consider this disposition a disease?
> LYDIA: No, what do you mean?
> INTERVIEWER: Yes, because I asked about genetics and then you came up with diseases.

LYDIA: Well, it's for me, yes! That's a disease for me, you can fall ill of something like that.
INTERVIEWER: Would you say that you are ill?
LYDIA: Me? No!

Does that mean that Lydia is healthy at home and ill in a genetic or clinical context? She seems to identify her state in the context of genetics as one of disease, whereas this seems not to be the case in her everyday reality. Are there other social contexts with a variational health identity?

Lisa (twenty-three) is Lydia's daughter. She is a student who is engaged to be married, and claims: "I do martial arts and that helps me, too, because I have the feeling I can fight it [cancer risk] ... even if I don't feel like it [martial arts training] I tell myself 'no, you have to go because it is for your body and against the cancer'." Lisa seems to be fighting cancer without being diagnosed. Is Lisa equating cancer with cancer risk? Has she therefore already fallen ill? Moreover, Lisa verbalizes her attitude by raising the eventual situation of developing cancer: "you are going to get healthy, you are not ill." Is this a paradoxical statement? Will Lisa never be ill even if she is officially diagnosed as "diseased"? How does she manage not to be ill if diagnosed but to be (more or less) ill if she is not? What meaning is given to "being ill" in this case?

Ursula is a twenty-seven-year-old physician who has just started gynaecological training. She has a boyfriend and describes how she deals with fear:

> sometimes, it [the fear of cancer] comes up a bit and then you have to tell yourself "ok, that's not fatal, it's not acute, calm down, nothing is happening" ... it happens, of course, more often if you are alone at home and somehow there has been something similar in the clinic that I am then, or when my sister had the operation [prophylactic removal of the breast] ... especially if I go to the check-ups ... you are worried, afraid.

Recalling social situations seems to (re-)connect Ursula to her fear of cancer, and she seems to be moving in and out of illness. Should that lack of constant awareness be understood as "repression"? In other words: how real is her "health" in between such episodes?

The explicit fuzziness of health-related self-definitions in these examples can be read both as a symptom and a characteristic of contemporary uncertainty about health and disease, with the infiltration of a broadened understanding of disease into the space of health (Bogner 2005; Wehling & Viehöver 2011). In this situation, the person who is labelled as being at risk needs to reduce the complexity of her health identity and develop a self-definition in this overlapping spectrum of health and illness before she is able to decide on practical consequences. The quotations indicate that this complex situation is dealt with in a flexible and contextualized way on the basis of a personal evaluative process.

The question I should like to pose is therefore: how can this be conceptualized? Or rather: what conceptual approaches to health exist, and are they able to capture this phenomenon?

THE EXPLANATORY CAPACITY OF DIFFERENT THEORIES OF HEALTH

In this section I discuss different theories of health, namely, the biostatistical theory, the holistic theory and a definition by public health scientist Klaus Hurrelmann who develops the concept of salutogenesis.

The biostatistical theory of health

According to the biostatistical definition (Boorse 1977), perfect health is the complete absence of disease (as statistically defined). Disease itself is understood as "the inability to perform all typical physiological functions with at least typical efficiency" (Boorse 1977: 542).

The crucial problem with BRCA-positive women is that, looking at the actual state of health, no one in the sample is diseased according to the biostatistical theory of health (BST), as the physiological functionality of the DNA repair mechanism that the BRCA gene product is contributing to is maintained because of the gene products of the remaining allele. Even the outcomes of psychological surveys done after BRCA testing return to "normal" results about one year post testing. But it nonetheless seems that most of the women feel ill at least sometimes. This illness is a personal experience that the BST does not even consider because it keeps to symptomatic diseases. So if one takes this experience of illness seriously, it can be concluded that the health spectrum is more diverse and unstable than the BST is capable of covering. Its lack of flexibility becomes obvious if you consider the future. Here, statistics point out a risk of a decrease in physical efficiency. The BST allows only two options, and so those at risk must be thought of as either healthy or diseased. One would probably hesitate to regard all those at increased risk of developing disorders to be as healthy. But thinking of risk as a "disease" is also untenable; then everybody is "diseased" because everybody is at risk, but this is not true. As there is no such thing as a "perfect genome" and most people possess quite a few dispositions for disease, a variety of future diseases can be anticipated. But not every disposition will lead to disease; the possibility of disease will not always be actualized. Hence a functional limitation referred to as a risk is not the same as a certainly emergent disease and the person in question will not inevitably be actually diseased. Concerning the future, an either–or perspective does not seem to be suitable. The phenomenon of diffuse health identities cannot, therefore, be adequately described by the BST.

The holistic theory of health

The holistic definition of health (HTH) states: "A person P is completely healthy if, and only if, P is in a bodily and mental state such that he has the ability to realise all his vital goals given his standard environment" (Nordenfelt 1991: 18) with disease being something that at least "tends to reduce" (Nordenfelt 2010) the health of P.

The suitability of this definition to the BRCA-positive women case is at the very least questionable. First of all, different parts of the women's standard environment (time, culture, setting) seem to accentuate different self-evaluations. This does not seem to be allowed for in the HTH where the standard environment seems to be understood as fixed. At that point a lack of flexibility and diversity in incorporating these environmental differences into the definitional space of the HTH becomes apparent.

Second, it is uncertain how a changing health definition is represented by the flexibility of the vital goals concept as the major indicator of health. Are goals understood as compromised in episodes of felt ill-health? Do they "return to normal" and therefore lead to "health" after such episodes? Or are they generally compromised by the BRCA diagnosis, which would mean that the women are always and irreversibly affected? The women do in all cases have to face a high probability of being declared ill because of a (time-limited) problem in realizing vital goals (the term "declaration" is appropriate here because of the evaluative perspective of the HTH). As the HTH contains a third-person perspective, it is not the woman herself who decides, but someone else who evaluates the possibility of goal realization. This stands in tension with the experiences voiced in the quotations given above, where the women themselves (try to) label their health status. Moreover, the question arises as to how goal-defined health is related to the defect-defined health in a clinical situation and maybe becomes influenced by the latter.

Third, if the tendency to reduce health is considered, it seems that this is a definite reason for describing these women as ill, which, again, does not capture the experiences described by the women. In any case, we can note that on the HTH account the actual experiences of ill-health and well-being are omitted and will always be hard to comprehend from a third-person perspective. Moreover, an appreciation of the flexibility and context-relatedness expressed in the quotations is missing.

Salutogenesis

In this approach health is understood as balancing constantly changing stimuli that may lead to a movement towards health or illness, which are understood as forming a continuum. The situation is evaluated by the "sense of coherence", a feeling of confidence derived from personal beliefs of the comprehensibility, manageability and meaningfulness of situations. These beliefs support coping with new challenges and are based on generalized resistance resources such as intelligence, body features and even social support or cultural stability (Antonovsky 1987). This concept is popular in parts of German public health and has been elaborated by Hurrelmann into a definition linked with the WHO definition, which thus focuses on every aspect that may influence personal health:

> Health indicates the state of the objective and subjective condition of a person which is given if this person's physical, psychological and social development is in accord with possibilities and aims, as well as the given external living conditions. Health is affected if demands occur in one or several of these fields, which cannot be fulfilled by the person at the particular stage of his lifecycle.
> (Hurrelmann 2000: 8, my translation)

Two objections and an additional question arise. In the definition, demands that need to be fulfilled are mentioned. This points to a latent understanding of health as performance and affected health as failure. This is a normative notion that places pressure on the BRCA-positive women because they are told they should be "in charge" of their genes, which are generally defined as a potential, in this case a potential that reaches from DNA repair to HBOC (Lemke 2004). Additional questions about the nature of the BRCA demand and the women's possibility to fulfil it arise. On the basis of participant observation during genetic counselling sessions, the demand can be summarized as follows: "know your risk and control it so that you are able to remain healthy." Because of a difference between the communicated genetic risk in the counselling session and the inherited danger to their health as how this information is experienced by the woman (Bogner 2005), a conceptual problem occurs. A risk is understood to be calculable and controllable by the individual, whereas danger is experienced as imposed on that person. She will be exposed to this danger and not be able to control it.[3]

Counsellors (who inform about risks) and counsellees (who experience danger) therefore refer to different concepts. This indicates that both groups are affected in different ways and the task of controlling cannot be fulfilled by the counsellees simply because it is no option for someone who is in danger. Because of this referential difference, living with chronic risk means not being able to fulfil all demands, but still finding a way of dealing with the situation. According to Hurrelmann, this means that the women's health is by definition affected; this does not sit well with the quotations.

As with the other theories, the BRCA-positive women's health identities are in danger of being defined and combined with behavioural obligations and the expectations of others in a way that neither matches the women's own identification, nor their way of dealing with the test result. As Schmidt (2010) says, more responsibility for oneself should not be confounded with more self-determination in the field of health promotion and prevention because of the phenomenon of "healthism" (Rose 1999), a generalized personal responsibility for one's own health that is to be fulfilled in a certain, approved way without taking into account personal ideas. Hence the challenge posed to the health theories is a subjective and relational one based on a societal way of defining health in a normative way.

The second objection focuses on the expression *physical, psychological and social development*. This classification of health-relevant or even determining factors leads to a "factor-analytic health concept" regarding the three areas, soma, psyche and society, as fields of development, and promotes a logic of control by promoting the idea that a checklist-style way of dealing with health demands guarantees personal health. The more "Brownie points" you collect on a list which contains everything from "eating more vegetables" to "exercising at least twice a week", the better your health will be and the safer you are from disease. Enhancing different physical, psychological and social factors can be seen as the most prominent action-guiding principle in health promotion and prevention but it does not work for BRCA-positive women, not only because genetic sequences cannot be influenced by that, but also because there is no known correlation between those "lifestyle factors" and the development of cancer in this specific case (Kollek & Lemke 2008).

An additional question is related to external living conditions: is this term flexible enough to cover the constant movement in and out of illness that at least some women experience? Although the term may cover this, it could very easily be misunderstood as a solid aggregate that assigns one, not several, definitions to one health condition.

All definitions seem to have problems capturing the diffuse and changing states of health under the terms of chronic risk and describing how the subjective status definitions in the examples are generated. In this context, flexibility and context-relatedness prove as especially problematic for understanding, description and acceptance of the ever-changing health status of BRCA-positive women. Especially Hurrelmann's "factorized health", which is an example of the leading view in public health, is too focused on the feasibility of good health, not on the evaluative process that seems to be central to one's health identity. All in all, the difficulties discussed here demonstrate the problem of the definitional coverage of different theories of health and are therefore symptomatic of the inability to account for health identities and provide an understanding of the situation of BRCA-positive women as an example of chronic risk.

To conclude this section, none of the discussed theories is able to account for the personal experience of illness in the case of BRCA-positive women who have a genetic condition that is treated as a disease in surveillance medicine.

A PROPOSAL FOR A CONSTRUCTIVIST HEALTH CONCEPT

In this section I develop what I take to be an adequate general definition of health in surveillance medicine. I shall attempt to take into account the challenges that arose from the data on BRCA-positive women and the examination of different health theories. I will aim to:

- refrain from using a central metaphor, term or "content" such as "vital goals" or "physical functionality" as an external marker for the evaluation of health, thereby focusing on the personal experience of the woman in question;
- consider the embeddedness of health in different social, situational contexts and the flexibility that seems to accompany it;
- reject the discourse of feasibility and control in favour of a personal, yet often reactive, discourse of creativity and evaluation.

This approach is based on several theoretical notions.

I understand the identity of a person to be essentially relational: "a person is a person through other persons" (Louw 2001: 15). Identity is intersubjective and emerges as dialogically mediated from mutual exposure in personal encounters of two or more persons in intricate networks of interrelatedness.

The constructivist approach to health that I will sketch has been inspired by feminist and queer theory (Jagose 1996; Wilchins 2004), especially the concept of "doing gender" (Becker-Schmidt & Knapp 2000) and the performative theory of Judith Butler (1990, 1993; cf. Bublitz 2002), as well as the work of Michel Foucault ([1976] 1998, 1990; cf. Lemke 2001). All of these theorists regard (gender) reality as something that is done according to latent structuring and question the implicitness of categories. According to this broad approach, biological, psychological and social factors are understood as culturally (co-)constructed.

These considerations stand in the tradition of social constructivism (Berger & Luckmann 1966) and of medical ethnology, prominent in the 1980s, when Good and Delvicchio-Good (1981) and Kleinman (1988) discussed a meaning-centred model of disease and illness that understood both disease and illness as socially constructed, rather than naturally given, realities.

"Filtered health"

As a consequence of these notions, I propose a definition of "filtered health" as a constructivist approach: "*Health* (in its complex and overlapping reality) *is a context-related label that is interactively realized and re-actualized in performative acts.*"

- The term "label" describes the more or less conscious decision to interpret a certain life situation as a certain health status that is based on an "evaluative filter".
- This "evaluative filter" consists of health characteristics, principles, rules, explanatory models, and so on, in short: interpretational and operational dispositions and competences concerning health that have been learned in different social systems during one's lifetime. The first and most important educational system is the primary social context, often the family. Hence, socialization appears as the basic source of the evaluative filter.
- "Performative acts" include the expressions (utterances, acts, accessories) that represent and (re-)produce identity in the course of continuous re-enactments.
- The term "life situation" is intentionally left vague. This term opens up a space for the influence of all the factors of factorized health, which are not irrelevant but given the experiences of BRCA-positive women, do not seem to be crucial for understanding a person's self-defined health status. This also allows for a decision to change perspective and put evaluation in centre stage. In order to influence one another, information derived from life situations and the evaluative filter must relate to the same interpretational logic, that is, "speak the same language". If someone who for example believes that "cosmic energy" is the only thing that influences their health status is told about the influence of DNA, they will hardly be impressed by this.

Having given a definition of evaluation-based filtered health, I will now describe the process of the formation of a health-related self-definition.

The process of health labelling

Process-related conceptual thoughts
My account of the process of health labelling is based on the *labelling model* (Franke 2006). It was originally postulated to account for psychosomatic and mental illness and has been used since to account for other aberrations of social norms such as "the outsider" or "the criminal" (Mercer 1973; Moncrieffe & Eyben 2007).

According to this model, these aberrational roles are formed by a three-step process:

(a) A certain behaviour is regarded as breaking rules of conduct by the social environment. This is called "primary aberration".
(b) A representative of an expert system (e.g. a medical professional) confirms this evaluation as an aberration and thereby labels the person as abnormal.
(c) The person in question adapts his/her identity to this judgement, which is called "second aberration". As an outcome the person is labelled a patient if medical conditions or roles are negotiated.

This approach has several minor problems. To begin with, this approach contains a disease orientation because it focuses on how aberrations from the norm emerge. This requires that the model is amended and thereby opened up to the broader spectrum of health/illness. Second, the term "behaviour" is under-determined, which is why "behaviour" will be specified as performative acts in my proposal. Third, the term "social environment" seems to be too vague and all-embracing thus obscuring a distinction between different social contexts and their norms. Therefore, I will instead use the term "specific social context" to indicate these distinctions.

In the original model, the person in question has no choice but to adapt to the shared opinion of this social context and the expert. However, labelled people possess relational autonomy and are able to (more or less consciously) decide whether to accept the labelling or not.

Moreover, in the original labelling model there is no option to self-label as the labelling agent is always someone else. To address this I will introduce the Foucauldian concept of governmentality. Governmentality describes a technique of self-regulation by internalized knowledge, which is used to control, guide, identify and judge oneself in the same way as one does with others. In this case, the person uses the same evaluative dispositions and competences to label themselves and others.

Finally, there is no longer a two-step process of social labelling needed to develop a "vulnerable identity"; because of the amount of information available there is often no need for an expert to confirm an "aberration", as the self-labelling and the acknowledging social context are sufficient to achieve this effect. This may be called the "expertization" of lay-people. On the other hand, self-labelling in conjunction with the opinion of an expert may also be understood as sufficient for a change of label independent of everyday social contexts. The latter is often seen in the BRCA context and initiates translational efforts between the clinic and the complex of different social contexts in the women's everyday lives.

The resulting new labelling approach can be depicted as follows:

(a) In a health-related context, a certain already self-labelled personal behaviour consisting of various performative acts is regarded as either conforming to or breaking rules of conduct that are viewed by a specific social context as representations of a certain identity. This is then acted upon by the participants of this context. This is called the "primary environmental health identification".
(b) This identification is an option that can be accepted or not by the individual, which then leads to a "secondary personal health identification" (which can be enhanced in other social contexts, e.g. an expert system).

Every such experience of a health identifying incident leaves "evaluative traces" that constantly build and rebuild the evaluative filter.

Consequences

The construction of health can therefore be understood as an on-going, creative and subjective process. Health identifications will vary with the specific context as well as a person's viable and intelligible abilities, that is, their personally imaginable interpretations and the capability to match them with a certain situation. The process of health identification can thus be called "doing health" in terms of its emphasis on health as the result of an (re-)active productive process. As such, health is a co-production of a socially embedded and situated person with a special biography and the respective context the person is in at a given moment. It is therefore possible that a person may have different "healths" in different contexts. The "doing" in "doing health" is only partly conscious, though. Health may therefore be described as always personal, but never individual.

Health is always personal (or subjective) because a person translates "health information" into meaning by contextualizing it on the basis of her or his special biographical situation, experience and relations, which function as a personal evaluative filter. The person then acts in a "self-determined" manner on that basis. But health is at the same time never individual because this health-related meaning and self-definition is dependent on socially determined contexts, too, so that "self-determination" is always a relational task.

Given not only the phenomenon of chronic risk but also that of health promotion or enhancement, the underlying paradigm of an exploitable potential and its ensuing compulsory responsibility becomes obvious. As the starting point for this improvement needs to be known before the potential can be exploited, Leriche's famous verdict of the "silence of the organs"[4] is obsolete because the organs are forced to tell in order to get started. Two practices that are required to fulfil a personalized health task become apparent: outing and passing. "Outing" describes the process of creating awareness of the existing health-related body (in) relation, its renegotiation in the light of "new information" and holding that view in public and private contexts. "Passing" describes a performative practice in situations with possible discrimination. The practice contains the conscious or unconscious choice of characteristics of the dominant (health) identity that are visibly displayed and publicly confirmed. This includes the fear of outing as not fully fitting and the possibility of failure. Passing is directed at the assumption of status or normality (Walker 2001).

Although the outing process brings out the once silent organs into consciousness, constructing health or disease is a task that includes work on multiple levels so that this silent "nothing" becomes a perceptible and action-guiding "something". Taking into account the nature of that construction, health resembles Butler's idea of gender including the notion that health is a copy without an original. Even Butler's "tripartite" notion of gender in her heterosexual matrix seems to some extent applicable. For Butler, gender is a conglomerate of sex, gender and desire; in a similar manner, health can be viewed as a socially constructed complex of body, patient status (healthy non-patient, at-risk unpatient, patient) and the good life. The body appears as a material that becomes meaningful by labelling. This labelling is realized performatively in the context of the role of the (non-, un-) patient, which includes a certain identity-based status and societal expectations. This is linked to an unquestionable desire for the good life, the promise related to health that is societally fixed and morally charged. In the interaction of those three levels, the identity of a healthy, ill, vulnerable, handicapped, and so on person is built. This identity is relatively flexible because of the flexibility of bodily labels and practices when compared with the gender category. Health identity is therefore a flowing identity. Like the gendered body, the healthy body is "called to life" (Bublitz 2002: 56, my translation) in a performative and discursive way.

CONCLUSION: ADVANTAGES OF THE CONSTRUCTIVIST APPROACH

Like any other theory of health, this constructivist approach needs to demonstrate its usefulness.

First of all, a change of perspective is suggested that highlights construction and creativity instead of objective data and a checklist approach to health. This may reduce the pressure of the normative assumption that only good health is the right health or that health can only be good if it is medically defined as such, and the resulting task of optimizing health. This perspective also aims to understand a person's own health-related logic, which may aid the understanding of the self-labelled health identity of the person and its flexibility. An increased understanding may then support positive resource orientation and a focus on competences instead of deficiencies, and therefore emphasize personal competence instead of incompetence. This attitude brings along a change of hierarchy: experts no longer meet lay-people; now medical and everyday experts exchange views and create a common reality in which they can act together. Last but not least, such an encounter includes the notion of relational autonomy, in which medical experts as well as other persons from different social contexts are seen as active parts of the health construction. This may then lead to a more complex overall picture of what "personal health" means for a certain person.

NOTES

1. In surveillance medicine, attention is paid to multiple interlinked risk factors in everyday life, society and lifestyle. Thereby medicine gains influence in non-medical fields. Diseases are no longer regarded as single events but as links in a chain of ill-health, with each link increasing the risk for a new disease.
2. The following quotations are derived from interviews that have been carried out in the course of my dissertation project.
3. Evidence for this is the fact that BRCA-positive women often experience affected health and a loss of control in situations that are meant to enable control and guarantee health. For example, medical screenings may be experienced as extremely challenging to a woman's health identity because of their potential to remind the BRCA-positive woman of her disposition and actualize the state of uncertainty, not just because of their diagnostic potential.
4. According to Labisch (2002), the quotation can be ascribed to Renè Leriche and was first cited by George Canguilhem ([1966] 1989) before other authors such as Gadamer ([1993] 1996) discussed it.

12. BEAUTY AND HEALTH AS MEDICAL NORMS: THE CASE OF NAZI MEDICINE

Sophia Efstathiou

THE QUESTION

This chapter deals with the entanglement of health and beauty. I discuss how concepts and states of "health" are entwined with concepts and states of "beauty", and in particular what problems this creates for medical practice.

My analysis is grounded in a historical case study: Nazi medicine (Efstathiou 2012). I argue that Nazi medicine conflated notions of health with notions of beauty and pursued aesthetic standards using medical means. The political exception of Jews, among other civilian populations, was a means to realizing the vision of a "healthy German race", where "health" was understood within a particular aesthetic ideological frame as equated to "purity" and "beauty".

Nazi medicine may seem too extreme to be an example of anything but horror, but it exemplifies the consequences of conflating health and beauty, a common and indeed live issue, as well as several broader philosophical issues.

Our notions of health and beauty overlap; the ambiguity can prove profitable for some and injurious to others. Consider the covers of magazines devoted to "healthy living": such publications present models of "health" that are rarely unattractive, seemingly implying that securing health is tantamount to a particular beautiful look. The popular media are not the only ones to identify health and beauty. Various conditions are classed as medical disorders purely for cosmetic reasons: for example, birthmarks, hair loss or common psoriasis. Conversely, descriptors of "health" often equivocate between saying that an organism is beautiful and healthy; for example, when we talk about an animal's "glossy coat" or "bright eyes".

Disabled bodies have only very recently been considered appropriate objects for art,[1] and disabled people have only recently been able to compete in sporting events[2] (the quintessential showcase of the "healthy" human). Using available associations between our notions of beauty and health, while reinforcing them, public health campaigns deploy images of "ugly" diseases to avert people from unhealthy behaviours, and pretty colours to promote "healthy" behaviours.

Further general lessons follow from the example of Nazi medicine. First, cultural aesthetic norms can impact science policy (in this case health care policy) and influence our account of "health". Nazi "eugenics" relied on concept(s) of the "*eu*" (Greek, meaning "good") as well as the ideas of "genus", or race. Important aesthetic (and so traditionally speaking "non-rational") standards lay at the heart of Nazi ideology, yet their realization was pursued via rational argument and bioscientific means as well as public health campaigns.

More broadly, biomedical concepts can be powerful political tools. The exercise of power on "bare life", that is, on the bodies and the lifecycle of particular individuals, or what Foucault ([1976] 1998) called "biopower", is likely to recruit biological and medical scientific ideas for its purposes, giving rise to various biopolitical paradigms. Nazi "culture of action" supplemented with notions in holistic biological theory served as a vehicle for Nazi totalitarian ideology.

Finally, the Nazi conflation of vital norms of physical health with aesthetic norms reverberates with attitudes relevant to (if not prevalent in) contemporary biopolitics. Even when the level at which health is defined is the individual as opposed to the "race", it seems that the duty to be healthy is still respected and enforceable, and still managed by cultural aesthetic means.[3]

NAZI CULTURE OF ACTION AND NAZI CULTURE IN ACTION

The 1991 film *The Architecture of Doom*, directed and researched by Peter Cohen, highlights the ties between National Socialism and the arts (Cohen 1991). As Cohen notes, almost half of the Nazi government were professional or aspiring artists. The stunning images captured in the films of Lenny Riefenstahl were partly her creation but partly that of a broader Nazi aesthetic vision. Propaganda minister Joseph Goebbels was a novelist and poet; Alfred Rosenberg, founder of the first Nazi Society for Culture, was a painter and novelist; and Adolph Hitler failed his entrance exams to study architecture in Vienna. Despite this setback in his career as an architect, Hitler's artistic inclinations did find expression in the "staging" of the drama that was Nazism.

Culture can have a dual role within collective actions: that of a product and that of a producer. That is, culture can be produced by social collective action and used to fashion collective action. Sociologist Maren Klawiter (1999) has introduced the notion of a "culture *of action*" to describe how "systems of *embodied* meaning" emerge from activist demonstrations (Klawiter 1999: 106, emphasis added). A culture of action is produced as *embodied* through *bodies* that are painted, marching, dancing, tied up or dressed in pink as part of parades, interventions or other actions. Ann Swidler (1986), on the other hand, argues that culture can function as "a 'tool kit' of symbols, stories, rituals, and world-views, which people may use in varying configurations to solve different kinds of problems" (Swidler 1986: 273). She introduces the notion of "culture *in action*" to describe culture used to *shape* social action repertoires and strategies, for instance in deciding how to design and perform a demonstration (Swidler 1986).

National Socialism presents us with an arguably distinctive culture of action. This is what makes parodies of Nazi actions so recognizable: the trademarked salute, the walk, look and music. As the Nazi movement was organized according to the "*Führerprinzip*", the recognition of one *Führer* (leader) as guiding party members and officials, Nazi collective action was fashioned following the Führer's aesthetic fixations. According to Cohen (1991), National Socialist public actions were distal outcomes of Hitler's culture in action.

Hitler points to the first time he saw the performance of Wagner's opera *Rienzi* as the hour when "it all began" (Cohen 1991). This opera tells the tale of Rienzi, a popular Roman leader, who leads the Romans to reunite and reinstate the Roman Empire but who, due to a malicious conspiracy, suffers a tragic yet glorious death before the wrecks of ancient Rome. The figure of the heroic popular leader, the historical setting in antiquity and Wagner's nationalism and anti-Semitism inspired Hitler and were partly reflected in the culture of Nazi action.

Hitler designed the party standard himself in 1923, to closely resemble ancient Roman standards, and he borrowed the symbol of the swastika from ancient Minoan art (Cohen 1991). Images of National Socialist mass rallies depict precise arrangements of disciplined, masculine bodies in synchronic motion, taking their positions around the Führer. Their faces are shaved, their hair cut, their uniforms clean; only the bent cross set against red hints at their impassioned purpose. These episodes of collective action feature Hitler as director and leading actor. The "body" of the "new" German *Volk*, clean, disciplined and masculine, orients itself in attention to its Führer.

The monumental scale of these actions, the emblazoning of ancient symbols on young bodies and the centring of it all around the Führer publicly produced and performed the culture of National Socialism: the nostalgia for the *ancient* and *pure*, the reverence for the *masculine* and *monumental*, and the vision of a united German *Volk* marching as one towards the realization of its purpose. Themes we see reflected in Germanic thought from Goethe and Nietzsche to Heidegger are here realized with a particular aim in mind. If this is an attempt at a complete aesthetic experience, following Wagner's operas, Hitler will go beyond the "total artwork" to produce a tragedy that will play out in world history.[4]

Yet Nazi actions could say more than their intended message. The "body" of the German *Volk* is staged and inherently unnatural. The uniformity in the motions and appearance of Nazi soldiers is a mere artefact of scale. Lock step cannot stifle the thoughts of these men, nor the private rumblings of their organs. The insincerity that comes with the pre-production of demonstrations of this scale mocks the oneness of their presumed purpose. (Admittedly, the effects of a "culture of action" seem to be dynamic, varying with the sensibilities of the action's audience: to us footage of Nazi social action may seem sinister, although to contemporary audiences it arguably did not.)

The aesthetic standards of Nazi culture were performed in more ways than one. First, art itself was made to conform to Nazi standards of beauty. Museum collections were actively purged of avant-garde pieces, which, supposedly, bore the marks of a cultural Bolshevism instigated by the Jews. Modernism was rejected, as well as experimental techniques such as impressionism, expressionism and some realism. Cohen's film contains footage from public exhibitions of so-called "degenerate" art, which took place in major German cities. Echoing Agamben's ([1966] 1998, 2003) discussion of political camps, one may say that these exhibitions functioned as *art* camps; that is, as spaces of *cultural* exception where "unfit" art was crammed, hung over doors and next to windows and left as the designated fodder of public disgust.

In juxtaposition to "degenerate" modern art, the annual Great German Art Exhibition (*Grosse Deutsche Kunstausstellung*), which was inaugurated in 1937, presented art pieces that captured the aesthetic of Nazism. The great museum halls holding pieces from the Bismarck era, alpine landscapes and images of strong German bodies at work, constituted Nazi culture in action. Sculpture was to become the national art form. Using the preferred art medium of the ancient Greeks and Romans, Nazi sculptors like Thorak and Brecker carved rock into muscular male bodies, erecting the vision of the new German man. Corresponding visions of the ideal woman pictured her as hard-working, fertile and strong, bearing Aryan features and mothering the next generation of Germans (Cohen 1991).

Perhaps this distinctive style was, though polemically asserted, a matter of taste that had no real import in the politics of Nazism? Hitler's opening speech for the Great German Art Exhibit of 1939 testifies otherwise. In celebration of the acquisition of the ancient Greek statue of the discus thrower by Menon, Hitler urges his audience:

Let us perceive how splendid Man's *physical beauty* once was and how we may only speak of *progress* when we have not only achieved such beauty, but even surpassed it. May we find here a *measure* of the tasks which confront us in our time! May we strive as one for *beauty and elevation* such that both our *race* and our *art* will withstand the judgement of the millennia.
(Quoted in Cohen 1991, emphasis added)

Hitler's words are stunning to modern ears. Could the achievement of physical beauty be this politician's idea of progress? Is the beautification of the German race and German art the way to make history? Surely, the achievement of "physical beauty" cannot be a political end.

It is crucial to grasp that the standards of beauty that Nazi culture produced and imposed were taken to capture the real essence of racial health. *Cultural* aesthetic standards were assumed to actually reflect *vital*, biological essences. The selected art of ancient Greece and Rome was thought to document the reality of a once pure and uncorrupted healthy Aryan race. As Hitler exclaimed, "Our first principle of beauty is health!" (Cohen 1991).

A stark example of this practice of conceptual conflation is found in a slide show created by the Nazi art theoretician Paul Schultze Naumburg (Cohen 1991; also see Barron 1991). In January 1931, Schultze Naumburg toured Germany with what he claimed was a demonstration that modern art showed signs of mental illness. The slide show consisted of modern art portraits placed alongside photos of mentally ill or physically disfigured patients. The similarities between the paired images were supposed evidence of a link between "physical degeneration and artistic perversion" (Cohen 1991).

Nazi art had to be rid of the so-called Jewish, Bolshevist degeneracy in its midst, and this was done by excluding modern art pieces from public spaces of art appreciation, by exhibiting them in "art camps" and eventually by destroying such pieces. In the words of Schultze Naumberg: "In the world of German art, a struggle *to the death* rages not unlike the struggle in politics and it must be fought with the same gravity and singleness of mind" (recorded in Cohen 1991, emphasis added). This example of Nazi aesthetics in action, the rhetoric and practice of "art hygiene", mirrors the racial purges that were to occur once the Nazis seized power.

At this point it is worth contemplating, along with Elaine Scarry (1999), the power that beauty exerts over us. Scarry observes that our attraction to beauty carries with it a conviction, similar to often visceral reactions to moral truth. The fairness of a face and the fairness of a situation are often similarly compelling – though possibly subjective.

The Beauty Myth by Naomi Wolf claims that modern society believes in a "myth": that there is such a thing as beauty, and that women must want to be beautiful and men must want to possess beautiful women (Wolf 1991: 12). Wolf says that this myth has been definitive of feminine culture and pursued as a surrogate to religious doctrine to exert excess financial and psychological oppression on modern women and prevent them from challenging male dominance. Nancy Etcoff (2000) disagrees with this; in *Survival of the Prettiest* she argues that humans' pursuit of beauty has evolved to favour the reproductive success of our species, not to oppress women. So, for example, humans tend to find strange-looking and very needy human babies "cute" so that we care and protect them; and we find human characteristics that associate with reproductive ability attractive so that we are likely to have offspring when we have sex.

It is possible that both views have some truth to them. Edouard Machery and Luc Faucher (2005) argue that racism may ride on evolved tendencies to recognize "ethnies": groups or tribes of humans of different origin than one's own. So, although racism is socially constructed, it latches onto existing and compelling tendencies humans have with respect to sorting through human diversity. Similarly, there may be social, economic and cultural reasons why we adhere to beauty myths, but some myths may be more compelling than others because they piggyback on pre-existent tendencies. Currently oppressive ideologies of beauty could bank on our tendency to pick out "beauty" traits that were once evolutionarily advantageous to our species.

Irrespective of the reasons why we are compelled by beauty, the legitimization of aesthetic/ideological standards through biomedical means can lead to questionable biopolitics. If for whatever reasons we tend to think that beauty is healthy and fair, we need to be cautious about the slippery slope we may be standing on. Nazi propaganda consistently blurred the line between "the beautiful" and "the healthy", and presented visions of health and beauty as "just" political ends. It was in this way that the achievement of physical beauty was legitimized as an end in itself and Nazi biopolitics became a biopolitics of culture.

At the same time, one cannot but wonder about the *biological* conceptions of health and race that legitimized art objects as representations of healthy Aryan-raced bodies. How could Hitler point to the statue of the discus thrower and assume that the physical beauty of the athlete was due to his racial purity, rather than long hours spent in discus practice?

Nazi culture's aesthetic norms were articulated within the life sciences and Nazi medical practice, specifically within the paradigms of racial hygiene and biological holism.

NAZI BIOMEDICINE: RACIAL HYGIENE

> National Socialism is politically applied biology.
> (Hans Schemm, Founder and Head of the
> National Socialist Teachers Association)

One could identify two biological theories that functioned as what Mehrtens calls "vehicles of transport" of Nazi ideology (Harrington 1996: 193): eugenic theories of "racial hygiene" and holism. According to historian Robert Proctor (1988), one can trace the intellectual origins of Nazi racial hygiene to the theory of Social Darwinism developed in the late nineteenth century.

Social Darwinists took the theory of natural selection introduced by Darwin in *On the Origin of Species* (1859) to apply within human societies. In 1895, in what has come to be considered the founding document of racial hygiene, or eugenics, Alfred Ploetz warned of the degeneration of the German race. Providing medical care to the "weak" was "counterselecting" the "unfit" elements in the race and was thus causing the weak to multiply at faster rates than the talented and the gifted (Proctor 1988: 15). Other mechanisms of counterselection included war and revolution, which resulted in the death or injury of the young and able-bodied, while the provision of welfare to the misfits and the poor further impoverished the genetic stock of the race.

What was the solution? Racial hygiene (*Rassenhygiene*), a term coined by Ploetz, put forth the health of the race as more important than that of the individual. It was suggested that "intelligent racial hygiene might eliminate the need for a struggle for existence altogether" (cited in Proctor 1988: 15). The program of racial hygiene was sympathetic to socialism but objected to the procreation of the "weak". Unlike Malthusians, racial hygienists did not propose birth control for all members of a population but suggested that we promote the procreation of the "fit" while refraining from "counterselecting" the "unfit".

At the heart of racial hygiene was Social Darwinists' assumption that societies function like natural environments and that social forces act like natural forces in the formation of the objective categories of "fit" and "unfit" individuals. The fact that an individual was "weak" (e.g. an alcoholic or a criminal) reflected a biologically real trait that *would* be eliminated by natural selection and hence *should* be eliminated by social selection – or at least should not be privileged by social protectionism. Genes were supposed to differ at the level of individuals, races and race mixtures, and genetic traits were considered fixed and inherited rather than learnt or environmentally influenced.

Particular political programmes have been associated with what are commonly distinguished as "Darwinist" and "Lamarckian" theories of selection.[5] Popular readings saw Darwinism as moving genetic potential away from the realm of the social and into the realm of the private: the natural and social environment could not shape an organism's genetic traits and fitness in some direct or intentional way. Rather, chance genetic mutations caused traits to be expressed that then could prove to be advantageous or injurious, given the environment; but social or environmental solutions to inherited problems were only temporary. Organisms were *born* fit or unfit, as a matter of chance, and did not all start off on the same footing in their struggle for survival. Lamarckianism was on the other hand understood to emphasize the importance of environmental factors for evolution: organisms could and did respond and adapt to the parameters of their environments and those adaptations could be passed down and persist across generations. Exporting these notions into human societies made Darwinism sympathetic to more liberal politics that assumed inequalities were unavoidable and natural, whereas Lamarckianism was associated with a socialist emphasis on supplying all with adequate environmental support to ensure theirs and their offspring's prosperity.

Especially influential in the nineteenth century was the thinking of Joseph-Arthur Comte de Gobineau, a French aristocrat who worked as secretary of Alexis de Toqueville in 1849. De Gobineau's race theory advanced the thesis that the "Aryan" race, the Germanic people, were the peak of civilization. He was read by Nietzsche, Wagner, and later Chamberlain and Hitler, and his theory of racial mixing confused biological concepts like "blood" with political ones like "nation".

De Gobineau argued that during the growth of a group of people from a "tribe" to a "civilization" racial mixtures were inevitable. Indeed, according to de Gobineau, it was the more advanced tribe that could overcome a natural "law of repulsion" towards crossing blood with other tribes and be instead compelled by a "law of attraction", which embodied the need (and rational decision) to join resources with other neighbouring tribes in order to expand and sustain power.

> Thus mankind lives in obedience to two laws, one of repulsion, the other of attraction; these act with different force on different peoples. The first is fully respected only by those races which can never raise themselves above the elementary completeness of the tribal life, while the power of the second, on the contrary, is the more absolute, as the racial units on which it is exercised are more capable of development.
> (De Gobineau [1853–55] 2000: 49, emphasis added)

The flipside of expansion, however, was degeneration. What enabled civilization was also its downfall, according to de Gobineau. The mixing of people enabled a nation to rule, be structured and organized and function over a larger territory. But it implied that the numbers of leaders would become increasingly smaller and the nature of leaders increasingly tolerant. The mixing of people would cause the stock of the leading race to degenerate, become broken up and polluted with the weaker race's stock, and the characteristics that had initially enabled their rule disappear. De Gobineau's advice for sustained rule was purity: conquer but do not mix.

> The word *degenerate*, when applied to a people, means (as it ought to mean) that the people has no longer the same intrinsic value as it had before, because it has no longer the same blood in its veins, continual adulterations having gradually affected the quality of that blood. In other words, though the nation bears the name given by its founders, the name no longer connotes the same race; in fact, the man of a decadent time, the *degenerate* man properly so called, is a different being, from the racial point of view, from the heroes of the great ages.
> (De Gobineau [1853–55] 2000: 45, emphasis added)

In 1905, Alfred Ploetz, together with psychiatrist Ernst Rudin, lawyer Anastasius Nordenholz and anthropologist Richard Thurnwald, founded the Society for Racial Hygiene to further promote the racial hygiene of the human race. It must be noted that the aim of this programme was not stated in racist terms. Racial hygiene, or eugenics, aimed to improve the human race *in general* – or at least all Western *Kulturrassen*. In 1895 Ploetz called anti-Semitism a "useless ploy", maintained that there are no pure races and that racial mixing between races that were not "too far apart" was a mechanism that would increase fitness (quoted in Proctor 1988: 21). One of the first members of the society for racial hygiene, Wilhelm Schallmeyer, explicitly distinguished between what he called Nordic superiority "race propaganda" and the value-free, objective goals of racial science (Proctor 1988: 21).

However, as Proctor remarks, the line separating the Nordic movement and racial hygiene became increasingly blurred. In the early 1920s the Society for Racial Hygiene contained a Nordic division organized by Ploetz. It now denounced anti-Semitism on the basis that Jews were not "really" Semitic anymore: racial intermarriage meant that Jews were mostly Aryan by now; a different proposition altogether. Already in 1907, Ploetz, Fritz Lenz and F. Wollny had established a secret Nordic Ring, which cultivated German racial character through training and sports, and popularized de Gobineau's vision of "the German Volk, last bastion of the Nordic race" (Proctor 1988: 25).

In the 1920s racial hygiene became identified with the Nordic movement. Ploetz was appointed honorary professor of racial hygiene in Munich and won the Goethe Medallion in 1936. He was also awarded the Nobel Peace Prize in 1936 for his pacifist ideas: Ploetz claimed that war was bad for the race as it interfered with the selection of the fittest. Hitler himself agreed. He maintained that the Nazis were "profoundly and philosophically committed to peace" (quoted in Proctor 1988: 29). In 1937 Ploetz joined the Nazi party.

Racial hygiene provided National Socialism with the conceptual tools it needed to articulate the urgency and importance of ridding the German "germ plasm" of degenerate elements. Racial hygiene legitimated the aims of the genetic doctor to improve the health of the whole race at the cost of individuals' health. The need for a new kind of doctor to take care of the race presupposed that the health of a race was of a different quality than individual health. It was not a simple sum of individual "healths" that determined the health of a race but rather something *about* the individuals, their "blood" or genetic heritage, that added to the health of the race. Whether or not an individual's "blood" was that of a sovereign race made no difference to his or her health, yet a race of people with degenerate blood was deemed unhealthy, and soon to see the end of its strength, whether political, economic or cultural. A trait that was not correlated with health on an individual level emerged as a critical measure of health on the level of the race.

Schultze Naumberg's slide show and the Nazis' ways of purging art from "Jewish Bolshevist degeneracy" foreshadowed the fate of the mentally ill and physically deformed patients, as well as that of communists and Jews. The perverse elements that Nazi racial hygiene focused on ridding the German race of included so-called mental and sexual degenerates, as well as Jews. The method adopted was "racial" exclusion by means of controlled reproduction and eventually extermination.

Nazi policy on racial hygiene progressed from the sterilization of supposed "homozygous" carriers of genetic diseases (Sterilization Law – 14 July 1933) and the Nuremberg Laws of 1935 preventing so-called "inter-racial" marriage between Jews and non-Jews, to the extermination of mentally ill patients starting in August 1939 (Operation T4), two weeks before the Polish invasion, and the "Final Solution" to exterminate all Jews at the start of 1941 (Operation 14 f 13 to destroy all concentration camp inmates not willing or able to work; Proctor 1988).

At the same time as exterminating the unfit, German social medicine made some truly progressive steps towards benefitting the fit. Nazi propaganda movies stressed the importance of diet for health, promoting the consumption of wholegrain bread and "natural" foods, speaking against additives and preservatives, and even making connections between diet and cancer. (Hitler himself was a vegetarian and abstained from alcohol, as did many Nazi officials.) The Nazis launched the first anti-tobacco campaigns, and a Nazi researcher was the first to publish statistical results linking smoking to lung cancer and to mouth and lip cancer (Proctor 1999: esp. 183–6). Nazi scientists were the first to talk of environmental health hazards and link asbestos to carcinogenesis, and they were progressive in protecting the health of mothers and the foetus, speaking against smoking and drinking during pregnancy.

NAZI BIOMEDICINE: GERMAN HOLISM

The theoretical framework that enabled Nazi rhetoric about the collective body of the German *Volk* and suggested both a return to nature and the importance of environmental health hazards was *holism*. "Holistic" science had a long history in Germany emerging in opposition to what was thought to be the "mechanistic" (and British) science of Newton.

Anne Harrington (1996) traces holistic thinking back to the early nineteenth century, to the *Naturphilosophie* of scientists and philosophers influenced by the Romantic impulse of their times. These thinkers felt that Newton:

> had been born into a universe of color, quality, and spontaneity and had proceeded ruthlessly to transform it into a cold, quality-less and impersonal realm of homogeneous and three-dimensional space, where particles of matter danced like marionettes to mathematically calculable laws. (Harrington 1996: 4)

Instead of this atomized and fragmented view of nature, natural philosophers like Fichte, Hegel, Schiller and Schelling argued for a sense of wholeness and synthesis in the realms of mind and nature. These neo-Kantian philosophers found a great resource in Kant's argument in the *Critique of Judgment* (Kant [1790] 2000) that although our innate categories of reasoning of mechanistic causality were sufficient to explain and analyse non-living reality, for the purposes of explaining living phenomena an extra principle of teleological causality had to be introduced: the principle of a "natural purpose" (*Naturzweck*). This principle was meant to capture the sense of "purposiveness" that organismic processes seemed to possess for the organism as a whole.

More suggestive for our study of how notions of health and beauty are related is a parallel that Kant drew between "teleological judgement" and what he called "aesthetic judgement." Kant suggested that similar forms of reasoning were involved in understanding the nature of *living phenomena* as were involved in grasping the nature of the *beautiful* or *sublime* (Kant [1790] 2000). In a move implicitly endorsing this Kantian thesis, the Nazis used a propaganda of aesthetics – rallies, films and exhibitions of beautiful bodies juxtaposed with degenerate ones – to argue about the organization of human life.

The Nazi spectacle aimed to recruit German aesthetic judgement on the side of Nazi rhetoric regarding the phenomenon of the (living) German race. The beauty inherent in the biological purity of the German race was first sensed – *seen* in paintings, *heard* in operas, *tasted* in wholewheat bread, *felt* to be the case – and thus presented as a goal: an ideal that could be sought by means of racial purification. Nazi rhetoric found a vehicle in both a long tradition of German philosophical thought and in German cultural life.

One of the intellectuals most revered by the Nazis was Johann Wolfgang von Goethe, who found in Kant an inspiration for his aesthetic–teleological vision of living nature. Observing and comparing different plants and processes of growth or metamorphosis in nature, Goethe concluded that the apparent chaos in the multiplicity of natural forms could in fact be classed under fewer fundamental forms or *Gestalten*. Much as Platonic forms could be accessed by our intuition, one could deduce the fundamental *Gestalten* from their observed expressions by using the pure judgement of mind to classify and abstract from one's observations. In Goethe's words:

> In every living being, we find that those things which we call parts are inseparable from the Whole to such an extent, that they can only be conceived in and with the latter; *and the parts can neither be the measure of the Whole, nor the Whole be the measure of the parts.* So [in turn] a circumscribed living being [an organismic Whole] takes part in the Infinite [the all-encompassing Whole]; it has something of infinity within itself.
>
> (Quoted in Harrington 1996: 5)

Compare this with the words of Karl Zimmerman, who would later be appointed Reich representative for racial education, soon after the Nazi seizure of power in 1933:

> All in all, the National Socialistic conception of state and culture is that of an organic whole. As an organic whole, the volkisch state is *more than the sum of its parts*, and indeed because these parts, called individuals, are fitted together to make a higher unity, within which they in turn become capable of a higher level

of life achievement, while also enjoying an enhanced sense of security. The individual is bound to this *sort of freedom* through the fulfillment of his duty in the service of the whole.
(Quoted in Harrington 1996: 176, emphasis added)

The new holistic way of approaching biology did not apply one theory uniformly across cases, but rather emerged in opposition to mechanistic or atomistic thinking; holism included a family of different biological theories. What holistic approaches had in common was "[T]he need to do justice to organismic purposiveness or teleological functioning – to questions of 'what for?' and not merely 'how?'" (Harrington 1996: xvii).

Among the different kinds of holism, some were concerned with finding ways to describe organismic processes in terms of their role for the whole organism, some were concerned with an integrated theory of the function of the mind and body of humans (the inception of modern psychosomatics) and some attempted to make sense of individual organisms as part of a greater whole, whether on the level of their immediate environment or the general evolutionary process. Another kind of holism was what Harrington calls "clinical holism", which attempted to integrate naturopathic and traditional forms of medicine with modern biomedical medicine.[6]

Holism helped legitimize the hierarchical, centralized organization of the Nazi party. Metaphors like the one cited above by Zimmerman, describing the body of the German *Volk* being led by its "brain", the Führer, suggested Nazism was a natural form of governance. Just as organisms functioned according to their *Naturzweck*, organizing their processes to realize their natural purpose, so should the German people organize according to the *Führerprinzip* to realize their higher purpose.

This usurpation of the power of biological talk by a political ideology makes one wonder: are there special aspects of biological concepts that enable such abuse? The life sciences do seem to concern and address humans in a more direct way than, say, physics. Bioscientific language has available to it a vocabulary of body, of feeling, of function that addresses us at a most intuitive, primary level. Thus analogies between humans and biological organisms or life processes could be compelling on a more basic level than comparisons with mechanical or information systems (even if living systems are sometimes understood in terms of mechanical ones).

In particular, medical science is value-based and action-inducing. It discusses the health and disease of organisms distinguishing the "bad" from the "good". Discussions of illness from a philosophical perspective may seek to understand its nature and the extent and significance of the conditions that result from it (Carel 2008). But if we are to think about ordinary responses, what is qualified as healthy or unhealthy comes with *value* and suggests an *action* – it is something to be pursued or avoided. Clinical medicine explores different *methods* to achieve health corresponding to different conceptions of a disease.

If we follow Georges Canguilhem ([1966] 1989), the history of medicine contains two kinds of conceptions of disease: *ontological* conceptions of disease that see disease as caused by a foreign agent, a "germ" that invades the body, and *dynamic* conceptions of disease that see disease as a state of disequilibrium, a loss of harmony between the organism and its environment and in particular, as an attempt by nature to establish a new equilibrium in the organism. Canguilhem calls both sorts of disease conceptions "optimistic": in the first case, the cause of disease is seen as something ontologically real that could hence be physically isolated and destroyed. The second conception assumes that "the way of nature" and medical techniques that reinforce or imitate natural therapeutic reactions could restore an organism's health.

In the case of the Nazis, the metaphor of the body of the *Volk*, given in holistic terms, allowed an ontological definition of disease to be mobilized: disease was thought to be caused by some "germ" (the Jew, the insane, the homosexual, the Gypsy) infiltrating this body. Following such an "optimistic" conception of disease Nazi doctors could devise ways to get rid of the "parasites" that had invaded the body of the *Volk*. Indeed Zyklon B, the poisonous gas used in the final most "efficient" stages of 14 f 13, was a pesticide.

Perhaps unsurprisingly, there was a movie made by the Nazis in 1938 to promote the use of this gas. The theme of the movie was "pest control"; the images shown were of vermin, rats and insects chewing away on pristine sacks of flour and burrowing into wooden statues of classic male bodies. Compare this with another propaganda movie, *The Eternal Jew*, premiered on 28 November 1940 in one of Berlin's largest cinemas (reproduced in Cohen 1991). Images of the Jewish ghetto in Warsaw likened Jews to vermin, pictured them eating from rubbish bins, and aimed to show Jews "as they really are ... The civilized Jews that we know in Germany give us only an incomplete picture of their racial character. This is how Jews really look before they conceal themselves behind the masks of civilized Europeans" (recorded in Cohen 1991).

Once more, Nazi propaganda horribly hints at the method by which Nazi goals would be articulated. In the words of Himmler addressing the SS in the April of 1943: "Anti-Semitism is like getting de-loused. Getting rid of lice is hardly a philosophical issue; it is a matter of cleanliness ... We shall soon be de-loused. There are now only 20,000 left. They will soon be extinct in all of Germany" (recorded in Cohen 1991).

Although holism was employed in Nazi theorizing, it is worth noting that holism also seems able to articulate explicitly anti-authoritarian perceptions of the organism. Several advocates of holistic biology were explicitly opposed to Nazi politics, even some with anti-Semitic feelings.[7] An example worthy of mention is the idea of organismic freedom articulated by holistic neuropsychiatrist Kurt Goldstein.

Kurt Goldstein was a Jew who had published a monograph on race hygiene in 1913 and was prosecuted by the Nazis for being Jewish and a member of the Democratic Socialist Party (SPD). After being expelled from his practice on 1 April 1933, along with all Jewish doctors, losing his position at the University of Berlin, being imprisoned and tortured, he succeeded in escaping to Amsterdam where he worked for a year at a local university. He eventually immigrated to the United States in 1935 and published the book he had dictated to his secretary while in exile in Amsterdam.[8] The book was based on his studies of patients that had suffered brain injuries in the First World War. Goldstein's work is quite philosophical – indeed Goldstein originally wanted to become a philosopher.[9]

Goldstein's notion of health is especially interesting. For Goldstein health was a matter of the relation between an organism and its milieu. A "milieu" was an environment that the organism can *select* and *modify*. An organism's environment could include social or physical entities and relations – an idea still pursued in thinking about medicine such as in what Carel calls the social world and geography of illness (Carel 2008: chapters 1–2).

Goldstein called an organism "normal" or "healthy" if it was able to respond to the demands placed on it by an "adequate" milieu. A milieu was adequate to a human if it enabled her to actualize her essential nature. What was a human's essential nature, according to Goldstein? Freedom. Goldstein thought one of the essential characteristics of humans is that we have an abstract, rather than concrete, attitude, that is, we are able to entertain the possible rather than the actual (Goldstein [1935] 1963: 44). An adequate milieu thus provided one with enough freedom to entertain the possible.

Goldstein noticed that injured people would tend to rearrange, or "shrink" their milieu to be able to meet its demands, and some formerly lost performances would thus be compensated for. Medical interventions could shrink a patient's milieu – by putting her in a hospital room, or numbing her sensations through, say, painkillers. But doctors had to keep in mind that with interventions that limited suffering came limited freedom and with limited freedom came diminished humanity. If we consider this definition in the context of Nazism we can see its subversiveness. These commitments led Goldstein to explicitly dismiss human eugenic breeding.

SOPHIA EFSTATHIOU

PHILOSOPHICAL INSIGHTS

Medicine has been perceived since antiquity as performing – or at least as aspiring to perform – a positive service to humanity. Plato describes medicine as a craft carried out for the purpose of *healing*. The ancient Greek word for medicine, *iatrike*, comes from the verb *iatreuo*, which means "to cure". Healing involves establishing or preserving the health of the patient and getting rid of disease. As discussed, medicine is necessarily value-based, oriented by a prior understanding of what constitutes health (which is to be pursued) and of what constitutes disease (which is to be avoided), and what technologies can effectively move us from the latter to the former. The cruelty of Nazi medicine is shocking because we do not expect physicians to be cruel.

Nazi medicine is still medicine because it, too, aimed to secure health and cure disease. Nazi notions of health and disease reflected the cultural standards of Nazi ideology more accurately than any biologically real, vital norms. Indeed, the conflation of social-aesthetic norms of beauty with biological norms of health was a most powerful propaganda tool for the "naturalization" and "beautification" of a political regime that was unjust and certainly now seen as deeply ugly and morally repulsive.

Why is this case still relevant? Nazi eugenics was, in some respects, ambitious and visionary (Proctor 1999). It reconceived health following "the latest" evolutionary science, and it sought to enhance and protect health by, in some cases, forward-looking public awareness campaigns and social interventions.

We still aim to enhance health. But how is "health" to be understood? Is it in terms of beauty or in terms of some other good? Philosophers and medical theorists have articulated *naturalist* notions of health, which posit health as some natural, biological state that is in one way or another helpful for the evolutionary and functional success of an organism; these naturalist conceptions of health are dissociated from *constructivist* understandings that define health based on some socio-culturally imposed idea of what it means for an individual to be "well", within a particular cultural milieu.

When we consider notions of beauty and their relation to notions of health, the boundaries of the "natural" and "constructed" start to come apart. There is, no doubt, cultural variation as to what is taken to be beautiful, but as a socially interpreted signal "beauty" could increase the mating and thus reproductive success of an organism, and so have a direct impact on the organism's fitness considered within a naturalist framework.

Conversely, even if we take notions of disease to have radically varied through the ages following a constructivist frame, some commonality in what we call "diseased", across societies, could be anchored by the intense emotional–aesthetic reactions that sickness or death tend to arouse. Looks are at once "natural" and socially "appraised"; humans' attraction to (often functionally irrelevant) features was after all the most compelling reason Darwin found for the existence of human "subspecies" or "races" (Darwin [1871] 2000).

Add debates on the definition of beauty to debates on the definition of health, and the situation gets more complicated. There are formalist, pluralist and naturalist accounts of beauty. As we saw, feminists warn against subscribing to a "beauty myth" and evolutionary psychologists justify the difficulty of ignoring beauty, saying it is an adaptive psychological trait, dating back to the time when women were mainly gatherers, men hunters and contraception non-existent.

Rather than trying to settle debates about the nature of health and beauty and the relations between them, I would like to draw attention to the consequences of underestimating their power. The Nazis created a culture that found ideas of beauty and goodness – or health – exemplified in the presumed form of an ancient, Nordic race and thus deemed the means of achieving such health to be just. By appealing to the inherent value of health while conflating the concept itself with a social–aesthetic norm of Germanness the Nazis succeeded in what Emanuel Todd has called the only successful revolution of the twentieth century (Levi & Rothberg 2003). It is still the case that medicine can be driven by and aimed at values that include beauty. And like aesthetic ideas, medical concepts are highly susceptible to misuse by ideologues who want to structure human behaviour and serve purposes that people may object to.

NOTES

1. Tobin Siebers argues that disability has been kept invisible in discussions of aesthetics as well as historiographies of art – he proposes "disability aesthetics" as an approach to aesthetics that keeps in sight the influence of the disabled, unnatural or disharmonious as well as of the beautiful, harmonious or healthy (Siebers 2006: 64). Indeed he proposes that good art often involves an element of "disability", broadly conceived as irregularity, which has a powerful emotive–aesthetic effect that kitsch Nazi art lacks (2006: 64–7).
2. The first sports event for disabled people was organized by the English physician Ludwig Guttmann in 1948, and aimed mainly at soldiers injured in the Second World War. The first Paralympic Games were held in Rome in 1960.
3. Note that public health fields such as epidemiology study variation across "groups" of humans. Bioinformatics tools in population genetics and genetic epidemiology also consider clusters of humans or "populations".
4. See Wagner's ([1849] 1993) discussion of the future of the artwork and Nietzsche ([1872] 1999) on Greek tragedy.

5. These two schools of thought should perhaps not be tagged by these authors' names as their work is not distinct from each other in these traditionally supposed and clear but crude ways. Still, I am assuming Proctor's discussion here for consistency.
6. This form of holism was also popular in the early pre-war years of Nazism. There was a law passed to allow natural healers to practice – and have them register their occupation – while the Ministry of the Interior formed in 1933 a Healers' League of Germany. For more detail see Proctor (1988: 228–9).
7. Consider the example of Hans Driesch, a vitalist embryologist and philosopher (Harrington 1996: 189), whose work was of interest to the Nazis, but who was himself opposed to Nazi politics and one of the first non-Jewish professors retired by the Nazis in 1933. Another example would be behavioural biologist Jacob Johann von Uexcull (or Uexkull) who had stark anti-Semitic feelings and corresponded in private with English race-theorist Houston Stewart Chamberlain, but criticized Alfred Rosenberg as an ideologue who distorted Chamberlain's basic message (Harrington 1996: 68). Chapters 2 and 6 of Harrington's *Re-enchanted Science* (1996) discuss the relation of von Uexcull's and Driesch's work to Nazism.
8. Harrington dedicates chapter 5 of *Re-enchanted Science* to a discussion of Goldstein (Harrington 1996: 140–74).
9. Goldstein wanted to become a philosopher but his father deemed philosophy a "*brotlose Kunst*" ("breadless art") and prevented him from doing so. His work, especially on aphasia, inspired later phenomenological thinking, in part through his cousin Ernst Cassirer, and directly through Merleau-Ponty.

BIBLIOGRAPHY

Abbott, H. P. 2008. *The Cambridge Introduction to Narrative*. Cambridge: Cambridge University Press.
Agamben, G. [1966] 1998. *Homo Sacer: Sovereign Power and Bare Life*, D. Heller-Roazen (trans.). Stanford, CA: Stanford University Press.
Agamben, G. 2003. "What is a Camp?" In *The Holocaust: Theoretical Readings*, N. Levi & M. Rothberg (eds), 252–6. New Brunswick, NJ: Rutgers University Press.
Agich, G. J. 1983. "Disease and Value: a Rejection of the Value-Neutrality Thesis". *Theoretical Medicine* **4**: 27–41.
Ahlzén, R. 2007. "Medical Humanities – Arts and Humanistic Science". *Medicine, Health Care and Philosophy* **10**: 385–93.
Aigner, M. & M. Bach 1999. "Clinical Utility of DSM-IV Pain Disorder". *Comprehensive Psychiatry* **40**: 353–7.
Alghrani, A. 2007. "The Legal and Ethical Ramifications of Ectogenesis". *Asian Journal of WTO & International Health Law and Policy* **2**(1): 189–212.
American Psychiatric Association 1952. *Diagnostic and Statistical Manual: Mental Disorders*. Washington, DC: American Psychiatric Association. 2nd edn 1968, 3rd edn 1980, 4th rev. edn 2000.
American Psychiatric Association 1973. "Homosexuality and Sexual Orientation Disturbance: Proposed Change in the DSM-II, 6th Printing, page 44". APA Document reference *no.* 730008. Washington, DC: American Psychiatric Association.
American Psychiatric Association 2000. *Diagnostic and Statistical Manual of Disorders*, 4th rev. edn. Washington, DC: American Psychiatric Association.
American Psychiatric Association 2010. "Complex Somatic Symptom Disorder", www.dsm5.org/ProposedRevisions/Pages/proposedrevision.aspx?rid=368 (accessed 6 September 2011).
Amundson, R. 1992. "Disability, Handicap and the Environment". *Journal of Social Philosophy* **23**(1): 105–19.
Amundson, R. 2000. "Against Normal Function". *Studies in History and Philosophy of Biological and Biomedical Sciences* **31**(1): 33–53.
Andreasen, R. O. 1998. "A New Perspective on the Race Debate". *British Journal for the Philosophy of Science* **49**: 199–225.

BIBLIOGRAPHY

Andreasen, R. O. 2000. "Race: Biological Reality or Social Construct?" *Philosophy of Science* **67**: 653–66.

Angermeyer, M. C. & H. Matschinger 2004. "Public Attitudes to People With Depression: Have There Been Any Changes Over the Last Decade?" *Journal of Affective Disorders* **83**: 177–82.

Antoniou, A., P. D. P. Pharoah, S. Narod, H. A. Risch, J. E. Eyfjord, J L. Hopper, N. Loman *et al.* 2003. "Average Risks of Breast and Ovarian Cancer Associated with BRCA1 or BRCA2 Mutations Detected in Case Series Unselected for Family History: A Combined Analysis of 22 Studies". *American Journal of Human Genetics* **72**: 1117–30.

Antonovsky, A. 1987. *Unravelling the Mysteries of Health: How People Manage Stress and Stay Well.* San Francisco, CA: Jossey-Bass.

Appiah, K. A. 1993. *In My Father's House: Africa in the Philosophy of Culture.* New York: Oxford University Press.

Appiah, K. A. 1998. "Race, Culture, Identity: Misunderstood Connections". In *The Political Morality of Race*, K. A. Appiah & A. Guttmann (eds), 30–105. Princeton, NJ: Princeton University Press.

Aristotle 1984. "Nicomachean". In *Complete Works of Aristotle*, The Revised Oxford Translation, J. Barnes (ed.), book 1, ch. 4, 20–25. Princeton, NJ: Princeton University Press.

Aristotle 2004. *The Nicomachean Ethics.* J. A. K. Thomson (trans.). London: Penguin.

Armstrong, D. 1995. "The Rise of Surveillance Medicine". *Sociology of Health and Illness* **17**(3): 393–403.

Árnason, V. 2000. "Gadamerian Dialogue in the Patient–Professional Interaction". *Medicine, Health Care and Philosophy* **3**(1): 17–23.

Aronova, E. 2009. "In Search of the Soul in Science: Medical Ethics' Appropriation of Philosophy of Science in the 1970s". *History and Philosophy of the Life Sciences* **31**: 5–34.

Aronowitz, R. A. 2009. "The Converged Experience of Risk and Disease". *The Milbank Quarterly* **87**(2): 417–42.

Atkinson, P. 2010. "The Contested Terrain of Narrative Analysis – an Appreciative Response". *Sociology of Health and Illness* **32**: 661–7.

Atran, S. 1999. "Folk Biology". In *The MIT Encyclopedia of the Cognitive Sciences*, R. A. Wilson and F. C. Keil (eds). Cambridge, MA: Bradford/The MIT Press.

Aydede, M. & G. Güzeldere 2002. "Some Foundational problems in the Scientific Study of Pain". *Philosophy of Science* **69**: 265–83.

Ballantyne, J. C., S. M. Fishman & J. P. Rathmell (eds) 2010. *Bonica's Management of Pain.* Philadelphia, PA: Lippincott Williams & Wilkins.

Bamberg, M. 2006. "Stories: Big or Small: Why Do We Care?" *Narrative Inquiry* **16**: 139–47.

Barnard, C. J. & J. L. Hurst 1996. "Welfare by Design: the Natural Selection of Welfare Criteria". *Animal Welfare* **5**: 405–33.

Barron, S. (ed.) 1991. *Degenerate Art: The Fate of the Avant-Garde in Nazi Germany.* New York: Harry N. Abrams.

Basaglia, F., N. Scheper-Hughes & A. Lovell 1987. *Psychiatry Inside Out: Selected Writings of Franco Basaglia.* New York: Columbia University Press.

Baszanger, I. 1998. *Inventing Pain Medicine: from the Laboratory to the Clinic.* I. Baszanger (trans.). New Brunswick, NJ: Rutgers University Press.

Battersby, J. L. 2006. "Narrativity, Self, and Self-representation". *Narrative* **14**: 27–44.
Bayer, R. 1981. *Homosexuality and American Psychiatry: the Politics of Diagnosis*. New York: Basic Books. Reissued 1987 (Princeton, NJ: Princeton University Press).
Bayne, T. & N. Levy 2005. "Amputees by Choice: Body Integrity Identity Disorder and the Ethics of Amputation". *Journal of Applied Philosophy* **22**(1): 75–86.
Beauchamp, T. L. & J. F. Childress [1979] 2008. *Principles of Biomedical Ethics*, 6th edn. New York: Oxford University Press.
Becker-Schmidt, R. & G.-A. Knapp 2000. *Feministische Theorien zur Einführung. [An Introduction into Feminist Theories]*. Dresden: Junius.
Berger, P. L. & T. Luckmann 1966. *The Social Construction of Reality: a Treatise in the Sociology of Knowledge*. New York: Anchor Books.
Bergsma, J. and D. C. Thomasma 2000. *Autonomy and Clinical Medicine: Renewing the Health Professional Relation with the Patient*. Norwell, MA: Kluwer.
Bering, J. 2011. *The Belief Instinct: the Psychology of Souls, Destiny and the Meaning of Life*. New York: W. W. Norton.
Biley, F. C. & J. Champney-Smith 2003. "'Attempting to Say Something Without Saying It . . .': Writing Haiku in Health Care Education". *Medical Humanities* **29**: 39–42.
Bird, A. 2004. "Kuhn, Naturalism and the Positivist Legacy". *Studies in the History and Philosophy of Science* **35**: 337–56.
Blazer, D. G., R. C. Kessler, K. A. McGonagle & M. S. Swartz 1994. "The Prevalence and Distribution of Major Depression in a National Community Sample: the National Comorbidity Survey". *American Journal of Psychiatry* **151**: 979–86.
Bochner, A. P. 2010. "Resisting the Mystification of Narrative Inquiry: Unmasking the Real Conflict between Story Analysts and Storytellers". *Sociology of Health and Illness* **32**: 661–7.
Bogner, A. 2005. *Grenzpolitik der Experten. Vom Umgang mit Ungewissheit und Nichtwissen in pränataler Diagnostik und Beratung*. [Border politics of experts: about the handling of uncertainty and not-knowing in prenatal diagnostics and counselling]. Weilerswist: Velbrück Wissenschaft.
Bolton, D. 2008. *What is Mental Disorder? An Essay in Philosophy, Science, and Values*. Oxford: Oxford University Press.
Bolton, D. & J. Hill 1996. *Mind, Meaning, and Mental Disorder: the Nature of Causal Explanation in Psychology and Psychiatry*. Oxford: Oxford University Press.
Boorse, C. 1975. "On the Distinction between Disease and Illness". *Philosophy and Public Affairs* **5**(1): 49–68.
Boorse, C. 1976. "What a Theory of Mental Health Should Be". *Journal for the Theory of Social Behaviour* **6**(1): 61–84. Reprinted in *Psychiatry and Ethics*, R. Edwards (ed.), 29–48 (Buffalo, NY: Prometheus Books, 1982).
Boorse, C.1977. "Health as a Theoretical Concept". *Philosophy of Science* **44**(4): 542–73.
Boorse, C. 1987. "Concepts of Health". In *Health Care Ethics: an Introduction*, D. Van de Veer & T. Regan (eds), 359–93. Philadelphia, PA: Temple University Press.
Boorse, C. 1997. "A Rebuttal on Health". In *What is Disease?* J. M. Humber & R. F. Almeder (eds), 3–134. Totowa, NJ: Humana Press.
Boorse, C. 2011. "Concepts of Health and Disease". In *Philosophy of Medicine*, F. Gifford (ed.), 13–64. Oxford: Elsevier.
Borgerson, K. 2009. "Valuing Evidence: Bias and the Evidence Hierarchy of Evidence-Based Medicine". *Perspectives in Biology and Medicine* **52**(2): 218–33.

Brain, C. E., S. M. Creighton, I. Mushtaq, P. A. Carmichael, A. Barnicoat, J. W. Honour & V. J. C. Achermann 2010. "Holistic Management of DSD". *Best Practice and Research Clinical Endocrinology and Metabolism* **24**: 335–54.

Brennan, J. 2001. "Adjustment to Cancer: Coping or Personal Transition?" *Psycho-Oncology* **10**: 1–18.

Brennan, J. 2004. *Cancer in Context: A Practical Guide to Supportive Care*. Oxford: Oxford University Press.

Brennan, J. 2007. "Counselling: Distress, Transitions, and Relationships". In *Enhancing Cancer Care: Complementary Therapy and Support*, J. Barraclough (ed.), 127–40. Oxford: Oxford University Press

Brewer, W. & A. Samarapungavan 1991. "Children's Theories vs. Scientific Theories: Differences in Reasoning or Differences in Knowledge?" In *Cognition and the Symbolic Processes: Applied and Ecological Perspectives*, R. R. Hoffman & D. S. Palermo (eds). 209–32. Hillsdale, NJ: Lawrence Erlbaum Press.

Brewer, W., C. Chinnand & A. Samarapungavan 2000. "Explanations in Scientists and Children". In *Explanation and Cognition*, F. Keil & R. Wilson (eds), 279–98. Cambridge, MA: Bradford/MIT Press.

Broadbent, A. 2009. "Causation and Models of Disease in Epidemiology". *Studies in History and Philosophy of Biological and Biomedical Sciences* **40**(4): 302–11.

Brody, H. 1987. *Stories of Sickness*. New Haven, CT: Yale University Press.

Broom, D. 1998. "Welfare, Stress and the Evolution of Feelings". *Advances in the Study of Behaviour* **27**: 371–403.

Bruner, J. 1990. *Acts of Meaning*. Cambridge, MA: Harvard University Press.

Bruner, J. 1991. "The Narrative Contruction of Reality". *Critical Inquiry* **18**: 1–21.

Bublitz, H. 2002. *Judith Butler zur Einführung* [An introduction to Judith Butler]. Dresden: Junius.

Bunt, L. 2010. "Music Therapy as a Resource for People Living with Cancer". Paper presented at the Concepts of Health and Illness Conference, Bristol, 1–3 September.

Butler, J. 1990. *Gender Trouble: Feminism and the Subversion of Identity*. New York: Routledge.

Butler, J. 1993. *Bodies that Matter: on the Discursive Limits of "Sex"*. New York: Routledge.

Butler, J. 2004. *Undoing Gender*. New York: Routledge.

Campaner, R. 2011. "Understanding Mechanisms in the Health Sciences". *Theoretical Medicine and Bioethics* **32**(1): 5–17.

Campbell, J. 1969. *The Hero with a Thousand Faces*. Princeton, NJ: Princeton University Press.

Campbell, J. 1994. *Past, Space, and Self*. Cambridge, MA: MIT Press.

Canguilhelm, G. 1978. *On the Normal and the Pathological*. Dordrecht & Boston, MA: D. Reidel.

Canguilhem, G. [1966] 1989. *The Normal and the Pathological*. New York: Zone Books.

Caplan, A. L., H. T. Engelhardt & J. J. McCartney (eds) 1981. *Concepts of Health and Disease: Interdisciplinary Perspectives*. Reading, MA: Addison-Wesley.

Carel, H. 2008. *Illness: The Cry of the Flesh*. Stocksfield: Acumen.

Carel, H. 2009. "A Reply to 'Towards an Understanding of Nursing as a Response to Human Vulnerability' by Derek Sellman: Vulnerability and Illness". *Nursing Philosophy* **10**: 214–19.

Carel, H. 2010. "Phenomenology and its Application in Medicine". *Theoretical Medicine and Bioethics* **32**(1): 33–46.

Carel, H. 2012. "Phenomenology as a Resource for Patients". *Journal of Medicine and Philosophy* **37**(2): 96–113.
Carel, H. 2013. "Bodily Doubt". *Journal of Consciousness Studies*. In press.
Casado, A. 2009a. "Back to Basics in Bioethics: Reconciling Patient Autonomy with Physician Responsibility". *Philosophy Compass* **4**(1): 56–68.
Casado, A. 2009b. "Towards a Comprehensive Concept of Patient Autonomy". *American Journal of Bioethics* **9**(2): 37–8.
Cassell, E. J. 1982. "The Nature of Suffering and the Goals of Medicine". *New England Journal of Medicine* **306**: 639–45
Cassell, E. 2010. *The Person as the Subject of Medicine*. Barcelona: Víctor Grífols i Lucas Foundation.
Chambers, T. 2009. "The Virtue of Incongruity in the Medical Humanities". *Journal of Medical Humanities* **30**: 151–4.
Charon, R. 2006. "The Self-Telling Body". *Narrative Inquiry* **16**: 191–200.
Charon, R. 2007. "Listening for the Self-telling Body". Presented at Caring for the Caregiver: Literature and Medicine National Conference, Manchester, New Hampshire, 9 May.
Charon, R. 2008. *Narrative Medicine: Honoring the Stories of Illness*. New York: Oxford University Press.
Chinn, C. & W. Brewer 1994. "Psychological Responses to Anomalous Data". In *Proceedings of the Biennial Meeting of the Philosophy of Science Association, Volume One: Contributed Papers* 304–13. Chicago, IL: University of Chicago Press.
Chochinov, H. M. 2004. "Dignity and the Eye of the Beholder". *Journal of Clinical Oncology* **22**(7): 1336–40.
Churchland, P. M. 1993. "Evaluating our Self-Conception". *Mind and Language* **8**: 211–22. Reprinted in *On the Contrary: Critical Essays, 1987–1997*, P. M. Churchland & P. S. Churchland (Cambridge, MA: Bradford/MIT Press, 1998).
Churchland, P. M. 1996. "Folk Psychology". In *Companion to the Mind*, S. Guttenplan (ed.), 308–37. Oxford: Blackwell. Reprinted in *On the Contrary: Critical Essays 1987–1997*, P. M. Churchland & P. S. Churchland (Cambridge, MA: Bradford/MIT Press, 1998).
Clouser, K. D., C. M. Culver & B. Gert 1981. "Malady: a New Treatment of Disease". *The Hastings Center Report* **11**: 29–37.
Clouser, K. D., C. M. Culver & B. Gert 1997. "Malady". In *What is Disease?* J. M. Humber & R. F. Almeder (eds), 173–218. Totowa, NJ: Humana Press.
Coakley, S. & K. Kaufman Shelemay (eds) 2007. *Pain and its Transformations: The Interface of Biology and Culture*. Cambridge, MA: Harvard University Press.
Cohen, P. (dir.) [1989] 1991. *The Architecture of Doom*. Research of P. Cohen. POJ Filmproduktion AB, Filminstitutet.
Conrad, P. 2007. *The Medicalization of Society*. Baltimore, MD: John Hopkins University Press.
Cooper, D. G. 1967. *Psychiatry and Anti-Psychiatry*. London: Tavistock Publications.
Cooper, R. 2002a. "Disease". *Studies in History and Philosophy of Biological and Biomedical Sciences* **33**: 263–82.
Cooper, R. 2002b. "Can it Be a Good Thing to Be Deaf?" *Journal of Medicine and Philosophy* **32**: 563–83.
Cooper, R. 2005. *Classifying Madness: a Philosophical Examination of the Diagnostic and Statistical Manual of Mental Disorders*. Dordrecht: Springer.

Cooper, R. 2007. *Psychiatry and Philosophy of Science*. Stocksfield: Acumen.
Cooper, R. In press. "Mental Health and Disorder". In *Arguing About Human Nature*, E. Machery and S. Downes (eds). London: Routledge.
Cooper, R. & C. Megone 2007. "Introduction". *Philosophical Papers* **36**: 339–41.
Cornford, C. S., A. Hill, & J. Reilly 2007. "How Patients with Depressive Symptoms View Their Condition: a Qualitative Study". *Family Practice* **24**: 358–64.
Costelloe, T. M. 2001. "Constructivism Dissected". Review of *Social Constructivism and the Philosophy of Science*, A. Kukla. *Social Studies of Science* **31**: 469–72.
Craig, K. D. 1984. "The Psychology of Pain". *Postgraduate Medical Journal* **60**: 835–40.
Craik, K. 1948. *The Nature of Explanation*. Cambridge: Cambridge University Press.
Crawford, J. M., G. Warne, S. Grover, B. R. Southwell & J. M. Hutson 2009. "Results from a Pediatric Surgical Centre Justify Early Intervention in Disorders of Sex Development". *Journal of Pediatric Surgery* **44**: 413–16.
Creighton, S. M., S. M. Greenberg, K. Roen & D. L. Volcano 2009. "Intersex Practice, Theory and Activism". See Morland (2009b), 249–60.
Culver, C. M. & B. Gert 1982. *Philosophy in Medicine: Conceptual and Ethical Issues in Medicine and Psychiatry*. Oxford: Oxford University Press.
Daniels, N. 1985. *Just Health Care*. New York: Cambridge University Press.
Darwin, C. [1859] 1996. *The Origin of Species*. Oxford: Oxford University Press.
Darwin, C. [1871] 2000. "On the Races of Man". In *The Idea of Race*, R. Bernasconi & T. L. Lott (eds), 54–87. Indianapolis, IN: Hackett.
Dawkins, M. S. 1990. "From an Animal's Point of View: Motivation, Fitness and Animal Welfare". *Behavioral and Brain Sciences* **13**: 1–9.
De Gobineau, J. A. [1853–55] 2000. "The Inequality of Human Races". In *The Idea of Race*, R. Bernasconi & T. L. Lott (eds), 45–53. Indianapolis, IN: Hackett.
Deleuze, G. & F. Guattari [1972] 2004. *Anti-Oedipus*. R. Hurley, M. Seem & H. R. Lane (trans.). London & New York: Continuum.
Demazeux, S. 2010. "Le concept de fonction dans le discours psychiatrique contemporain". *Matière Première, Revue d'Épistémologie* **1**: 31–74.
DeVito, S. 2000. "On the Value-Neutrality of the Concepts of Health and Disease: Unto the Breach Again". *Journal of Medicine and Philosophy* **25**(5): 539–67.
Dinos, S., S. Stevens, M. Serfaty, S. Weich & M. King 2004. "Stigma: the Feelings and Experiences of 46 People with Mental Illness". *British Journal of Psychiatry* **184**: 176–81.
Donnellan, K. S. 1983. "Kripke and Putnam on Natural Kind Terms". In *Carl Ginet*, S. Shoemaker (ed.), 84–104. New York: Oxford University Press.
Dragulinescu, S. 2012. "On 'Stabilising' Medical Mechanisms, Truth-Makers and Epistemic Causality: a Critique to Williamson and Russo's Approach". *Synthese* **187**(2): 785–800.
Dreger, A. D. 1998. *Hermaphrodites and the Medical Invention of Sex*. Cambridge, MA: Harvard University Press.
Dreger, A. D. 1999a. "A History of Intersex: From the Age of Gonads to the Age of Consent". See Dreger (1999b), 5–22.
Dreger, A. D. (ed.) 1999b. *Intersex in the Age of Ethics*. Hagerstown, MD: University Publishing Group.
Dreger, A. D. 2004. "'Ambiguous Sex' – or Ambivalent Medicine". In *Health, Disease and Illness*, A. L. Caplan, J. J. McCartney, D. A. Sisti (eds), 137–52. Washington, DC: Georgetown University Press.

Dreger, A. D. & C. Chase 1999. "A Mother's Care". See Dreger (1999b), 83–9.
Dreger, A. D. & A. M. Herndon 2009. "Progress and Politics in the Intersex Rights Movement". See Morland (2009b), 199–224.
Dumesnil, H. & P. Verger 2009. "Public Awareness Campaigns About Depression and Suicide: A Review". *Psychiatric Services* **60**(9): 1203–13.
Duncan, I. J. H. 1996. "Animal Welfare Defined in Terms of Feelings". *Acta Agriculturae Scandinavica. Section A, Animal Science. Supplementum* **27**: 29–35.
Dupré, J. 1993. *The Disorder of Things: Metaphysical Foundations of the Disunity of Science*. Cambridge, MA: Harvard University Press.
Dworkin, R. 1988. *The Theory and Practice of Autonomy*. New York: Cambridge University Press.
Eckert, L. 2009. "'Diagnosticism': Three Cases of Medical Anthropological Research into Intersexuality". See Holmes (2009b), 41–71.
Elliott, C. 2003. *Better than Well: American Medicine Meets the American Dream*. New York: W. W. Norton.
Engelhardt, H. T. 1975. "The Concepts of Health and Disease". In *Evaluation and Explanation in the Biomedical Sciences*, H. T. Engelhardt & S. F. Spicker (eds), 125–42. Dordrecht: Reidel.
Engelhardt, H. T. 1976. "Ideology and Etiology". *Journal of Medical Philosophy* **1**: 256–68.
Engelhardt, H. T. 1981. "The Concepts of Health and Disease". In *Concepts of Health and Disease: Interdisciplinary Perspectives*, A. L. Caplan, H. T. Engelhardt & J. J. McCartney (eds), 31–45. Reading, MA: Addison-Wesley.
Engelhardt, H. T. 1986. *The Foundations of Bioethics*. New York: Oxford University Press.
Etcoff, N. 2000. *Survival of the Prettiest: The Science of Beauty*. New York: Anchor Books.
Efstathiou, S. 2012. "The Nazi Cosmetic: Medicine in the Service of Beauty". *Studies in History and Philosophy of Biological and Biomedical Sciences* **43**: 634–42.
Etxeberria Agiriado, A. & A. Casado 2008. "Autonomía, vida y bioética". *Ludus Vitalis* **30**: 213–16.
Evans, H. M. & J. Macnaughton 2004. "Should Medical Humanities be a Multidisciplinary or an Interdisciplinary Study?" *Medical Humanities* **30**: 1–4.
Fausto-Sterling, A. 1998. "The Five Sexes: Why Male and Female are Not Enough". In *Questions of Gender*, D. L. Anselmi & A. L. Law (eds), 24–8. Boston, MA: McGraw-Hill.
Feder, E. K. 2006. "In Their Best Interests. Parents' Experience of Atypical Genitalia". In *Surgically Shaping Children: Technology, Ethics and the Pursuit of Normality*, E. Parens (ed.), 189–210. Baltimore, MD: Johns Hopkins University Press.
Felsen, G. & P. B. Reiner 2011. "How the Neuroscience of Decision Making Informs our Conception of Autonomy". *The American Journal of Bioethics – Neuroscience* **2**(3): 3–14.
Fields, H. L. 2007. "Setting the Stage for Pain. Allegorical Tales from Neuroscience". In *Pain and its Transformations: The Interface of Biology and Culture*, S. Coakley & K. Kaufman Shelemay (eds), 36–61. Cambridge, MA: Harvard University Press.
Fine, C. 2010. *Delusions of Gender*. New York: W. W. Norton.
Finkelstein, V. 1980. *Attitudes and Disabled People*. New York: World Rehabilitation Fund.
Finkler, K. 2000. *Experiencing the New Genetics: Family and Kinship on the Medical Frontier*. Philadelphia, PA: University of Pennsylvania Press.

Fletcher, G. & G. Thomas 1996. "Close Relationship Lay Theories: Their Structure and Function". In *Knowledge Structures in Close Relationships: a Social Psychological Approach*, G. Fletcher & J. Fitness (eds), 3–24. Hillsdale, NJ: Lawrence Erlbaum Press.

Foot, P. 2001. *Natural Goodness*. Oxford: Clarendon Press.

Fordyce, W. E. 1978. "Learning Processes in Pain". In *The Psychology of Pain*, R. A. Sternbach (ed.), 49–72. New York: Raven Press.

Foucault, M. 1961. *Madness and Civilisation: a History of Insanity in the Age of Reason*, R. Howard (trans.). London: Tavistock.

Foucault, M. 1963. *The Birth of the Clinic: an Archaeology of Medical Perception*, A. M. Sheridan Smith (trans.). London: Tavistock.

Foucault, M. 1976. "The Social Extension of the Norm". In *Foucault Live: Collected Interviews 1961–1984*, S. Lotringer (ed.), L. Hochroth (trans). Newbould: Semiotext[e].

Foucault, M. 1980. *Herculine Barbin. Being the Recently Discovered Memoirs of a Nineteenth-century Hermaphrodite*, M. Foucault (introd.), R. McDougall (trans.). New York: Vintage Books. Originally published in French as *Herculine Barbin dite Alexina B* (France: Editions Gallimard, 1978).

Foucault, M. 1990. *Discipline and Punish: The Birth of the Prison*. Harmondsworth: Penguin.

Foucault, M. [1976] 1998. *The History of Sexuality Vol. 1: The Will to Knowledge*, R. Hurley (trans.). Harmondsworth: Penguin.

Frank, A. 1995. *The Wounded Storyteller: Body, Illness, and Ethics*. Chicago, IL: University of Chicago Press.

Frank, A. 2000. "The Standpoint of the Storyteller". *Qualitative Health Research* **10**: 354–65.

Frank, A. 2002. *At the Will of the Body: Reflections on Illness*. New York: Houghton Mifflin.

Frank, A. 2010. "In Defence of Narrative Exceptionalism". *Sociology of Health and Illness* **32**: 661–7.

Franke, A. 2006. *Modelle von Gesundheit und Krankheit* [Models of health and illness]. Bern: Verlag Hans Huber.

Frankfurt, H. G. 1971. "Freedom of the Will and the Concept of a Person". *The Journal of Philosophy* **68**(1): 5–20.

Freeman, M. 2006. "Life 'on Holiday?' In Defense of Big Stories". *Narrative Inquiry* **16**: 131–8.

Fuchs, T. 2000. *Psychopathologie von Leib und Raum: Phänomenologisch-empirische Untersuchungen zu Depressiven und Paranoiden Erkrankungen*. Darmstadt: Steinkopff.

Fuchs, T. In press. "Temporality and Psychopathology". *Phenomenology and the Cognitive Science* (doi:10.1007/s11097-010-9189-4).

Fulford, K. W. M. 1989. *Moral Theory and Medical Practice*. Cambridge: Cambridge University Press.

Fulford, K. W. M. 1999. "Nine Variations and a Coda on the Theme of an Evolutionary Definition of Dysfunction". *Journal of Abnormal Psychology* **108**(3): 412–20.

Fulford, K. W. M. 2002. "Report to the Chair of the DSM-VI Task Force". In *Descriptions and Prescriptions: Values, Mental Disorders and the DSMs*, J. Z. Sadler (ed.), 323–62. Baltimore, MD: Johns Hopkins University Press.

Furnham, A. & R. Malik 1994. "Cross-Cultural Beliefs about 'Depression'". *International Journal of Social Psychiatry* **40**(2): 106–23.

Gabriel, Y. 2004. "The Voice of Experience and the Voice of the Expert: Can They Speak to Each Other?" In *Narrative Research in Health and Illness*, B. Hurwitz, T. Greenhalgh & V. Skultans (eds), 168–86. Oxford: Blackwell.

Gadamer, H. G. [1993] 1996. *The Enigma of Health: The Art of Healing in a Scientific Age*, J. Gaiger & N. Walker (trans.). Stanford, CA: Stanford University Press.

Gallagher, S. 2003. "Self-Narrative in Schizophrenia". In *The Self in Neuroscience and Psychiatry*, T. Kircher & A. David (eds), 336–58. Cambridge: Cambridge University Press.

Gallagher, S. 2005. *How the Body Shapes the Mind*. Oxford: Oxford University Press.

Gammelgaard, A. 2000. "Evolutionary Biology and the Concept of Disease". *Medicine, Health Care and Philosophy* 3: 109–16.

Garvey, B. 2007. *Philosophy of Biology*. Durham: Acumen.

Georgakopoulou, A. 2006. "Thinking Big with Small Stories in Narrative and Identity Analysis". *Narrative Inquiry* 16: 122–30.

Gerhardus, A., H. Schleberger, B. Schlegelberger & F. W. Schwarz (eds) 2005. *BRCA – Erblicher Brust- und Eierstockkrebs. Beratung – Testverfahren – Kosten* [BRCA – hereditary breast and ovarian cancer. Counselling – test procedure – costs]. Heidelberg: Springer.

Gillon, R. 2003. "Ethics Needs Principles – Four Can Encompass the Rest – and Respect for Autonomy Should Be 'First Among Equals'". *Journal of Medical Ethics* 29: 307–12.

Goffman, E. 1959. *The Presentation of Self in Everyday Life*. New York: Doubleday.

Goldney, R. D., L. J. Fisher & D. H. Wilson 2001. "Mental Health Literacy: An Impediment to the Optimum Treatment of Major Depression in the Community". *Journal of Affective Disorders* 64: 277–84.

Goldstein, K. [1935] 1963. *The Organism: a Holistic Approach to Biology Derived from Pathological Data in Man*. Boston, MA: Beacon Press.

Good, B. J. 1992. "A Body in Pain: The Making of a World of Chronic Pain". In *Pain as a Human Experience: an Anthropological Perspective*, M. Delvecchio Good, P. E. Brodwin, B. J. Good & A. Kleinmann (eds), 29–48. Berkeley, CA: University of California Press.

Good, B. & M.-J. Delvicchio-Good 1981. "The Meaning of Symptoms: A Cultural Hermeneutic Model for Clinical Practice". In *The Relevance of Social Science for Medicine*, L. Eisenberg & A. Kleinman (eds), 165–96. Dordrecht: Reidel.

Goodman, M. P. 2009. "Female Cosmetic Genital Surgery". *Obstetrics and Gynaecology* 113(1): 154–9.

Goosens, W. 1980. "Values, Health and Medicine". *Philosophy of Science* 47: 100–15.

Gordijn, B. & R. Chadwick (eds) 2008. *Medical Enhancement and Posthumanity*. Dordrecht: Springer.

Greenberg, J. A. 2006. "International Legal Developments Protecting The Autonomy Rights of Sexual Minorities: Who Should Determine the Appropriate Treatment for an Intersex Infant?" See Sytsma (2006), 87–101.

Greenberg, P. E., L. E. Stiglin, S. N. Finkelstein & E. R. Berndt 1993. "The Economic Burden of Depression in 1990". *Journal of Clinical Psychiatry* 54: 405–18.

Greenhalgh, T. & B. Hurwitz (eds) 1998. *Narrative Based Medicine: Dialogue and Discourse in Clinical Practice*. London: BMJ Books.

Greer, G. 2000. *The Whole Woman*. London: Anchor.

Grene, M. 1977. "Philosophy of Medicine: Prolegomena to a Philosophy of Science". In *Proceedings of the 1976 Biennal Meeting of the PSA*, vol. 2, F. Suppe & P. D. Asquith (eds), 77–93. East Lansing, MI: Philosophy of Science Association.
Griffin, J. 1986. *Well-being*. Oxford: Clarendon Press.
Gruber, J. & A. Kring 2008. "Narrating Emotional Events in Schizophrenia". *Journal of Abnormal Psychology* **17**: 520–33.
Guibert, H. 1995. *To the Friend Who Did Not Save My Life*. London: Quartet Books. Originally published in French as *A l'ami qui ne m'a pas sauvé la vie* (Paris: Editions Gallimard, 1990).
Hacking, I. 1991. "The Making and Molding of Child Abuse". *Critical Inquiry* **17**: 253–88.
Hacking, I. 1995. "The Looping Effects of Human Kinds". In *Causal Cognition: A Multidisciplinary Debate*, D. Sperber, D. Premack & A. J. Premack (eds), 351–94. Oxford: Clarendon Press.
Hacking, I. 1998. *Mad Travellers: Reflections on the Reality of Transient Mental Illness*. Charlottesville, VA: University Press of Virginia.
Hacking, I. 1999. *The Social Construction of What?* Harvard, MA: Harvard University Press.
Hacking, I. 2007. "The Contingencies of Ambiguity". *Analysis* **67**: 269–77.
Hardcastle, G. V. 1999. *The Myth of Pain*. Cambridge, MA: MIT Press.
Harper, C. 2007. *Intersex*. Oxford: Berg.
Harrington, A. 1996. *Reenchanted Science: Holism in German Culture from Wilhelm II to Hitler*. Princeton, NJ: Princeton University Press.
Haslam, N., L. Ban & L. Kaufmann 2007. "Lay Conceptions of Mental Disorder: The Folk Psychiatry Model". *Australian Psychologist* **42**: 129–37.
Hausman, D. 2011. "Is an Overdose of Paracetamol Bad for One's Health?" *British Journal for the Philosophy of Science* **62**: 657–68.
Hawbecker, H. 1999. "Who Did This to You?". See Dreger (1999b), 111–13.
Hawkins, A. H. 1999. *Reconstructing Illness: Studies in Pathography*. West Lafayette, IN: Purdue University Press.
Healy, D. 1997. *The Anti-depressant Era*. Cambridge, MA: Harvard University Press.
Heidegger, M. [1927] 1996. *Being and Time*, J. Stambaugh (trans.). Albany, NY: SUNY Press.
Heidegger, M. [1954] 1977. *The Question Concerning Technology and Other Essays*, W. Lovitt (trans.). New York: Harper & Row.
Hempel, C. 1965. "Fundamentals of Taxonomy". In *Aspects of Scientific Explanation and other Essays in the Philosophy of Science*, C. G. Hempel (ed.), 137–54. New York: Free Press.
Henrich, J., S. J. Heine & A. Norenzayan 2010. "The Weirdest People in the World?" *Behavioural and Brain Sciences* **33**: 61–83.
Heyes, C. J. 2007. *Self-Transformations: Foucault, Ethics, and Normalized Bodies*. Oxford: Oxford University Press.
Hofmann, B. 2002. "On the Triad Disease, Illness and Sickness". *Journal of Medicine and Philosophy* **27**(6): 651–73.
Holmes, M. 2008. *Intersex. A Perilous Difference*. Selinsgrove, PA: Susquehanna University Press.
Holmes, M. 2009a. "Introduction: Straddling Past, Present and Future". See Holmes (2009b), 1–12.
Holmes, M. (ed.) 2009b. *Critical Intersex*. Farnham: Ashgate.

Horwitz, A. & J. Wakefield 2007. *The Loss of Sadness: How Psychiatry Transformed Normal Sadness into Depressive Disorder*. Oxford: Oxford University Press.
Howick, J. 2009. "Questioning the Methodologic Superiority of 'Placebo' over 'Active' Controlled Trials". *American Journal of Bioethics* **9**(9): 34–48.
Hoyningen-Huene, P. 1993. *Reconstructing Scientific Revolutions: Thomas S. Kuhn's Philosophy of Science*. Chicago, IL: University of Chicago Press.
Hughes, I. A. 2010. "The Quiet Revolution". *Best Practice and Research Clinical Endocrinology and Metabolism* **24**: 159–62.
Hughes I. A., C. Houk, S. F. Ahmed & P. A. Lee 2006. "Consensus Statement on Management of Intersex Disorders". *Archives of Diseases of Childhood* **91**: 554–63.
Hurrelmann, K. 2000. *Gesundheitssoziologie. Eine Einführung in sozialwissenschaftliche Theorien von Krankheitsprävention und Gesundheitsförderung* [Health sociology: An introduction in socioscientific theories of disease prevention and health promotion]. Weinheim: Juventa.
Hurwitz, B., T. Greenhalgh & V. Skultans (eds) 2004. *Narrative Research in Health and Illness*. Oxford: Blackwell.
Hutto, D. D. 2007a. "Narrative and Understanding Persons". In *Narrative and Understanding Persons*, D. D. Hutto (ed.), 1–16. Cambridge: Cambridge University Press.
Hutto, D. D. (ed.) 2007b. *Narrative and Understanding Persons*. Cambridge: Cambridge University Press.
Hutto, D. D. 2008. *Folk Psychological Narratives: the Sociocultural Basis of Understanding Persons*. Cambridge, MA: MIT Press.
Hydén, L.-C. 1997. "Illness and Narrative". *Sociology of Health and Illness* **19**: 48–69.
Hyvärinen, M. 2006. "Towards a Conceptual History of Narrative". In *The Travelling Concept of Narrative*, M. Hyvärinen, A. Korhonen & J. Mykkänen (eds), 20–41. Helsinki: Helsinki Collegium for Advanced Studies.
Hyvärinen, M., L.-C. Hydén, M. Saarenheimo & M. Tamboukou (eds) 2010. *Beyond Narrative Coherence*. Amsterdam: John Benjamins.
Illich, I. 1975. *Medical Nemesis. The Expropriation of Health*. London: Calder & Boyars.
Illich, I. 1977. "Disabling Professions". In *Disabling Professions*, I. Illich, I. K. Zola, K. Irving, J. McKnight, J. Caplan & H. Shaiken (eds), 11–39. London: Marion Boyars Publishers.
Imperato-McGinley, J., R. E. Peterson, T. Gautier & E. Sturia 1979. "Androgens and the Evolution of Male-Gender Identity Among Male Pseudohermaphrodites With 5 Alpha-Reductase Deficiency". *New England Journal of Medicine* **300**(22): 1233–7.
International Association for the Study of Pain: Task Force on Taxonomy 1994. *Classification of Chronic Pain: Descriptions of Chronic Pain Syndromes and Definitions of Pain*, 2nd edn. Seattle, WA: IASP Press.
Intersex Society of North America 2007. "Dear ISNA Friends and Supporters", www.isna.org/farewell_message (accessed 20 December 2010).
Jackson E. J. 1992. "After a While No One Believes You". In *Pain as a Human Experience: an Anthropological Perspective*, M. Delvecchio Good, P. E. Brodwin, B. J. Good & A. Kleinmann (eds), 138–68. Berkeley, CA: University of California Press.
Jackson E. J. 1994. "Chronic Pain and the Tension Between the Body as Subject and Object". In *Embodiment and Experience: the Existential Ground of the Self*, T. J. Csordas (ed.), 201–28. New York: Cambridge University Press.
Jackson E. J. 2005. "Stigma, Liminality, and Chronic Pain: Mind–Body Borderlands". *American Ethnologist* **32**: 332–53.

Jagose, A, 1996. *Queer Theory: an Introduction*. New York: New York University Press.
Janoff-Bulman, R. 1992. *Shattered Assumptions: Towards a New Psychology of Trauma*. New York: Free Press/Macmillan.
Jennings, B., D. Callahan & A. L. Caplan 1988. "Ethical Challenges of Chronic Illness". *The Hastings Center Report* **18**(1): 1–16.
Jonsen, A. R., S. J. Durfy, W. Burke & A. G. Motulsky 1996. "The Advent of the 'Unpatients'". *Nature Medicine* **2**(6): 622–4.
Kant, I. [1790] 2000. *Critique of Judgment*. J. H. Bernard (trans.). New York: Prometheus Books.
Karkazis, K. 2008. *Fixing Sex: Intersex, Medical Authority and Lived Experience*. Durham, NC: Duke University Press.
Kass, L. R. 1975. "Regarding the End of Medicine and the Pursuit of Health". *The Public Interest* **40**: 11–42.
Kehler, J., K. Hübner, S. Garrett & H. R. Schöler 2005. "Generating Oocytes and Sperm from Embryonic Stem Cells". *Seminars in Reproductive Medicine* **23**(3): 222–33.
Kemp, S. F. 2006. "The Role of Genes and Hormones in Sexual Differentiation". See Sytsma (2006), 1–16.
Kendell, R. E. 1975. "The Concept of Disease and its Implications for Psychiatry". *British Journal of Psychiatry* **127**(4): 305–15.
Kenen, R., A. Arden-Jones & R. Eeles 2003. "Living with Chronic Risk: Healthy Women with a History of Breast/Ovarian Cancer". *Health Risk and Society* **5**(3): 315–31.
Kessler, S. 1990. "The Medical Construction of Gender: Case Management of Intersexual Infants". *Signs* **16**(1): 3–26.
Khan, S., S. Bhaskar, W. Lam & R. Donat 2011. "Establishing a Reference Range for Penile Length in Caucasian British men: a Prospective Study of 609 Men". *British Journal of Urology International* **109**(5): 740–44.
Khushf, G. 2007. "An Agenda for Future Debate on Concepts of Health and Disease". *Medicine, Health Care and Philosophy* **10**(1): 19–27.
Kingma, E. 2007. "What Is It to Be Healthy?" *Analysis* **67**(2): 128–33.
Kingma, E. 2010. "Paracetamol, Poison and Polio: Why Boorse's Account of Function Fails to Distinguish Health and Disease". *British Journal for the Philosophy of Science* **61**: 241–64.
Kitcher, P. 1996. *The Lives to Come: the Genetic Revolution and Human Possibilities*. New York: Simon & Schuster.
Kitcher, P. 1999. "Race, Ethnicity, Biology, Culture". In *Racism*, L. Harris (ed.), 87–117. Amherst, NY: Humanity Books.
Kitcher, P. 2007. "Does 'Race' Have a Future?" *Philosophy and Public Affairs* **35**: 293–317.
Klawiter, M. 1999. "Racing For the Cure, Walking Women, and Toxic Touring: Mapping Cultures of Action within the Bay Area Terrain of Breast Cancer". *Social Problems* **46**(1): 104–26.
Klein, D. F. 1978. "A Proposed Definition of Mental Illness". In *Critical Issues in Psychiatric Diagnosis*, R. L. Spitzer & D. F. Klein (eds), 41–70. New York: Raven Press.
Kleinman, A. 1988. *The Illness Narratives: Suffering, Healing and the Human Condition*. New York: Basic Books.
Kleinman, A. 1995. *Writing at the Margin*. Berkeley, CA: University of California Press.
Kleinman, A. 2004. "Culture and Depression". *New England Journal of Medicine* **651**(10): 951–3.

Kollek, R. & T. Lemke 2008. *Der medizinische Blick in die Zukunft: gesellschaftliche Implikationen prädiktiver Gentests* [The medical gaze into the future: Societal implications of predictive genetic tests]. Frankfurt: Campus.

Kopelman, L. 1975. "On Disease: Theories of Disease and the Ascription of Disease: Comments on 'the Concepts of Health and Disease'". In *Evaluation and Explanation in the Biomedical Sciences*, H. T. Engelhardt & S. F. Spicker (eds), 143–50. Dordrecht: Reidel.

Kraus, W. 2006. "The Narrative Negotiation of Identity and Belonging". *Narrative Inquiry* **16**: 103–11.

Krell, D. F. 1996. *Infectious Nietzsche*. Bloomington, IN: Indiana University Press.

Kripke, S. 1972. *Naming and Necessity*. Cambridge, MA: Harvard University Press. Reprinted 1980.

Kristiansen, K., S. Vhamas & T. Shakespeare 2009. *Arguing about Disability: Philosophical Perspectives*. Abingdon: Routledge.

Kugelmann R. 1996. "A Phenomenological Analyses of Mental and Physical Pain". In *Problems of Theoretical Psychology: Proceedings of the Sixth Biennial Conference of the International Society for Theoretical Psychology Carleton University, Ottawa, Ontario, Canada, 21–26 May 1995*, C. W. Tolman *et al.* (eds), 342–50. North York, Ontario: Captus University.

Kuhn, T. 1962. *The Structure of Scientific Revolutions*. Chicago, IL: University of Chicago Press. Reprinted 1970.

Kuhn, T. S. 1990. "Dubbing and Redubbing: the Vulnerability of Rigid Designation". In *Scientific Theories*. C. Wade Savage (ed.), 298–318. Minnesota Studies in the Philosophy of Science, volume 14. Minneapolis, MN: University of Minnesota Press.

Kukla, A. 2000. *Social Constructivism and the Philosophy of Science*. London: Routledge.

Kukla, R. 2005. "Conscientious Autonomy: Displacing Decisions in Health Care". *Hastings Center Report* **35**(2): 34–44.

Kurzban, R. & M. R. Leary 2001. "Evolutionary Origins of Stigmatisation: the Functions of Social Exclusion". *Psychological Bulletin* **127**(2): 187–208.

Kuukkanen, J.-M. 2008. *Meaning Changes: a Study of Thomas Kuhn's Philosophy of Science*. Saarbrücken: VDM Verlag Dr. Mueller.

Labisch, A. 2002. "Health in the Era of Molecular Medicine: A Historical Perspective". In *Health and Quality of Life: Philosophical, Medical, and Cultural Aspects*, A. Gimmler, C. Lenk & G. Aumüller (eds), 199–220. Munich: LIT.

Lai, Y. M., C. P. H. Hong & C. Y. I. Lee 2001. "Stigma of Mental Illness". *Singapore Medical Journal* **42**(3): 111–14.

Laing, R. D. 1960. *The Divided Self: an Existential Study in Sanity and Madness*. Harmondsworth: Penguin.

LaPorte, J. 1996. "Chemical Kind Term Reference and the Discovery of Essence". *Noûs* **30**: 112–32.

LaPorte, J. 2004. *Natural Kinds and Conceptual Change*. Cambridge: Cambridge University Press.

Leder, D. 1990. *The Absent Body*. Chicago, IL: University of Chicago Press.

Lemke, T. 2001. "Gouvernmentalität" [Governmentality]. In *Michel Foucault. Eine Einführung in sein Denken* [Michel Foucault: An introduction into his thoughts], M. S. Kleiner (ed.), 108–22. Frankfurt: Campus.

Lemke, T. 2004. *Verantwortung und Veranlagung. Genetische Diagnostik zwischen Selbstbestimmung und Schicksal* [Responsibility and predisposition. Genetic diagnostics between self-determination and fate]. Bielefeld: Transcript Verlag.

Leriche, R. 1940. *The Surgery of Pain*, A. Young (trans. and ed.), 2nd edn. Baltimore, MD: Williams & Wilkins.

Leventhal, H., D. Meyer & D. Nerenz 1980. "The Common Sense Representation of Illness Danger". *Medical Psychology* **2**: 7–30.

Levi, N. & M. Rothberg (eds) 2003. *The Holocaust: Theoretical Readings*. New Brunswick, NJ: Rutgers University Press.

Levin, I., R. Sielger, S. Druyan & R. Gardosh 1990. "Everyday and Curriculum-based Physics Concepts: When Does Short-term Training Bring Change Where Years of Schooling Have Failed to Do So?" *British Journal of Developmental Psychology* **8**: 269–79.

Lewis, B. E. 1998. "Reading Cultural Studies of Medicine". *Journal of Medical Humanities* **19**: 9–24.

Lilienfeld, S. O. & L. Marino 1995. "Mental Disorder as a Roschian Concept: A Critique of Wakefield's 'Harmful Dysfunction' Analysis". *Journal of Abnormal Psychology* **104**(3): 411–20.

Lings, J. 2010. "Motor Neurone Disease: The Experience of Illness Expressed Through Song-writing" Presented at Concepts of Health and Illness Conference, 1–3 September, Bristol.

Loeser, D. J. & R. Melzack 1999. "Pain: an Overview". *Lancet* **353**: 1607–9.

Long, L. S. 2006. "DSD vs Intersex". *Archives of Diseases in Childhood* **91**(7): 554–63.

Louw, D. J. 2001. "Ubuntu and the Challenges of Multiculturalism in Post-Apartheid South Africa". *Question: an African Journal of Philosophy* **XV**(1–2): 15–36.

Lupton, D. 1997. "Foucault and the Medicalisation Critique". In *Foucault, Health and Medicine*, A. Petersen & R. Bunton (eds), 94–110. Abingdon: Routledge.

Machery, E. & L. Faucher 2005. "Social Construction and the Concept of Race". *Philosophy of Science* **72**: 1208–19.

MacIntyre, A. 1981. *After Virtue*. London: Duckworth.

Mackenzie, C. & J. Poltera 2010. "Narrative Integration, Fragmented Selves, and Autonomy". *Hypatia* **25**: 32–54.

Macmillan Cancer Support 2006. *Worried Sick: The Emotional Impact of Cancer*. London: Macmillan Cancer Support

Maitland, S. 2008. *A Book of Silence*. London: Granta.

Mallon, R. 2004. "Passing, Travelling and Reality: Social Constructionism and the Metaphysics of Race". *Noûs* **38**: 644–73.

Mallon, R. 2007. "A Field Guide to Social Construction". *Philosophy Compass* **2**: 93–108.

Margolis, J. 1976. "The Concept of Disease". *The Journal of Medicine and Philosophy* **1**: 238–55.

McAdams, D. 2005. *The Redemptive Self*. Oxford: Oxford University Press.

McKloskey, M. 1983. "Intuitive Physics". *Scientific American* **248**: 114–22.

Megone, C. 1998. "Aristotle's Function Argument and the Concept of Mental Illness". *Philosophy, Psychiatry and Psychology* **5**: 187–201.

Megone, C. 2000. "Mental Illness, Human Function and Values". *Philosophy, Psychiatry and Psychology* **7**: 45–65.

Megone, C. 2007. "Mental Illness, Metaphysics, Facts and Values". *Philosophical Papers* **36**: 399–426.

Melzack, R. 1999. "From the Gate to the Neuromatrix". *Pain* **6** (supplement): S121–6.
Melzack, R. & D. P. Wall 1965. "Pain Mechanism: a New Theory". *Science* **150**: 971–9.
Menzel, P. 1992. "Oregon's Denial: Disabilities and Quality of Life". *Hastings Center Report* **22**(6): 21–5.
Mercer, J. R. 1973. *Labelling the Mentally Retarded: Clinical and Social System Perspectives on Mental Retardation*. Berkeley, CA: University of California Press.
Mergenthaler, D. 2004. "Medicine as Task: Karl E. Rothschuh's Philosophy of Medicine". *Medicine, Health Care and Philosophy* **7**: 253–60.
Merleau-Ponty, M. [1945] 1962. *Phenomenology of Perception*, C. Smith (trans.). London: Routledge.
Mills, C. W. 1998. *Blackness Visible: Essays on Philosophy And Race*. Ithaca, NY: Cornell University Press.
Mitchell, A. & M. Cormac 1998. *The Therapeutic Relationship in Complementary Health Care*. London: Churchill Livingstone.
Mollon, P. 2002. *Releasing the Self: The Healing Legacy of Heinz Kohut*. Chichester: Wiley.
Moncrieffe, J. & R. Eyben 2007. *The Power of Labelling: How People are Categorized and Why it Matters*. London: Earthscan.
Money, J. 2002. *A First Person History of Pediatric Psychoendocrinology*. New York: Kluwer Academic/Plenum Publishers.
Money, J. & A. A. Ehrhardt 1972. *Man and Woman, Boy and Girl*. Baltimore, MD: Johns Hopkins University Press.
Moreno, A. 1999. "In Amerika They call Us Hermaphrodites". See Dreger (1999b), 137–40.
Moreno Bergareche, A. & A. Casado da Rocha 2011. "Autonomy Beyond the Brain: What Neuroscience Offers to a More Interactive, Relational Bioethics". *The American Journal of Bioethics – Neuroscience* **2**(3): 54–6.
Morland, I. 2009a. "What Can Queer Theory Do for Intersex?" See Morland (2009b), 285–312.
Morland, I. (ed.) 2009b. "Intersex and After". *A Journal of Lesbian and Gay Studies* **15**(2): 191–356.
Morris, D. B. 1991. *The Culture of Pain*. Berkeley, CA: University of California Press.
Morris, D. B. 1999. *Illness and Culture in the Postmodern Age*. Berkeley, CA: University of California Press.
Mukherjee, S. 2011. *The Emperor of All Maladies*. New York: Fourth Estate.
Murphy, D. 2006. *Psychiatry in the Scientific Image*. Cambridge, MA: MIT Press.
Murphy, D. 2008. "Concepts of Disease and Health". In *The Stanford Encyclopedia of Philosophy*, Edward N. Zalta (ed.) http://plato.stanford.edu/archives/sum2009/entries/health-disease (accessed on 31 May 2012).
Murphy, D. & R. L. Woolfolk 2000a. "The Harmful Dysfunction Analysis of Mental Disorder". *Philosophy, Psychiatry, and Psychology* **7**(4): 241–52.
Murphy, D. & R. L. Woolfolk 2000b. "Conceptual Analysis Versus Scientific Understanding: An Assessment of Wakefield's Folk Psychiatry". *Philosophy, Psychiatry, and Psychology* **7**(4): 271–94.
Naik, A. D., C. B. Dyer, M. E. Kunik & L. B McCullough 2009. "Patient Autonomy for the Management of Chronic Conditions". *American Journal of Bioethics* **9**(2): 23–30.
National Pharmaceutical Council 2001. "Pain: Current Understanding of Assessment, Management, and Treatments", www.scribd.com/doc/7563609/Pain-Current-

Understanding-of-Assessment-Management-and-Treatments (accessed January 2012).
Nersessian, N. 2003. "Kuhn, Conceptual Change, and Cognitive Science". In *Thomas Kuhn*, T. Nickles (ed.), 178–211. Cambridge: Cambridge University Press.
Nettleton, S. 2006. *The Sociology of Health and Illness*. Cambridge: Polity Press.
Nicolás, P. & C. Romeo Casabona (eds) 2009. *Controles éticos en la actividad biomédica: Análisis de situación y recomendaciones* [Ethical supervision in biomedical activity: Analysis of the situation and recommendations]. Madrid: Instituto Roche.
Nietzsche, F. [1872] 1999. *The Birth of Tragedy and Other Writings*, R. Geuss & R. Spiers (eds), R. Spiers (trans.). Cambridge: Cambridge University Press.
Nisbett, R. E. & T. D. Wilson 1977. "Telling More Than We Can Know: Verbal Reports on Mental Processes". *Psychological Review* **84**(3): 231–59.
Nordenfelt, L. 1987. *On the Nature of Health*. Dordrecht: D. Reidel.
Nordenfelt, L. 1991. *Towards a Theory of Health Promotion: a Logical Analysis*. Linköping: CMT.
Nordenfelt, L. 1994. "On the Disease, Illness and Sickness Distinction: a Commentary on Andrew Twaddle's System of Concepts". In *Disease, Illness and Sickness: Three Central Concepts in the Theory of Health*, A. Twaddle & L. Nordenfelt (eds), 19–36. Studies on Health and Society no. 18. Linköping: Department of Health and Society, Linköping University.
Nordenfelt, L. 1995. *On the Nature of Health: an Action-Theoretic Approach*, 2nd rev. edn. Dordrecht: Kluwer Academic Publishers.
Nordenfelt, L. 1997. *Talking about Health: a Philosophical Dialogue*. Stockholm: Value Inquiry Book Series.
Nordenfelt, L. 2000. *Action, Ability and Health: Essays in the Philosophy of Action and Welfare*. Dordrecht: Kluwer Academic Publishers.
Nordenfelt, L. 2001. *Health, Science and Ordinary Language*. Amsterdam: Rodopi.
Nordenfelt, L. 2004. "The Logic of Health Concepts". In *Handbook of Bioethics: Taking Stock of the Field from a Philosophical Perspective*, G. Khushf (ed.), 205–22. Dordrecht: Kluwer Academic Publishers.
Nordenfelt, L. 2006. *Animal and Human Health and Welfare: A Comparative Philosophical Analysis*. Wallingford: CABI.
Nordenfelt, L. 2007 "The Concepts of Health and Illness Revisited". *Medicine, Health Care and Philosophy* **10**: 5–10.
Nordenfelt, L. 2008. *The Concept of Work Ability*. London: Peter Lang.
Nordenfelt, L. 2010. Keynote Address at the Concepts of Health and Illness conference, 1–3 September, Bristol.
Nordt, C., W. Rossler & C. Lauber 2006. "Attitudes of Mental Health Professionals Toward People With Schizophrenia and Major Depression". *Schizophrenia Bulletin* **32**(4): 709–14.
Office for National Statistics 2002. "Psychiatric Morbidity Among Adults Living in Private Households", www.statistics.gov.uk/pdfdir/mhaa1201.pdf (accessed September 2010).
Oliver, M. 1990. *The Politics of Disablement*. Basingstoke: Palgrave Macmillan.
Organisation for Economic Co-operation and Development 2011. "OECD Health Data 2011 – Frequently Requested Data", www.oecd.org/document/16/0,3746,en_2649_37407_2085200_1_1_1_37407,00.html (accessed 14 June 2012)
Padfield, D., B. Hurwitz & C. Pither 2003. *Perceptions of Pain*. London: Dewi Lewis Publishing.

Park, J. H., J. Faulkner & M. Schaller 2003. "Evolved Disease-avoidance Processes and Contemporary Anti-social Behavior: Prejudicial Attitudes and Avoidance of People With Physical Disabilities". *Journal of Nonverbal Behavior* **27**(2): 65–87.

Parker, G., G. Gladstone & K. T. Chee 2001. "Depression in the Planet's Largest Ethnic Group: the Chinese". *American Journal of Psychiatry* **158**: 857–64.

Parkes, C. 1971. "Psycho-social Transitions: A Field for Study". *Social Science and Medicine* **5**: 101–15.

Patterson, B. L. 2001. "The Shifting Perspectives Model of Chronic Illness". *Journal of Nursing Scholarship* **33**: 21–6.

Pattison, S. 2003. "Medical Humanities: a Vision and Some Cautionary Notes". *Medical Humanities* **29**: 33–6.

Paykel, E. S., D. Hart & R. G. Priest 1998. "Changes in Public Attitudes to Depression During the Defeat Depression Campaign". *British Journal of Psychiatry* **173**: 519–22.

Pellegrino, E. D. & D. C. Thomasma 1988. *For the Patient's Good: The Restoration of Beneficence in Health Care*. New York: Oxford University Press.

Peluso, E. T. P. & S. L. Blay 2009. "Public Stigma in Relation to Individuals with Depression". *Journal of Affective Disorders* **115**: 201–6.

Pennebaker, J. W. 1997. *Opening Up: the Healing Power of Expressing Emotions*. New York: Guildford Press.

Perry, B. L., B. A. Pescosolido, J. K. Martin, J. D. McLeod & P. S. Jensen 2007. "Comparison of Public Attributions, Attitudes, and Stigma in Regard to Depression Among Children and Adults". *Psychiatric Services* **58**(5): 632–5.

Pettit, P. 2001. *A Theory of Freedom: From the Psychology to the Politics of Agency*. New York: Oxford University Press.

Phelan, J. 2005. "Editor's Column: Who's Here? Thoughts on Narrative Identity and Narrative Imperialism". *Narrative* **13**: 205–10.

Phillips, J. 2003. "Schizophrenia and the Narrative Self". In *The Self in Neuroscience and Psychiatry*, T. Kircher & A. David (eds), 319–35. Cambridge: Cambridge University Press.

Pickering, N. 2006. *The Metaphor of Mental Illness*. Oxford: Oxford University Press.

Pill, R., L. Prior & F. Wood 2001. "Lay Attitudes to Professional Consultations for Common Mental Disorder: a Sociological Perspective". *British Medical Bulletin* **57**: 207–19.

Pinker, S. 1997. *How the Mind Works*. New York: W. W. Norton.

Piper, A. 1992. "Passing for White, Passing for Black". *Transition* **58**: 4–32.

Pörn, I. 1993. "Health and Adaptedness". *Theoretical Medicine* **14**: 295–304.

Power, M. & T. Dalgleish 1997. *Cognition and Emotion: From Order to Disorder*. Hove: Psychology Press.

Press, N., S. Reynolds, L. Pinsky, V. Murthy, M. Leo & W. Burke 2005. "'That's Like Chopping Off a Finger Because You're Afraid it Might Get Broken': Disease and Illness in Women's Views of Prophylactic Mastectomy". *Social Science and Medicine* **61**: S1106–17.

Preves, S. E. 1999. "For the Sake of the Children: Destigmatizing Intersexuality". In *Intersex in the Age of Ethics*, A. D. Dreger (ed.), 51–81. Hagerstown, MD: University Publishing Group Inc.

Priest, R. G., C. Vize, A. Roberts, M. Roberts & A. Tylee 1996. "Lay People's Attitude to Treatment of Depression: Results of Opinion Poll for Defeat Depression Campaign just Before its Launch". *British Medical Journal* **313**: 858–9.

Proctor, R. N. 1988. *Racial Hygiene: Medicine Under the Nazis.* Cambridge, MA: Harvard University Press.

Proctor, R. N. 1999. *The Nazi War on Cancer.* Princeton, NJ: Princeton University Press.

Putnam, H. 1973. "Meaning and Reference". *Journal of Philosophy* **70**: 699–711.

Putnam, H. 1975. "'The Meaning of 'Meaning'". In his *Mind, Language and Reality: Philosophical Papers, vol. II*, 131–93, Cambridge: Cambridge University Press. Also available in *Minnesota Studies in the Philosophy of Science* **7**: 131–93.

Raguram, R, M. G. Weiss, S. M. Channabasavanna & G. M. Devins 1996. "Stigma, Depression, and Somatisation in South India". *American Journal of Psychiatry* **153**(8): 1043–9.

Raingruber, B. & M. Kent 2003. "Attending to Embodied Responses: a Way to Identify Practice-Based and Human Meanings Associated with Secondary Trauma". *Qualitative Health Research* **13**(4): 449–68.

Ratcliffe, M. 2008. "The Phenomenological Role of Affect in the Capgras Delusion". *Continental Philosophy Review* **41**(2): 195–216.

Reif, F. & J. Larkin 1991. "Cognition in Scientific and Everyday Domains: Comparison and Learning Implications". *Journal of Research in Science Teaching* **28**(9): 733–60.

Reiner, W. G. 2006. "Prenatal Gender Imprinting and Medical Decision-Making". See Sytsma (2006), 153–63.

Reznek, L. 1987. *The Nature of Disease.* London: Routledge.

Ricoeur, P. 1990. *Time and Narrative*, vol. 1. Chicago, IL: University of Chicago Press.

Rimmon-Kenan, S. 2006. "What Can Narrative Theory Learn from Illness Narratives?". *Literature and Medicine* **25**: 241–54.

Roeloffs, C., C. Sherbourne, J. Unutzer, A. Fink, L. Tang & K. Wells 2003. "Stigma and Depression Among Primary Care Patients". *General Hospital Psychiatry* **25**: 311–15.

Roen, K. 2009. "Clinical Intervention and Embodied Subjectivity: Atypically Sexed Children and Their Parents". See Holmes (2009b), 15–40.

Rogers, C. 1951. *Client-Centered Therapy: Its Current Practice, Implications and Theory.* London: Constable.

Root, M. 2000. "How We Divide the World". *Philosophy of Social Science* **67**: S628–39.

Rosario, V. A. 2009. "Intersex and the Molecular Deconstruction of Sex". See Morland (2009b), 267–83.

Rose, N. 1999. *Powers of Freedom: Reframing Political Thought.* Cambridge: Cambridge University Press.

Ruse, M. 1997. "Defining Disease: the Question of Sexual Orientation". In *What is Disease?* J. M. Humber & R. F. Almeder (eds), 135–72. Totowa, NJ: Humana Press.

Russo, F. & J. Williamson 2007. "Interpreting Causality in the Health Sciences". *International Studies in the Philosophy of Science* **21**: 157–70.

Russo, F. & J. Williamson 2011. "Generic versus Single-Case Causation: the Case of Autopsy". *European Journal for the Philosophy of Science* **1**: 47–69.

Saavedra, J., M. Cubero & P. Crawford 2009. "Incomprehensibility in the Narratives of Individuals with a Diagnosis of Schizophrenia". *Qualitative Health Research Journal* **19**: 1548–58.

Sacks, O. 1984. *A Leg to Stand On.* London: Duckworth.

Samarapungavan, A. & R. Wiers 1994. "Do Children Have Epistemic Constructs About Explanatory Frameworks: Examples from Naïve Ideas About the Origin of Species". In *Proceedings of the 16th Annual Conference of the Cognitive Science Society*, A. Ram & K. Eiselt (eds), 778–83. Hillsdale, NJ: Lawrence Erlbaum Press.

Sanford, E. S. 2006. "My Shoe Size Stayed the Same: Maintaining a Positive Identity with Achondroplasia and Limb-Lengthening Surgeries". In *Surgically Shaping Children: Technology, Ethics and the Pursuit of Normality*, E. Parens (ed.), 29–42. Baltimore, MD: Johns Hopkins University Press.
Sartre, J.-P. [1943] 1956. *Being and Nothingness*, H. E. Barnes (trans.). New York: Washington Square Press.
Sartwell, C. 2000. *End of Story: Toward an Annihilation of Language and History*. Albany, NY: SUNY Press.
Sartwell, C. 2006. "Frankie, Johnny, Oprah and Me: the Limits of Narrative". *Narrative Inquiry* **16**: 156–63.
Scadding, J. G. 1967. "Diagnosis: the Clinician and the Computer". *Lancet* **290**: 877–82.
Scadding, J. G. 1988. "Health and Disease: What Can Medicine Do for Philosophy?" *Journal of Medical Ethics* **14**: 118–24.
Scadding, J. G. 1990. "The Semantic Problem of Psychiatry". *Psychological Medicine* **20**: 243–8.
Scarry, E. 1985. *The Body in Pain*. Oxford: Oxford University Press.
Scarry, E. 1999. *On Beauty and Being Just*. Princeton, NJ: Princeton University Press.
Schechtman, M. 2007. "Basic Survival: A Refinement and Defense of the Narrative View". In *Narrative and Understanding Persons*, D. D. Hutto (ed.), 336–60. Cambridge: Cambridge University Press.
Scheff, T. J. 1966. *Being Mentally Ill: A Sociological Theory*. Chicago, IL: Aldine.
Schiff, B. 2006. "The Promise (and Challenge) of an Innovative Narrative Psychology". *Narrative Inquiry* **16**: 19–27.
Schmidt, B. 2010. "Familiale Gesundheitsverantwortung im aktivierenden Sozialstaat" [Familial health responsibility in the activating welfare state]. In *Gesundheit als Familienaufgabe. Zum Verhältnis von Autonomie und staatlicher Intervention* [Health as a family task: About the relationship between autonomy and interventions by the state], H. Ohlbrecht & C. Schönberger (eds), 87–107. Munich: Juventa.
Schneewind, J. B. 1998. *The Invention of Autonomy*. Cambridge: Cambridge University Press.
Scholz, C. 1995. "Biographie und molekulargenetische Diagnostik" [Biography and molecular genetic diagnostics]. In *Welche Gesundheit wollen wir?* [Which health do we want?], E. Beck-Gernsheim (ed.), 33–72. Frankfurt: Suhrkamp.
Schramme, T. 2007. "A Qualified Defence of a Naturalist Theory of Health". *Medicine, Health Care and Philosophy* **10**: 11–17.
Schroeder, T. 2005. "Moral Responsibility and Tourette Syndrome". *Philosophy and Phenomenological Research* **71**(1): 106–23.
Seedhouse, D. 1986. *Health: the Foundations for Achievement*. Chichester: Wiley.
Shaw, C. M., F. Creed, B. Tomenson, L. Riste & J. K. Cruikshank 1999. "Prevalence of Anxiety and Depressive Illness and Help-Seeking Behaviour in African Caribbeans and White Europeans: Two Phase General Population Survey". *British Medical Journal* **318**: 302–6.
Siann, G. 1994. *Gender, Sex and Sexuality*. Hove: Psychology Press.
Siebers, T. 2006. "Disability Aesthetics". *Journal for Cultural and Religious Theory* **7**(2): 62–73.
Simon, J. 2010. "Advertisement for the Ontology of Medicine". *Theoretical Medicine and Bioethics* **31**: 333–46.

Simons, J. 2007. "Beyond Naturalism and Normativism: Reconceiving the 'Disease' Debate". *Philosophical Papers* **36**: 343–70.
Sims, A. 1993. "The Scar That is More Than Skin Deep: the Stigma of Depression". *British Journal of General Practice* **43**: 30–31.
Sokal, A. & J. Bricmont 1998. *Intellectual Impostors*. London: Profile Books.
Solomon, M. 2008. "Epistemological Reflections on the Art of Medicine and Narrative Medicine". *Perspectives in Biology and Medicine* **51**(3): 406–17.
Solomon, M. 2011. "Group Judgment and the Medical Consensus Conference". In *Philosophy of Medicine*, F. Gifford (ed.), 239–54. London: Elsevier.
Sontag, S. 1978. *Illness as a Metaphor*. New York: Farrar, Straus & Giroux.
SOU 2009. *Gränslandet mellan sjukdom och arbete* [The borderland between disease and work]. Official Report 2009:89. Stockholm: Swedish Government.
Spiegelberg, H. 1972. *Phenomenology in Psychology and Psychiatry*. Evanston, IL: Northwestern University Press.
Spiegelberg, H. 1982. *The Phenomenological Movement: A Historical Introduction*. The Hague: M. Nijhoff.
Spitzer, R. L. 1974. "In Defense of the New Nomenclature for Homosexuality". *Medical Worlds News Review* **1**(2): 16–18.
Spitzer, R. L. 1997. "Brief Comments from a Psychiatric Nosologist Weary from His Own Attempts to Define Mental Disorder: Why Ossorio's Definition Muddles and Wakefield's 'Harmful Dysfunction' Illuminates the Issues". *Clinical Psychology: Science and Practice* **4**(3): 259–61.
Spitzer, R. L. 1999. "Harmful Dysfunction and the DSM Definition of Mental Disorder". *Journal of Abnormal Psychology* **108**: 430–32.
Spitzer, R. L. & J. Endicott 1978. "Medical and Mental Disorder: Proposed Definition and Criteria". In *Critical Issues in Psychiatric Diagnosis*, R. L. Spitzer & D. F. Klein (eds), 15–39. New York: Raven Press.
Spitzer, R. L & P. T. Wilson 1975. "Nosology and the Official Psychiatric Nomenclature". In *Comprehensive Textbook of Psychiatry*, A. M. Freedman, H. I. Kaplan & B. J. Sadock (eds), 826–46. Baltimore, MD: Williams & Wilkins.
Spurgas, A. K. 2009. "(Un)Queering Identity: The Biosocial Production of Intersex/DSD". See Holmes (2009b), 97–122.
Stempsey, W. E. 2000. "A Pathological View of Disease". *Theoretical Medicine* **21**: 321–30.
Sternbach, R. A. 1974. *Pain Patients: Traits and Treatment*. New York: Academic Press.
Stirner, M. [1844] 1995. *The Ego and Its Own*, D. Leopold (ed. and intro.). Cambridge Texts in the History of Political Thought. Cambridge: Cambridge University Press.
Stoller, R. J., J. Marmor, I. Bieber, R. Gold, C. W. Socarides, R. Green & R. L. Spitzer 1973. "A Symposium: Should Homosexuality Be in the APA Nomenclature?" *American Journal of Psychiatry* **130**(11): 1207–16.
Strawson, G. 2004. "Against Narrativity". *Ratio* **17**: 428–52.
Strawson, G. 2007. "Episodic Ethics". In *Narrative and Understanding Persons*, D. D. Hutto (ed.), 85–115. Cambridge: Cambridge University Press.
Sulmasy, D. P. 2005. "Diseases and Natural Kinds". *Theoretical Medicine and Bioethics* **26**: 487–513.
Svenaeus, F. 2000a. "Das Unheimliche: Towards a Phenomenology of Illness". *Medicine, Health Care and Philosophy* **3**: 3–16.
Svenaeus, F. 2000b. *The Hermeneutics of Medicine and the Phenomenology of Health: Steps Towards a Philosophy of Medical Practice*. Dordrecht: Kluwer.

Svenaeus, F. 2000c. "The Body Uncanny: Further Steps towards a Phenomenology of Illness." *Medicine, Health Care and Philosophy* **3**: 125–37.
Svenaeus, F. 2003. "A Phenomenological Analysis of the Concepts of Handicap and Illness". In *Dimensions of Health and Health Promotion*, P.-E. Liss & L. Nordenfelt (eds), 97–109. Amsterdam: Rodopi.
Svenaeus, F. 2007. "A Heideggerian Defense of Therapeutic Cloning". *Theoretical Medicine and Bioethics* **28**: 31–62.
Svenaeus, F. 2009. "The Phenomenology of Falling Ill: An Explication, Critique and Improvement of Sartre's Theory of Embodiment and Alienation". *Human Studies* **32**: 53–66.
Svenaeus, F. 2010. "The Body as Gift, Resource, or Commodity: Heidegger and the Ethics of Organ Transplantation". *Journal of Bioethical Inquiry* **7**: 163–72.
Svenaeus, F. 2011. "Illness as Unhomelike Being-in-the-World: Heidegger and the Phenomenology of Medicine". *Medical Health Care and Philosophy* **14**: 333–43.
Swidler, A. 1986. "Culture in Action: Symbols and Strategies". *American Sociological Review* **51**(2): 273–86.
Sytsma, S. E. (ed.) 2006. *Ethics and Intersex*. Dordrecht: Springer.
Szasz, T. S. 1960. "The Myth of Mental Illness". *American Psychologist* **15**: 113–18.
Tammi, P. 2006. "Against Narrative ('A Boring Story')". *Partial Answers: Journal of Literature and the History of Ideas* **4**: 19–40.
Tauber, A. I. 1999. *Confessions of a Medicine Man: an Essay in Popular Philosophy*. Cambridge, MA: MIT Press.
Tauber, A. I. 2002. "The Ethical Imperative of Holism in Medicine". In *Promises and Limits of Reductionism in the Biomedical Sciences*, M. H. V. Van Regenmortel & D. L. Hull (eds), 261–78. Chichester: John Wiley.
Taylor, C. 1989. *Sources of the Self*. Cambridge: Cambridge University Press.
Taylor, P. W. 1976. *Respect for Nature: A Theory of Environmental Ethics*. Princeton, NJ: Princeton University Press.
Taylor, S. E. 1990. *Positive Illusions: Creative Self-Deception and the Healthy Mind*. New York: Basic Books.
Taylor, S. E. & J. D. Brown 1988. "Illusion and Well-being: a Social Psychological Perspective". *Psychological Bulletin* **103**: 193–210.
The Telegraph 2010. "Sex Change Dog Seeks New Home". *The Telegraph* (13 October). www.telegraph.co.uk/news/newstopics/howaboutthat/8060144/Sex-change-dog-seeks-new-home.html# (accessed 22 November 2010).
Thomas, C. 2010. "Negotiating the Contested Terrain of Narrative Methods in Illness Contexts". *Sociology of Health and Illness* **32**: 647–60.
Thomasma, D. 2000. "Moral and Metaphysical Reflections on Multiple Personality Disorder". *Theoretical Medicine and Bioethics* **21**(3): 235–60.
Thomasma, D. C. & E. D. Pellegrino 1981. "Philosophy of Medicine as the Source for Medical Ethics". *Theoretical Medicine and Bioethics* **2**(1): 5–11.
Toates, F. 1987. "The Relevance of Models of Motivation and Learning to Animal Welfare". In *Biology of Stress in Farm Animals: an Integrative Approach*, P. R. Wiepkema & P. W. M van Adrichen (eds), 153–86. Dordrecht: Martinus Nijhoff.
Toombs, S. K. 1987. "The Meaning of Illness: A Phenomenological Approach to the Patient–Physician Relationship". *Journal of Medicine and Philosophy* **12**: 219–40.
Toombs, S. K. 1988. "Illness and the Paradigm of the Lived Body". *Theoretical Medicine* **9**: 201–26.

Toombs, S. K. 1990. "The Temporality of Illness: Four Levels of Experience". *Theoretical Medicine* **11**: 227–41.
Toombs, S. K. 1992. *The Meaning of Illness: a Phenomenological Account of the Different Perspectives of Physician and Patient.* Dordrecht: Kluwer Academic Publishers.
Toombs, S. K. 1993. "The Metamorphosis: the Nature of Chronic Illness and its Challenge to Medicine." *Journal of Medical Humanities* **14**(4): 223–30.
Toombs, S. K. 1995. "The Lived Experience of Disability." *Human Studies* **18**: 9–23.
Toombs, S. K. (ed.) 2001a. *Handbook of Phenomenology and Medicine.* Dordrecht: Kluwer Academic Publishers.
Toombs, S. K. 2001b. "Introduction: Phenomenology and Medicine". In *Handbook of Phenomenology and Medicine*, S. K. Toombs (ed.), 1–26. Dordrecht: Kluwer Academic Publishers.
Travis, C. 2009. *Thought's Footing: a Theme in Wittgenstein's Philosophical Investigations.* Oxford: Oxford University Press.
Twaddle, A. 1994. "Disease, Illness and Sickness Revisited". In *Disease, Illness and Sickness: Three Central Concepts in the Theory of Health*, A. Twaddle & L. Nordenfelt (eds), 1–18. Linköping: Department of Health and Society, Linköping University.
US Food and Drug Administration 2010. "FDA clears Cymbalta to Treat Musculoskeletal Pain", www.fda.gov/NewsEvents/Newsroom/PressAnnouncements/ucm232708.htm (accessed September 2011)
van der Weij, M. 2010. "Beyond Words – Envisioning Experiences of People's Pain: Design of a Communication Tool to Help People to Express Experiences of Pain and Illness". Concepts of Health and Illness Conference, 1–3 September, Bristol.
Van Seters, A. P. & A. K. Slob. 1988. "Mutually Gratifying Heterosexual Relationship With Micropenis Of Husband". *Journal of Sex and Marital Therapy* **14**(2): 98–107.
Wagner, R. [1849] 1993. *The Art-Work of the Future and Other Works.* W. A. Ellis (trans.). Lincoln, NE: University of Nebraska Press.
Wakefield, J. C. 1992a. "The Concept of Medical Disorder: On the Boundary Between Biological Facts and Social Values". *American Psychologist* **47**: 373–88.
Wakefield, J. C. 1992b. "Disorder as Harmful Dysfunction: A Conceptual Critique of D.S.M-III-R's Definition of Mental Disorder". *Psychological Review* **99**: 232–47.
Wakefield, J. C. 1993. "Limits of Operationalization: A Critique of Spitzer and Endicott's (1978) Proposed Operational Criteria for Mental Disorder". *Journal of Abnormal Psychology* **102**(1): 160–72.
Wakefield, J. C. 2000. "Spandrels, Vestigial Organs, and Such: Reply to Murphy and Woolfolk's 'The Harmful Dysfunction Analysis of Mental Disorder'". *Philosophy, Psychiatry, and Psychology* **7**(4): 253–70.
Wakefield, J. C. 2007. "The Concept of Mental Disorder: Diagnostic Implications of the Harmful Dysfunction Analysis". *World Psychiatry* **6**(3):149–56.
Walker, L. 2001. *Looking Like What You Are: Sexual Style, Race, and Lesbian Identity.* New York: New York University Press.
Wang, J. & D. Lai 2008. "The Relationship Between Mental Health Literacy, Personal Contacts and Personal Stigma Against Depression". *Journal of Affective Disorders* **110**: 191–6.
Wartofsky, M. W. 1975. "Organs, Organisms and Disease: Human Ontology and Medical Practice". In *Evaluation and Explanation in the Biomedical Sciences*, H. T. Engelhardt & S. F. Spicker (eds), 67–84. Dordrecht: Reidel.

Wasserman, D., A. Asch, J. Blustein & D. Putnam 2011. "Disability: Definitions, Models, Experience". In *The Stanford Encyclopedia of Philosophy*, Edward N. Zalta (ed.), http://plato.stanford.edu/archives/win2011/entries/disability/ (accessed December 2011).

Wehling, P. & W. Viehöver 2011. "Entgrenzung der Medizin: Transformationen des medizinischen Feldes aus soziologischer Perspektive" [The de-limitation of medicine: Transformations of the medical field from a sociological perspective]. In their *Entgrenzung der Medizin. Von der Heilkunst zur Verbesserung des Menschen?* [The de-limitation of medicine: From the art of healing to the promotion of man?], 7–47. Bielefeld: Transcript.

Whitbeck, C. 1978. "Four Basic Concepts of Medical Science". *PSA: Proceedings of the Biennial Meeting of the Philosophy of Science Association* **1**: 210–22.

Whitbeck, C. 1981. "A Theory of Health". In *Concepts of Health and Disease: Interdisciplinary Perspectives*, A. L. Caplan, H. T. Engelhardt Jr & J. J. McCartney (eds), 611–26. Reading, MA: Addison-Wesley.

Wilchins, R. 2004. *Queer Theory, Gender Theory: An Instant Primer*. Los Angeles, CA: Alyson Publications.

Wilkes, K. 1984. "Pragmatics in Science and Theory in Common-Sense". *Inquiry* **27**: 339–61.

Wilson, T. D. 2002. *Strangers to Ourselves: Discovering the Adaptive Unconscious*. Cambridge, MA: Belknap Press (Harvard University Press).

Wittgenstein, L. 1953. *Philosophical Investigations*. Oxford: Blackwell.

Wittgenstein, L. 1958. *The Blue and Brown Books*. Oxford: Blackwell.

Wittgenstein, L. 1974. *On Certainty*. Oxford: Blackwell.

Wolf, N. 1991. *The Beauty Myth: How Images of Beauty Are Used Against Women*. London: Vintage.

Wolff, G., S. Pathare & C. Craig 1996. "Public Education for Community Care: A New Approach". *British Journal of Psychiatry* **168**: 441–7.

Woods, A. 2010. "Emotion and Narrative in *Schizophrenia Bulletin*'s First Person Accounts". Presented at the AHRC Emotions and Feelings in Psychiatric Illness Network Conference, 10 September, Durham, UK.

Woods, A. 2011a. "The Limits of Narrative: Provocations for the Medical Humanities". *Medical Humanities Journal* **37**: 73–8.

Woods, A. 2011b. "Post-narrative: An Appeal". *Narrative Inquiry* **21**: 399–406.

Woods, A. 2011c. "Temporality, Narrativity and Psychopathology". Presented at the 14th Annual International Network for Philosophy and Psychiatry Conference, 1–4 September, Gothenburg, Sweden.

World Health Organization 2010a. "Persistent Somatoform Pain Disorder" (F45.4), http://apps.who.int/classifications/apps/icd/icd10online (accessed 6 September 2011).

World Health Organization 2010b. "Symptoms, Signs and Abnormal Clinical Findings Not Elsewhere Classified" (Block R00-R99), http://apps.who.int/classifications/apps/icd/icd10online (accessed 6 September 2011).

World Health Organization 2010c. "Depression", www.who.int/mental_health/management/depression/definition/en/print.html (accessed January 2010).

Worrall, J. 2007. "Evidence in Medicine and Evidence-Based Medicine". *Philosophy Compass* **2**: 981–1022.

Wright, L. 1973. "Functions". *Philosophical Review* **82**: 139–68.

BIBLIOGRAPHY

Zahavi, D. 2003. *Husserl's Phenomenology*. Stanford, CA: Stanford University Press.
Zahavi, D. 2007. "Self and Other: The Limits of Narrative Understanding". In *Narrative and Understanding Persons*, D. D. Hutto (ed.), 174–209. Cambridge: Cambridge University Press.
Zaner, R. M. 1981. *The Context of Self: A Phenomenological Inquiry Using Medicine as a Clue*. Athens, OH: Ohio University Press.

INDEX

Accord Alliance 172
Agamben, G. 214
Amundson, R. 171
Angermeyer, M. 186
animal (health and disease) 32–5, 166, 211
anorexia 7
antipsychiatry 85
Aristotle 131
   Aristotelian accounts of the good life 6–7
autonomy 57–74

beauty 211–27
Beauchamp, T. 57, 63–5, 68
being-in-the-world 9, 102–4, 106–8, 124, 131, 133, 138
being-towards-death 105, 110–11
beneficence 66
bereavement *see* grief
bioethics 16, 57–74, 108
biostatistical theory of health *see* Boorse
body 101–2, 124, 140, 155
Boorse, C. 4–5, 23–36, 39–40, 53, 87–8, 161, 201–2
BRCA-positive 197–205
Broom, D. 33
Butler, J. 165, 209

cancer 1, 8, 16, 20, 105, 110, 119, 120, 129–42, 197–210
   of the breast 20, 132, 197–210

Canguilhem, G. 73, 145, 224
Carel, H. 8, 9, 66, 67, 69, 99, 125, 142, 174–6, 225
Charon, R. 113–14
Childress, J. 57, 63–5, 68
Chronic Fatigue Syndrome/myalgic encephalomyelitis 11–12
Churchland, P. 187
Cohen, P. 212, 214–15
conceptual analysis 77–84
   history of application to "mental disorder" 84–91
   limits of 84
   of natural kind terms 78–81
   ordinary understanding of 81–2
Congenital Adrenal Hyperplasia (CAH) 163–4, 166–9
Conrad, P. 13
constructivism 37, 43–55, 197–210
Cooper, R. 42, 89

Darwin, C. 217–18
Dawkins, M. 34
De Gobineau, J. 218
death 1, 7–8, 19, 26–8, 64, 105, 110–11, 138, 141, 170, 182, 198, 213, 217, 227
depression 153, 181–194
Diagnostic and Statistical Manual of Mental Disorders 148–9, 153
   definition of mental disorder 86–7, 89
   depression criteria 182–3

253

INDEX

disability 10–11, 13, 106–7, 211
Down's syndrome 40, 109
Dreger, A. 177
dualism (mind/body) 17, 99, 100, 144, 148, 155–7
Duncan, I. 34

embodiment 17, 100–102, 107, 111, 119, 122–6, 138–9, 179
Engelhardt, T. 41, 88
epistemology of medicine 10
Etcoff, N. 216

family resemblance term ("disease" as) 7, 81
Faucher, L. 216
Fausto-Sterling, A. 177
Feder, E. 166
folk reasoning 187, 189–93
Foucault, M. 171–2, 175, 205, 212
four principles (approach to ethics) 57–8, 63–5
Frank, A. 17, 118–24
Fuchs, T. 104, 123
function 4–5, 24, 39, 87, 89, 90

Gadamer, H. G. 9, 99, 102, 197
gender 165–6
Gender Recognition Act (2004) 165, 178
Goebbels, J. 212
Goethe, J. W. 222
Goldstein, K. 225
good life (accounts of the) 6–7
Goosens, W. 41–2
Great German Art Exhibition 214
Greer, G. 163
grief 2, 29–32

HIV 12
Hacking, I. 44, 46
harm (accounts of) 6–7
Harrington, A. 221, 223
Haslam, N. 81
Heidegger, M. 9, 98, 102–4, 109–11, 131, 135, 139, 213
Henrich, J. 193
hermeneutics 9, 101, 111

Heyes, C. 173
Hitler, A. 212–13, 220–21
Hofmann, B. 61–3, 70
holism (German) 221–5
holistic theory of health 6, 23–36, 202–3
Holmes, M. 178
homosexuality 5–6, 13, 53, 86–7, 172
Hughes, I. 169
Hurrelmann, K. 203, 205
Husserl, E. 9, 98–9, 135

ICD-10 149, 151
identity 207–8
Illich, I. 143, 171–72
Imperato-McGinley, J. 174
informed consent 69–70
intersex 161–80
Intersex Society of North America 170

jade 47–9
justice 65

Kant, I. 57, 221–2
Karkazis, K. 175–7
Kessler, S. 177
Klawiter, M. 212
Kuhn, T. 187–9
Kukla, A. 44

labelling model 207–8
Lamarckianism 218
Leder, D. 99
Leriche, R. 209
Lilienfeld, S. 83
lived body 8, 104, 118, 123, 131, 138

Machery, E. 216
Marino, L. 83
medical humanities 17, 113–14, 118, 124–6
medical technology 108–10
medicalization 2, 12–14, 28–9, 173–7
mental disorder 79–93
Merleau-Ponty, M. 8–9, 98–9
metaphysics of medicine 10

micropenis 168–9
milieu 225
Money, J. 167
Morland, I. 176

Naik, A. 70–71
narrative 17, 72, 113–126, 155, 173, 190, 198
naturalistic theory of health *see* Boorse
Nietzsche, F. 110, 213, 218
non-maleficence 64
Nordenfelt, L. 6, 23–36, 42, 61, 84, 133, 202

organ transplantation 110

pain 143–57
paradigm
  Kuhnian 188–9
  Pollyanna proto-paradigm 190–93
partial androgen insensitivity 174
patients (as political force) 11–12
Pellegrino, E. 58
performativity 165, 206, 210
Pettit, P. 71
phenomenology 8, 9, 17, 98–9, 124–6
phenomenology of illness 8, 10, 131–2, 135, 185
phenomenology of medicine 97–111
philosophy of medicine defined 2–3
Piaget, J. 137
placebo effect 156
Ploetz, A. 217, 219
Pollyanna principle 190
pregnancy 29–32
problems in living 12–13
Proctor, R. 217

race 44–5, 218–20
racial hygiene 217–21
Riefenstahl, L. 212
risk factors 1, 12, 197–205
Roen, K. 179
Rogers, C. 132, 137
Rosario, V. 164–5
Rosenberg, A. 212
Rothschuh, K. 59

salutogenesis 203
Sartre, J.-P. 9, 98, 101, 110
Scarry, E. 215
Schallmeyer, W. 219
Schmidt, B. 204
Schramme, T. 28–9
sex 162–5
social constructivism *see* constructivism
Society for Racial Hygiene 219
Solomon, M. 10
Spitzer, R. 86–90
Stirner, M. 85
Strawson, G. 17, 114–23, 122–3
suffering 1, 8, 13, 17, 19, 27, 31, 33–4, 67, 87, 89, 97–8, 100, 103, 105, 111, 120–21, 123–5, 129, 143, 145, 147, 154, 157, 161, 182, 185, 192, 198, 225
surgery
  cosmetic 173
  genital 166–9, 172–3, 176–8
survival (conceptual link to "disease") 26–8
Svenaeus, F. 9, 17, 23, 27, 99, 131, 134–5, 139
Swidler, A. 213
Szasz, T. 85–8, 150

Tauber, A. 63
Taylor, P. 35
Thomasma, D. 58–9
Todd, E. 227
Toombs, S. K. 8–9, 99, 123, 175
treatment (conceptual link to "disease") 41–3
Twaddle, A. 61
twin earth 47

vital goal 24–5, 34–5

Wakefield, J. 6, 53, 80, 89
water 47
Wittgenstein, L. 7, 78, 81–3
Wolf, N. 216

Zaner, R. 99
Zimmerman, K. 222